HUNTERS, FISHERS AND
FARMERS OF EASTERN EUROPE
6000–3000 B.C.

Archaeology

Editor

JOHN M. COLES
MA, PH.D

Lecturer in *Archaeology*
in the University of Cambridge

HUNTERS, FISHERS AND FARMERS OF EASTERN EUROPE

6000-3000 B.C.

Ruth Tringham

Assistant Professor of Archaeology
Department of Anthropology
Harvard University

HUTCHINSON UNIVERSITY LIBRARY
LONDON

HUTCHINSON & CO (*Publishers*) LTD
3 Fitzroy Square, London W1

London Melbourne Sydney Auckland
Wellington Johannesburg Cape Town
and agencies throughout the world

First published 1971

*The anthropomorphic pot (see Fig. 19) on the cover of the
paperback edition is reproduced by courtesy of the
Banatului Museum, Timişoara, Rumania*

*This book has been set in Times type, printed in Great Britain
on opaque wove paper by Anchor Press, and
bound by Wm. Brendon, both of Tiptree, Essex*
ISBN 0 09 108790 2 (cased)
0 09 108791 0 (paper)

To

my three mentors

and the memory of *V. Gordon Childe*

CONTENTS

CONTENTS

PLATES

FIGURES

ABBREVIATIONS

Acta Arch. et Ant. Acta Archaeologica et Antiqua (Szeged)
Acta Arch. Carp. Acta Archaeologica Carpatica (Krakow)
Acta Arch. Hung. Acta Archaeologica Hungarica (Budapest)
AJA American Journal of Archaeology (Princeton)
A Mora F. Muz. Evk. A Mora F. Muzeum Evkönyve (Szeged)
Arch. Aust. Archaeologica Austriaca (Vienna)
Arch. Ert. Archaeologiai Értesitő (Budapest)
Arch. Iug. Archaeologica Iugoslavica (Belgrade)
Arch. Mold. Archeologia Moldoviei (Iaşi)
Arch. Polski Archeologia Polski (Warsaw–Wroclaw)
Arch. Rozh. Archeologické Rozhledy (Prague)
Arh. Rad. i Raspr. Arheološki Radove i Rasprave (Zagreb)
Arh. Vestnik Arheološki Vestnik (Ljubliana)
Ausgr. u. Funde Ausgrabungen und Funde (E. Berlin)
BASPR Bulletin of the American School of Prehistoric Research
Ber. R.G.K. Bericht der Römisch-Germanisch Kommission (W. Berlin)
Dolg. Dolgozatok a M.Kir.Horthy M.–tudományegyetem régiségtudo-
mányi intézetéből (Szeged)
Glasnik Z.M. Sar. Glasnik Zemaljskog Muzeja (Sarajevo)
God. Nar. Arkh. Muz. Godištnik na Narodniya Arkheologičeski Muzej
(Plovdiv)
God. Nar. Bibl. i Muz. Godištnik na Narodnata Biblioteka i Muzej
(Plovdiv)
IAD Izvestia na Arkheologičeskoto Družestvo (Sofia)
IAI Izvestia na Arkheologičeski Institut (Sofia)
IPEK Jahrbüch fur Prähistorische und Ethnographische Kunst
JRAI The Journal of the Royal Anthropological Institute (London)
KSIA Kratkiye Soobščeniya Instituta Arkheologii AN SSSR (Moscow–
Leningrad)

KSIIMK Kratkiye Soobščeniya Instituta Istorii Materialnoi Kulturi (Moscow)
MAGW Mitteilungen der Anthropologischen Gesellschaft in Wien (Vienna)
Materiale Materiale şi cercetări arheologice (Bucharest)
Mat. Arch. Materialy archeologiczne (Krakow)
MIA Materialy i Issledovaniya po Arkheologii SSSR. (Moscow–Leningrad)
MIA YuZSSSR & RNR Materialy i Issledovaniya po Arkheologii Yugozapada SSSR i Rumunskoi Narodnoi Republiki (Kišinev)
Pam. Arch. Památky Archeologické (Prague)
PPS Proceedings of the Prehistoric Society (Cambridge)
Prähist. Zeitschr. Prähistorische Zeitschrift (W. Berlin)
Rc. Radiocarbon
SA Sovětskaya Arkheologiya (Moscow-Leningrad)
Sbornik N.M. Sbornik Narodniho Muzeja (Prague)
SCIV Studii şi Cercetări de Istorie Veche (Bucharest)
Slov. Arch. Slovenská Archeológia (Bratislava–Nitra)
Spraw. Arch. Sprawozdania Archeologiczne (Wroclaw–Krakow)
Stud. i Mat. Neol. Malopolski Studiow i Materialow do Badan nad Neoliticzne Malopolsky (Krakow)
Štud. Zvesti Študijné Zvesti (Nitra)
Wiad. Arch. Wiadomości Archeologiczne (Warsaw)
WPZ Wiener Prähistorische Zeitschrift (Vienna)
Zeitschr. für Arch. Zeitschrift für Archäologie (E. Berlin)

PRONUNCIATION

Much of the literature referred to in this book has been written in the Slavonic group of the Indo-European languages. The oldest of these languages were written in the Cyrillic script, and many (Russian, Bulgarian, Ukrainian, Serbian) still are. For the purposes of this book, however, they have been transliterated into the Latin script, as in modern Czech, Polish and Croatian. Some of the accents, etc., involved in this transliteration are explained below; in addition some of the special characteristics of the pronunciation of Rumanian, a Romance language, and Hungarian, a language belonging to an entirely different family (Finno-Ugrian), are noted.

Czech	Polish	Serbo-Croat	Rumanian	Hungarian	English equivalent
c	c	c	ţ	c	ts
t'	ć	ć	—	—	tsh
č	cz	č	ce, ci	cs	tch
ch	h, ch	h, ch	h	—	'ch' in 'loch' (translit. 'kh')
ď	dź, dzi	dj, đ		gy	'd' in 'dew'
j	j	j	i, ii, ie	j, ly	'y' in 'yet'
k	k	k	ca, co, cu, ch	k	'c' in 'cat'

Czech	Polish	Serbo-Croat	Rumanian	Hungarian	English equivalent
ň	ń	nj		ny	'n' in 'new'
ř	rz	—	—	—	simultaneous 'r' + French 'je'
s	s	s	s	sz	s
š	ś, sz	š	ş	s	sh
v	w	v	v	v	v
ž	ź, ż	ž	j	zs	's' in 'pleasure'
('u' translit. from Bulgarian)			ă	ö	'er' in bigger phonetic 'ə'
ě	je	ě	ie	je	ye
—	ą	—	—	—	French 'on'
—	ę	—	—	—	French 'in' in 'vin'
(translit. 'y' from Russian)			î	—	nearest equiv. is the 'i' in 'ill'
—	—	—	—	ő	'or' in 'word'
—	—	—	—	ü	cf. German ü

PREFACE

In this book I have chosen to discuss a series of subjects and problems which most interest me, rather than write a systematic description of prehistoric cultural development of east-central Europe and the Danube basin from *c.* 6000–3000 B.C. A prehistory of this part of Europe is badly needed both for students and researchers, because the last one to be attempted, Gordon Childe's *Danube in Prehistory* (1929), is now out of date. The chronological framework of the prehistoric cultures of this area and period has been set out in numerous studies, more recently with reference to radiocarbon dating evidence.[1]* The interpretation of some of the relevant evidence and its partial description does occur as part of Childe's *Dawn of European Civilisation* and Stuart Piggott's *Ancient Europe*.[2] To write a prehistory of east-central Europe, however, from 6000–3000 B.C., including details of the chronological framework, cultural development, primary sources of evidence and interpretation of this evidence in terms of prehistoric cultural processes, would be a lifetime's work, and one which has not been attempted here. The primary sources of the mass of evidence of east European prehistory are generally hidden behind a barrier of unfamiliar languages and illegible scripts. It was not my aim, however, merely to act as the transmitter or interpreter of this evidence to 'western Europe' through a familiarity with the material and a knowledge of the languages. Nor would I wish to duplicate the work of my east European colleagues, or presume to offer them new information or

* Superior figures refer to notes on p. 23 and subsequently to end-of-chapter notes.

evidence, or any different interpretation of the material in terms of cultural and chronological identification.

Instead, I have concentrated on the interpretation of the material in terms of prehistoric cultural processes, rather than its description or classification. I do not consider morphological classifications or typologies of pottery or stone tools, or the identification of cultures and their relative chronological position, to be the main end of prehistoric studies; they are rather the means to the interpretation of prehistoric material in terms of processes of social, economic and technological development and the reconstruction of as much as possible of the 'sum total of human activities'. In order that these processes may be intelligible to a wide audience, which includes not only students and specialist researchers in prehistory, but also those interested in every aspect of the study of Man, references to specific sites and finds and the discussion of complex archaeological problems of chronology and cultures have generally been kept out of the main text.

However, students seeking a guide to the complex material of prehistoric eastern Europe will find that this book exists on two levels in imitation of Stuart Piggott in his *Ancient Europe*. Details of the evidence and bibliographical references have been brought together at the end of each chapter. The general bibliography at the end of the book, containing works generally written in English, French and German, should be of interest to a wider audience. In general, all the bibliographical references have been chosen for their availability in 'western' libraries. For this reason, I hope I shall be forgiven for omitting certain references, especially of pre-war date, in rather more obscure journals. I hope that the notes and references may provide a useful starting-point for a number of research projects.

In addition, for those who prefer to read the ideas expressed in this book in their chronological and cultural context, I have provided a pull-out chart (Fig. 41) of the cultural framework of eastern Europe in this period and two tables of the relevant radiocarbon dates (Figs. 39, 40), all of which were up to date at the time of writing. It should be remembered, however, that the theoretical position of many specialists in this field and the available information changes each month.

My main aim in this book is to interpret the available evidence of eastern Europe *c*. 6000–3000 B.C. in terms of human activities and cultural responses to changing environmental conditions and the diffusion of innovations in their way of life; in terms of the potentialities of the environment and how these were exploited or rejected as sources of food and raw materials; and in terms of the factors responsible for the discovery, development, diffusion, acceptance and rejection of innovations, including factors such as environment, economy, technology and cultural choice. Many activities of pre-historic societies are probably (but not necessarily) beyond the limits of inference from archaeological evidence, including those con-nected with social structure and religion or beliefs. The interpretation of archaeological material, however, can be greatly enriched if the activities of modern 'ethnographic' small-scale societies are examined and used not in a one-to-one relationship, but to provide a range of possible interpretations of the material and to stimulate new questions and answers about the material.[3] Unfortunately the evidence available to a prehistorian is very much poorer than that available to an ethnographer. Whereas, for example, an ethno-grapher can concentrate his attention on isolating the factors which determine the form of an artefact including raw material, level of technological skill, the intended function of the artefact and cultural choice of preferred shape, the archaeologist must carefully analyse the artefact to reconstruct its original form and function and its method of manufacture, before he can begin to think of other factors. Such analyses of artefacts and excavations with these questions in mind have only very rarely been carried out in pre-historic studies in eastern Europe. For this reason, any such analyses which do exist, such as the excellent work done at Bylany and in Moldavia, have been excessively used and stressed in this book.

The dominant problem which runs through this book concerns the diffusion of the techniques and equipment associated with the domestication and exploitation of plants and animals and a food-producing economy from the Near East through south-east Europe and north-west through the Danube basin, through changing en-vironmental conditions, and finally reaching western Europe. Thus to understand the adoption of a food-producing economy in Europe as a whole, it is essential to understand the mechanisms and processes of the diffusion and non-diffusion of the techniques and associated economy in central and eastern Europe. I hope that this may suggest to my east European colleagues new approaches to their research and new forms of evidence to seek, leading to system-atic investigations and quantitative analyses on a larger scale in order to prove or disprove my hypotheses.

The absolute chronology followed here is based on radiocarbon dates quoted in the chart and the text as B.C. which have been calcu-lated according to the 'old half-life' of 5570 ± 30 years; if the dates were calculated according to the 'new half-life' they would be some 200–300 years older. A further calculation on the basis of Suess's curve for Bristlecone pine dating in order to bring the radiocarbon years in line with earth years would make the dates still older by

300–400 years. It is clear, therefore, that those who wish to think in terms of absolute dates will have to indulge in mathematics. This fact, however, should not belittle the value of radiocarbon dates, not least in the field of relative dating.

To acknowledge the valuable help of all my colleagues in eastern Europe and Great Britain and to express my gratitude to those whose precious time I took up in various Museums and Institutes of Archaeology throughout eastern Europe would fill a whole book. I am especially grateful, in Bulgaria, to Dr G. Georgiev, Dr N. Džambazov, Dr R. Katinčarov and Mr B. Nikolov; in Czechoslovakia, to Professor Dr J. Filip, Dr A. Točik, Dr J. Neustupny, Dr J. Lichardus, Dr E. Neustupny, Dr I. Pavlu, Dr J. Pavuk, Dr M. Zapotocka and Dr R. Tichy; in Hungary, to Dr S. Bökönyi, Dr N. Kalicz, Dr I. B. Kutzian, Dr J. Makkay and Dr O. Trogmayer; in Rumania, to Dr D. Berciu, Dr E. Comşa, Professor V. Dumitrescu, Mr A. Florescu, Mr I. Paul, Dr M. Petrescu-Dîmboviţa, Mr N. Vlassa and Mme E. Zaharia; in Russia, to Dr T. S. Passek whose tragic death was such a shock to us all, and to Dr E. K. Černyš, Dr V. N. Danilenko, Dr P. Dolukhanov, Dr N. N. Gurina, Dr G. F. Korobkova, Dr N. J. Merpert, Dr V. Masson, Mme T. A. Popova, Dr S. A. Semeonov and Dr D. J. Telegin; in Moldavia, to Dr V. I. Markyěvič; and, in Yugoslavia, to Dr A. Benac, Dr B. Brukner, Dr B. Jovanović, Dr D. Srejović, Dr L. Szekeres and their American colleague, Dr A. McPherron.

I am also grateful to Dr H. Quitta and Dr G. Kohl of E. Berlin for their helpful advice and their kind information about their radiocarbon dates; it is primarily due to their efforts that so much of the east European neolithic material is now supported by radiocarbon dates.

To my colleagues in Britain and west Europe I also express my thanks, in particular to Dr J. Alexander, Mr A. Ammerman, Mr R. Newell, Dr C. Renfrew, Mr M. Rowlands, Professor T. Sulimirski, and my editor Dr John Coles.

I am indebted to the British Council, the University of Edinburgh, and the Wenner-Gren Foundation for Anthropological Research whose grants-in-aid and research fellowships enabled me to visit the Museums and Institutes of Archaeology of Eastern Europe for long periods and gain the first-hand familiarity with the material without which this book could not have been written.

Finally, I should like to express my deep gratitude to Professor Stuart Piggott of the University of Edinburgh, Dr Bohumil Soudsky of the Institute of Archaeology in Prague, and Dr Peter J. Ucko of the Department of Anthropology at University College, London, the last of whom spent valuable time in correcting this manuscript until it read like intelligible English. I am dedicating this work to them because of the encouragement and stimulation which they have given me in my research and because they have been the most instrumental in the formulation of the ideas expressed in this book.

London   R.T.
January 1971

1. Milojčic, V. (1949a): without any Carbon 14 dates and now generally out of date; Neustupny, E. (1968a); id. (1969); Quitta, H. (1967); Ehrich, R. (1965).
2. Childe, V. G. (1957), 84–136; Piggott, S. (1965), 40–56.
3. Trigger, B. (1968); Ucko, P. (1968); id. (1969a), 262–3; id. (1969b), 27–31.

I

ENVIRONMENTAL BACKGROUND

The territory covered by this book has been variously described as Eastern Europe,[1] East Central Europe,[2] the 'Eastern Marchlands' and more recently the 'territory of the People's Democracies'. In this book, the region is not defined by any rigid physical or political boundaries and the material discussed is frequently compared to the evidence from neighbouring regions: the Baltic coast in the north, Greece, the east Mediterranean and the Near East in the south, the Rhine basin in the west, and the steppes and forests of the USSR in the east. The dominant drainage system of this region is the Danube, but not all the valleys studied in this book belong to rivers which drain into the Danube; some like the Dniester drain into the Black Sea, some like the Vardar and Maritsa drain into the Mediterranean, and others like the Elbe and Vistula drain into the Baltic. Thus the region discussed in this book cannot be said to comprise a single geographical or even political unit. Many different geographical areas, ecological zones and culture areas are contained within it.

In any investigation of the patterns and processes of cultural development of a human population, it is necessary to understand their natural environment, every aspect of its potentialities and its limitations. Ideally this would involve a detailed study of the geology, geomorphology, pedology, climatic and vegetational history, faunal and floral content, etc., of the micro-region of each settlement or group of settlements. Unfortunately this has only ever been attempted on a very limited scale in the prehistoric studies of eastern Europe. It is possible, however, to make a few general observations on the geology and structure and the vegetational and climatic history of

eastern Europe. Evidence of the physical structure of eastern
Europe is readily available since it has changed very little in the last
10,000 years. Pollen analysis has been useful in reconstructing the
postglacial vegetational history of Europe north and north-east
of the Carpathian mountains, for example in N. Germany, Poland,
the Baltic States and Byelorussia, where pollen of arboreal and non-
arboreal species has been preserved in waterlogged conditions of
bogs. In central and south-east Europe, however, the soil conditions
have not been favourable for the preservation of floral remains, and
pollen has rarely been collected or analysed.

Structure and relief

The area with which this book is concerned may be divided on the
basis of structure and relief into four main regions:[3]

   1. The Russo-Siberian platform formed by very old sediments
which were covered by deposits of Mesozoic Age. The platform
extends westwards to include much of N.W. Europe and forms the
underlying structure of the north European and east European
plains. Much of this area was directly affected by the Pleistocene
glaciations and shows glaciated features including lake-filled hollows,
drumlins, and morainic accumulations of boulders, boulder clay, etc.
South of the maximum advance of the ice-sheet, the Mesozoic
deposits were covered by alluvial and periglacial deposits, as in
S.E. Germany, S. Poland, N.E. Rumania, Moldavian and Ukraine
SSRs. The plains rarely rise above 250 m above sea-level and are
characterised by large rivers draining into the Baltic and Black Seas.

   2. Palaeozoic deposits which later subsided, forming basins.
These were later filled with deposits of Pleistocene age, in particular
the periglacial aeolian loess deposits. Basins, such as the Pannonian–
Hungarian and Walachian plains are drained by the Danube–Tisza
system; others such as the Bohemian plain are drained by the north-
ward-flowing Elbe system.

   3. The Hercynian mountain system was formed at the end of the
Carboniferous period comprising predominantly granites and
gneisses, and includes the Harz and Bohemian–Moravian mountains
in C. Europe, the Rhodope–Macedonian mountains in S.E. Europe
and the Urals in the east. The mountains have been very much
eroded, levelled, intruded and covered by later deposits in the
Tertiary and Quarternary periods, so that they generally form steep-
sided hills, 800–1,500 m.a.s.l. with level, rounded summits.

   4. The younger Alpine folds, formed mostly in the Tertiary period,
are often of very high elevation, are much more inhospitable and
form real barriers to communications. East of the Alps themselves

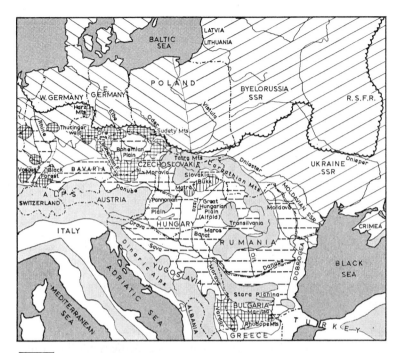

 Alpine mts

Hercynian mts

S. limit of ice-sheet

Volcanic massifs

Russo-Siberian platform

Platform and tabular region of secondary age

Basins partially covered with quaternary deposits (loess and alluvium)

Fig. 1

Map of the structural, physical and modern national divisions of E. Europe.

there are two main branches of Alpine mountains: towards the
north-east, the arc of the Carpathian mountains and the Transilvanian
Alps continues, south of the Danube, in the Balkan mountains or
Stara Planina. The Danube has cut its way through the mountains
in a series of gorges, the most famous of which is the Iron Gates.
The Carpathians formed the southern boundary of the north
European ice-sheet during the Pleistocene glaciations. The southern
extension of the Alpine system of mountains was along the western
part of the Balkan peninsula in the Dinaric Alps which are formed
mainly of Cretaceous limestone with characteristic karst scenery
and excessive drainage. In much of the eastern part of the Dinaric
Alps, in C. Yugoslavia the limestone has been eroded to reveal the
underlying Palaeozoic deposits resulting in more surface drainage.

Soils

On the basis of the present-day distribution of soils in eastern
Europe[4] and the evidence of buried soils on prehistoric sites it is
possible to make some general observations on the soils of the prehistoric settlements and their potentialities and limitations as
agricultural soils.

   Mountain soils are distributed in all upland regions regardless of
age. In every case their use is restricted at most to grazing, since they
are generally associated with cold and wet climatic conditions, occur
on steeply sloping ground and are rather shallow. These soils also
provide wood which may be used for charcoal and other fuel. In
many areas, for example the Dinaric Alps which are at present largely
without soil, there is vegetational and faunal evidence that in the
period with which this book is concerned there was a greater soil
covering. In addition there are pockets in these mountains, which
have fertile alluvial soil.

   North and east European plain soils are those of a cool and at
present humid climate. Leached or podsolised soils are characteristically formed under these climatic conditions and the degree of
podsolisation varies with the acidity of the bedrock, degree of
humidity, vegetation, drainage, etc. The highly podsolised soils
have been formed under coniferous forest on acid soils, the less
podsolised soils, such as grey-brown podsolic soils, have been formed
under deciduous forest from less acid rocks. In every case, however,
they are not very fertile and their cultivation is difficult without
deep ploughing and artificial fertilisers. The degree of podsolisation

Fig. 2
Map of the vegetation and hunting-gathering settlements of E. Europe
during the late Boreal vegetation period (Zone VI), *c.* 6500–5500 B.C.

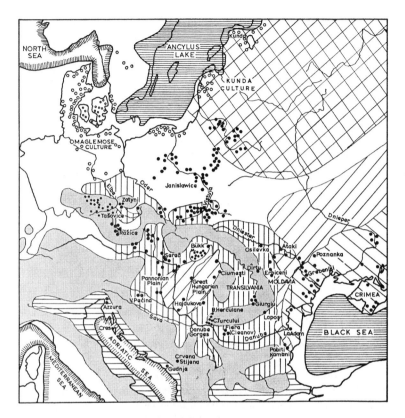

- •   Undated later postglacial hunter-gatherer sites

- ○   Hunter-gatherer sites dated to the Boreal vegetational period

Coastline

Semi-desert

Steppe

Forest-steppe

Oak-elm forest sub-Mediterranean vegetation

Mixed pine and deciduous forest

Mixed coniferous–birch forest

Mountain vegetation

Fig. 2

reached in the period with which this book is concerned is of course
very much open to question.

The *central European loess deposits* at present tend to have a less
leached brown forest soil, particularly on their periphery. These
have been formed under thick deciduous forest cover. They grade
into 'brunizems' and 'chernozems' which are very characteristic
of loess deposits although they may also be formed on sandy and
alluvial deposits. From the buried soils it would seem that the
'chernozems' were much more widespread in the prehistoric period
than at the present time. For instance, they occur in prehistoric
settlements of East Germany and west Czechoslovakia. It would
seem that they were formed in a temperate continental climate.
Whether they were formed under grassland or under forest cover is
still under discussion. They are very fine soils, fertile, easy to work
but are quickly eroded once their vegetational covering has been
removed. Although some alluvial deposits, particularly in south-
east Europe, for example in the Maritsa and Morava valleys, are
covered by brunizems and brown forest soils, in general alluvial soils
in eastern Europe were too poorly drained to be of any use to early
prehistoric agriculturalists, and were presumably covered by thick
gallery forests.

*Outline of the post-glacial climatic and vegetational history of
E. Europe*[5]

The most complete evidence of the climatic and vegetational history
comes, as mentioned above, from the north European plain. On the
basis of the pollen evidence from this area, the postglacial vegetational
history of northern Europe has been divided into vegetational zones
or periods.[6] The period with which this book is concerned involves
Zones VI–VIII. Naturally there are no sharp breaks between the
zones; they offer a rough guide to the vegetational and climatic
sequence of Europe.

Zone VI (*Late Boreal*). Dated by radiocarbon 6500–5500 B.C. The
evidence of the pollen indicates that over the continent of Europe
there was a tendency towards a more continental climate, that is
towards hot dry summers and cold dry winters. This involved an
increase in the glaciers in the mountains and shrinkage in the sea-
level which caused, among other things, the formation of a freshwater lake in the region of the present-day Baltic Sea. The extremes
of climate caused a general predominance of conifers and birch.
It is likely that mixed pine and oak forests, which at present form the
natural vegetation of the east Baltic, Byelorussia and central Europe
were distributed further south and west so that this type of forest
covered the north European plain and possibly the wetter non-

loess areas of central Europe. Pine and birch predominated on the drier podsolised and sandy soils and spruce on the boggier soils. On the more fertile brown forest soils it is likely that deciduous trees, such as oak, lime, hazel, birch, etc., predominated over conifers. Although there is no direct evidence of pollen remains from the loess deposits of central and east Europe, it has been inferred that the warm, dry summers of the Boreal period would have encouraged the growth of grassland, even true steppe on the dry permeable loess soils.[7] Similar conditions exist at the present time on the loess of north Pontic Russia. In this region trees grow only in the alluvial valleys. In south-east Europe there is pollen evidence from the Dalmatian coast which indicates that during this period the climate encouraged the growth of a mixed oak, hazel, elm and lime forest, of the type which occurs today in C. Europe but with the addition of certain sub-Mediterranean shrubs.[8] Pollen and malacological evidence from the lower Danube valley shows that at this time a forest/steppe vegetation predominated on the loess and alluvial deposits much the same as at present in that area.[9] Towards the mountains where the chernozems and brunizems graded into brown forest soils a more forested vegetation occurred, consisting in particular of deciduous trees. It is probable that a similar forest/steppe vegetation prevailed on the loess deposits as far as the Dniester valley.[10] East of this area, however, where forest/steppe grades into steppe grassland today, it is probable that in the Boreal period, with the greater aridity, steppe grassland graded into extreme steppe or even semi-desert.[11]

Zone VII (Atlantic). Dated by radiocarbon *c*. 5500–3000 B.C. As mentioned above there was no sudden increase of humidity, but from about 5500 B.C. there was a tendency for winters to be warmer and wetter, and summers to be cooler and wetter. The climate which is at present prevalent in the temperate maritime areas extended further east into European USSR. The Scandinavian and many Alpine glaciers disappeared completely. There was a general rise in the sea-level and in the area of the modern Baltic Sea the freshwater Ancylus Lake of the Boreal period was replaced by the salt-water Littorina Sea. In the north European plain there was an eastward spread of the maritime mixed oak forests although in the east Baltic area these were still mixed with a certain proportion of conifers, such as pine. On the more podsolised and acid soils these would have been lighter, but on the brown forest soils they must have been very dense with thick undergrowth. The forest tended to extend up the mountain sides *c*. 2–300 m higher than at present. The small amount of palaeobotanical evidence from the C. European loess deposits indicates that in this period they were covered by mixed oak, alder and spruce forest which varied in density according to the

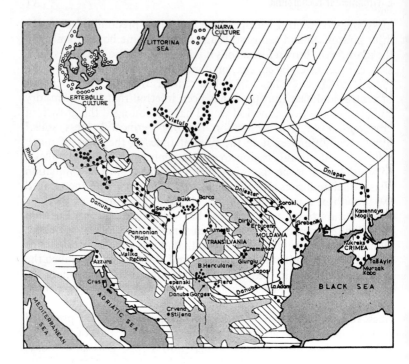

- Undated later postglacial hunter-gatherer sites
- Hunter-gatherer sites dated to the Atlantic vegetational period

Maritime oak forest

Forest-steppe

Oak–alder–spruce forest

Juniper and evergreen oak forest

Over 500 m.a.s.l. mountain vegetation

Mixed pine and deciduous forest

Steppe

Fig. 3
Map of the vegetation and hunting-gathering settlements of E. Europe
during the Atlantic vegetation period (Zone VIIa), *c.* 5500–3000 B.C.

underlying soil and the drainage of the loess. In general, however, they were lighter than the forests of the N. European plain. An increase in tree pollen can be seen in the lower Danube basin and Moldavia but this was of hazel, lime, elm and birch rather than oak and alder. The north Pontic area of the USSR would seem to have been rather more tree-covered than at present. On the Mediterranean coast evergreen forest including juniper predominated (as in present-day inland Mediterranean areas such as Anatolia and Africa) until the latter half of the Atlantic vegetational period. Everywhere in Europe there is evidence that the maximum growth of forest was reached *c.* 4000 B.C. after which the climate gradually became more continental and the present-day distribution of Mediterranean evergreen oak forest along the coast and of steppe and forest-steppe in the north Pontic area was reached.

In north-west and central Europe, however, the climate did not stabilise into its present-day conditions until much more recently.[12] Even now the climate is much less predictable in these regions. After the vegetational climax there is evidence in the temperate maritime areas of Europe that in the vegetational period known as *Zone VIII or VIIb (Sub-Boreal)* the climate became more continental and the maritime oak forests on the north European plain were replaced by the lighter beech woods on brown forest soils and mixed oak and hornbeam woods on the more podsolised and acid soils. A similar mixed oak and hornbeam forest occurred on the loess deposits of central and south-east Europe at this time. However, by 3000 B.C. a further factor was affecting the growth of forest and the vegetation apart from climate and geology. This was the effect of cultivation of the land and clearance of forest by an increasing human population. Even during the Atlantic period there is evidence in the loess plains of central and south-east Europe of intensive human activity which must have involved a certain amount of forest clearance. The area of sedentary settlements based on a food-producing economy was extended to the brown forest and podsolised soils of the N. European plain in a period which coincided with the Atlantic–Sub-Boreal transition. The dual effect of Man in clearing the forest and intensively collecting shoots and leaves for animal fodder and the increasingly continental climate caused a sudden decrease of various trees such as elm and hornbeam. This phenomenon, which has been referred to as the 'elm decline', may be seen in the palaeobotanical evidence from numerous sites in N.W. Europe.

C

1. Pounds, N. (1969).
2. Ehrich, R. (1965).
3. Pounds, N. (1969), 11–18.
4. Pounds, N. (1969), 34–7.
5. Butzer, K. (1965a); id. (1965b); Firbas, F. (1949); Waterbolk, T. (1968).
6. N.W. Europe: Kubitzki, K., 'Zur synchronisierung der nordwesteuropäischen Pollendiagramme', *Flora*, 150, Jena (1961); Kubitzki, K. and Munnich, K., 'Neue C 14 Datierung zur nacheiszeitlichen Waldgeschichte Nordwestdeutschlands', *Deutsche Botanische Gesellschaft*, 73, E. Berlin (1960). N.E. Europe: Dolukhanov, P. M., 'Poslelednikovaya istoriya Baltiki i khronologiya neolita', *Noviye Metode v Arkheologičeskikh Issledovaniyakh*, Moscow (1963), 57–76; Szafer, W., *The Vegetation of Poland*, Warsaw (1966), 561–93.
7. For a discussion of the vegetation of loess soils: Butzer, K. (1965a), 446; Garnett, A. (1945); Leimbach, W., 'Zur Waldsteppenfrage in der Sowjetunion', *Erdkunde*, II (1948), 238–56; Ložek, V., 'Die quatäre Klimaentwicklung in der Tschechoslowakei', *Quartär*, XVII (1966), 1–20; Wilhemy, H., 'Das Alter der Schwarzerde und der Steppen Mittel- und Ost-europas', *Erdkunde*, IV (1950), 5–34; Vadasz, E., 'Zur prähistorischen Siedlungs- und Klimageschichte des Bezirks von Kalocsa', *A Mora F. Muz. Evkönyve*, Szeged (1969), 83–92.
8. Beug, H.-J., 'Beiträge zur postglazialen Floren- und Vegetationsgeschichte in Süd-Dalmazien: Der Zee "Malo ezero" auf Mljet', *Flora*, 150 (1961), 601–56.
9. Leroi-Gourhan, A., Mateesco, C., et al, 'Contribution à l'étude du climat de la station de Vădastra du Paléolithique superieur à la fin du Néolithique', *Bull. Assoc. Française Étude Quatenaire*, 4, Paris (1967–8), 271; Protopopescu-Pake, E., Mateescu, C., Grosso, A., 'Formation des conches de civilisation de la station de Vădastra en rapport avec le sol, la faune palaeocologique et le climat', *Quartär*, 20 (1970), 135–62.
10. Markyevič, V. I., *Neolit Moldavii*, unpublished thesis for Kandidat Istoričeskikh Nauk degree in Inst. of Archaeology, ANSSSR, Moscow (1968).
11. Sulimirski, T. (1970), 27–8.
12. Frenzel, B., 'Climatic change in the Atlantic/sub-Boreal transition in the northern hemisphere: botanical evidence', *World Climate from 8000–0 B.C.*, Royal Met. Soc., London (1966), 99–123.

2

POSTGLACIAL HUNTING AND

GATHERING COMMUNITIES IN

EASTERN EUROPE

In the period immediately preceding the introduction of agriculture and a food-producing economy into south-east and central Europe there existed groups of food-gatherers scattered over a variety of terrains. They were distributed especially along the banks of rivers and lakes in areas of sand dunes, and the foothills of mountains, but avoided the loess plains of Europe. In some areas they survived alongside the earliest of the food-producing groups, but there is rarely any evidence to indicate that there was contact between the two. For most of the postglacial food-gathering, or mesolithic, settlements, dating evidence is lacking. In some cases it is possible to relate them to the climatic/vegetational periods of northern Europe from the evidence provided by the pollen remains in the habitation debris. For the most part, however, attempts to construct a chronological framework for these settlements have been based on the morphological classification of their chipped stone tools.

Not only is it often impossible to assign a more specific date to the mesolithic settlements than 'postglacial', but there is little more than sporadic evidence for their environment, means of subsistence, and material culture, apart from the chipped stone industry. The material from the mesolithic settlements, compared with that from the preceding Upper Palaeolithic settlements of the Late Pleistocene period, or the succeeding early neolithic settlements, is very poor. But this need not be explained by any 'cultural or economic degeneration' due to drastic climatic changes of the early postglacial period and the re-adaptation which these necessitated. Certainly these changes had their effects, but it was rather to encourage settlement of the sandy alluvial areas and limestone uplands. The former produces soils with a high acid content, and the latter produces very thin soil, and, as such, both are unfavourable to the preservation of organic material such as antler, bone and wood, or traces of habitations. The periglacial basins, in which rich debris of the Upper Palaeolithic settlements has been preserved in thick loess deposits, were completely abandoned by the mesolithic hunters and gatherers. Settlement in caves also became much rarer. In the cases where there are postglacial habitation layers inside caves, these provide some of the rare evidence of organic material.

The early postglacial background

In the final stages of the Würm glaciation and the early postglacial periods, from approximately 11,000–7000 B.C., the settlements in eastern Europe which are referred to as Late Palaeolithic or Epipalaeolithic, represent the successors of the various Upper Palaeolithic groups. Their chipped stone industries provide a link between the Upper Palaeolithic and later postglacial or mesolithic industries.[1]

In the western part of eastern Europe, along the valleys of the upper Elbe and upper Danube rivers, settlements of the successors of the Magdalenian reindeer hunters, referred to as the 'Epi-magdalenians', have been discovered, but in the majority of cases without any satisfactory dating evidence.[2] In the eastern part of east Europe, the early postglacial sites on river terraces and mountain foothills have chipped stone industries which have strong links with east Gravettian industry utilised by Upper Palaeolithic mammoth hunters. The sites are often referred to as 'Epigravettian'. These have been dated by Carbon 14 evidence to the 9th millennium B.C., and by palaeobotanical evidence to the Allerød and Younger Dryas climatic/vegetation periods.[3] The sites are characterised by small blades steeply retouched down one or both longitudinal edges to form narrow pointed or parallel-sided tools.

In north-eastern Europe, particularly in east Poland and west Byelorussia SSR, settlements are distributed predominantly on sand dunes with a chipped stone industry referred to as 'Swiderian'. Among the stone implements of these sites, there occur large numbers of tanged triangular pointed implements which have generally been interpreted as arrowheads. The animals on which the arrowheads were used, however, remain unknown due to the lack of preservation of bone material in the sandy soils. Arrowheads of 'Swiderian' type have been found as far east as the Oka river in the eastern part of European Russia. In these sites, however, they are associated with quite a different set of stone implements and are dated to a different period. It seems very unlikely that they represent the slow eastwards spread of a population. It is possible that this particular implement was diffused from the west, along with the method of hunting with a bow and arrow. It seems more likely, however, that the occurrence of 'Swiderian points' over such a widespread area represents a series of independent responses to particular environmental conditions.[4] 'Swiderian points' occur sporadically south of Poland, but only on two sites in any quantity.[5]

Evidence of food-gathering groups in the early postglacial period in south-east Europe occurs in cave-sites scattered in the limestone mountains but without any definite dating evidence. The Late Palaeolithic habitation layers of certain cave-sites in S.E. Europe contain a chipped stone industry which has morphological similarities to the 'Epigravettian' further north and east, in that the tools consist predominantly of narrow blades with one or both lateral edges blunted by deliberate retouch.[6] There is no evidence, however, to suggest that this is the result of widespread diffusion of the Epigravettian industry, but may be rather a local evolution from the industries of the late glacial Upper Palaeolithic settlements.

Later postglacial (mesolithic) settlements

The paucity of material from the mesolithic settlements of eastern Europe (Figs. 2, 3) has forced many prehistorians to divide them into spatial and chronological groups on the basis, for lack of any other criterion, of morphological stone types. The use of this basis for a classification to distinguish archaeological cultures, which are defined as consistently recurring assemblages of various artefact types representing a comprehensive picture of human activities, is questionable. It is a dangerous assumption that, because there is a certain amount of homogeneity in the form, and possibly the function and technology, of stone tools, there is therefore a similar uniformity in other aspects of behavioural patterns and material culture.

In eastern Europe it is possible to distinguish certain groups of settlements which have relatively uniform sets of stone tools, from the point of view of technology, form, and function. They may be described most accurately as belonging to various 'industries'. In most cases, it is dubious, considering the fact that the preserved archaeological material consists only of chipped stone, whether the accepted classification of mesolithic assemblages may be used or extended to define cultures, or even 'techno-complexes'. These latter terms imply artefacts in a greater range of materials and representing a more comprehensive range of activities, including an 'interlinked response to common factors in environment, economy and technology'.[7] However, the mesolithic settlements in the present

Baltic coastal area, often referred to as the 'Baltic forest culture', may well be interpreted as two successive techno-complexes. The waterlogged soils on which these settlements are situated have preserved evidence of the climate and vegetation at that time, of the means of subsistence, and artefacts in a variety of raw materials including wood and bone. Within the large techno-complex in this area, various smaller groups may be distinguished and have been classically interpreted as cultures (p. 58), including Maglemose and Ertebølle in the west Baltic and Kunda in the east.

It is much more difficult to accept the interpretation of the assemblages of predominantly 'geometric' microlithic stone implements, often referred to as the 'Tardenoisian', in terms of a techno-complex stretching 'from the Balkans to Britain and from Spain to Poland'.[8] It is even questionable whether the term 'industry' can be applied to these assemblages of stone tools in eastern Europe, since they do not form a 'continuous space-time area'; they are interspersed with 'non-geometric' microlithic as well as non-microlithic stone assemblages. Settlements with predominantly 'geometric' microlithic stone industries are not situated in a uniform topographical position. Some are at the bottom of river valleys, some on the high plateaus, and others on slopes and river terraces. From the lack of evidence, it is impossible to tell whether there was any uniformity in their means of subsistence beyond the fact that they were food-gathering, or whether there was a corresponding homogeneity in artefacts made in other raw materials which have not survived.

Thus, as far as the mesolithic settlement of eastern Europe is concerned, we have to be content with building up a picture of

---

Fig. 4

Mesolithic and neolithic stone techniques.

a Method of manufacturing microlithic blades by truncating large blades (after Bordaz, 1970).

b–c Method of manufacturing microlithic blades by striking bladelets from microcores. *b* Pencil-shaped micro-core from Erbiceni, N.E. Rumania (after Păunescu, 1970). *c* Method of retouching bladelet into required shape (after Bordaz, 1970).

d Microlithic blades slotted as barbs in an antler spearhead. Menturren, N.E. USSR (E. Prussia) Kunda culture (after S. Kozlowski, 1965).

e Microlithic blades slotted as knife edge in an antler handle. Raigorod, Ukraine SSSR. Dnieper-Donetz culture (after Telegin, 1968).

f Microlithic blades inserted as tip and barb in an arrowhead. Løshult, Sweden (after Clark, 1967).

g–h Reconstructions of microlithic blades inserted as tips in arrows (after Clark).

i–j Blades inserted in antler handle and used as a sickle. Karanovo, Bulgaria (after Georgiev, 1958). *i* the sickle as excavated. *j* Detail of the blade inserts. Dotted area denotes 'sickle-gloss'.

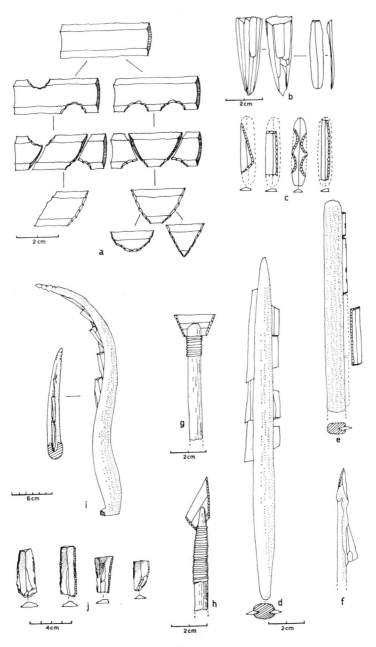

Fig. 4

industries, and of the settlement patterns connected with these, supplemented by sporadic evidence for the natural environment, economy, and habitations.

A widespread feature of the stone industries of all the mesolithic settlements of eastern Europe is the tendency towards diminution in the size of the blades. Microlithic blades are a distinctive feature of the mesolithic assemblages not only throughout eastern Europe, but as far east as the Urals, and throughout western Europe.[9] There are a few areas where they are much less common, in particular the Hungarian and inland Yugoslav cave-sites, and the Iron Gates settlements on the Danube. Microlithic blades occurred in the stone industry of several Upper Palaeolithic settlements of eastern Europe, such as Pavlov in Czechoslovakia, and the Crimean peninsula in southern USSR. They occur with increasing frequency in the Late Palaeolithic settlements and predominate in many of the mesolithic stone assemblages. Along the Baltic littoral they occur in association with heavy chipped and polished stone axes. In the rest of east Europe they occur in association with longer blades which may or may not have been retouched into different shapes.

There are two main techniques for producing microlithic blades,[10] and it is the distinction of these two techniques (Fig. 4), rather than any size criterion, which is important in the classification of microlithic blades. First, the blades may be struck directly off a microcore, in which case they are distinguished by their narrowness rather than their short length. These microblades were especially common in the area north of the Black Sea. The second method was to strike a long blade off a macrocore, and to snap this blade into short lengths; the truncated segments were finished off by deliberate retouch into a variety of shapes including trapezes, triangles, and lunates, which are referred to in general as 'geometric microliths'. They are distinguished by their short length in relation to their width. In western Europe 'geometric microlithic' blades characterise the latest mesolithic settlements. They occur all over eastern Europe, predominantly in undated contexts.

In the waterlogged settlements of the Baltic coastal region, microlithic blades are found inserted singly or compositely in antler, bone, and wooden hafts. They could act as a continuous cutting edge down one or both sides of the haft of a thrusting or projected weapon such as a spear, or of a curved or straight knife. The advantage of using microblades as inserts for cutting implements is that the microlithic segments were snapped off the middle sections of long blades where the maximum strength and sharpness is found; thus, once they were retouched to a regular shape and size, they could be inserted close together to form a continuous strong sharp edge of unlimited length. Similarly, a curved cutting edge could be produced more easily by inserting microlithic segments into a curved handle. If long blades were inserted into a curved haft, the edge would either be discontinuous or the blades would have to be inserted diagonally as with the later neolithic European sickles. Both methods would produce an edge of uneven strength and sharpness. Microlithic blades are also found inserted as barbs for spearheads, arrowheads, and harpoons, or inserted singly at the end of the arrowshaft to act as the actual piercing head. The advantage of using microlithic blades as inserts on projectile implements is that their light weight will not affect the speed or balanced path of flight, yet they will cause the weapon to penetrate deeply and hold firmly.

Although hafted microlithic blades have not been discovered outside the area of the 'Baltic forest culture' in eastern Europe, owing to the lack of preservation of organic material, it is presumed that they were all used for a similar variety of implements to those described above.

The majority of mesolithic assemblages in eastern Europe have not been excavated but are from surface collections. The sites which have been excavated show a very thin habitation layer, rarely thicker than 0·5 m, often very near the surface and partially destroyed. Traces of surface habitations are very rare. They are limited to hearths,[11] or concentrations of burnt flint and bones which are possibly related to habitation remains.[12] These are possibly the traces of light wooden constructions or tents. The only direct evidence for more substantial surface structures comes from Lepenski Vir in N.E. Yugoslavia, where a number of trapezoid plaster floors was excavated. These were surrounded by post-holes reinforced by stones which probably represent the basis of a solid wooden superstructure. Other traces of habitations are shallow pits.[13] The pits are of a long irregular ovaloid shape, ranging from 9 to 6 metres long, and 2 to 5 metres wide, and never more than 1 metre deep. Several of the pits have traces of hearths in and around them, and one of the pits at Tašovice had small post-holes surrounding it. This would suggest that some of the pits were used as habitations with a light wooden or skin superstructure. But it does not mean that all pits excavated on mesolithic sites should automatically be interpreted as dwelling places.

To talk of movements and diffusion of people, techniques or ideas with reference to the mesolithic population of eastern Europe, or the whole of Europe for that matter, is very dangerous in view of the limited material and evidence of relative or absolute dating of the settlements. There was an increasing tendency towards the manufacture of microlithic stone blades in many areas of Europe from about 8000 to 4500 B.C. It is not yet possible to decide whether these were the result of independent response to the same changes in the environment of Europe at this time, or whether they were the result of migration of the hunters and gatherers themselves, or of diffusion of the techniques associated with the manufacture of composite tools with small stone blades.

Evidence for the chronology of the mesolithic settlements of eastern Europe comes from two main sources, radiocarbon dating and the evidence of pollen analysis. Radiocarbon dates provide evidence of absolute dating from only four areas in eastern Europe:[14]

1. The east Baltic coastal area, from the sites of Kunda and Narva in Estonia. The dates range from 6500–3550 B.C. and come from samples representing at least two successive cultures, possibly corresponding to the Maglemosian and Ertebølle cultures of the west Baltic area.

2. Witow, central Poland, 6230 ± 140 B.C. The sample (K 954) was associated with a predominantly geometric microlithic stone industry, stratified above a Late Palaeolithic 'Swiderian' industry.

3. Soroki II, layers 2 and 3, Moldavia SSR. Two mesolithic layers dated c. 5500 B.C.

4. Lepenski Vir, layers I and II, N.E. Yugoslavia, series of dates c. 5500–4600 B.C.

In northern Europe it is possible, by analysis of the pollen remains from the mesolithic settlements, to reconstruct the surrounding vegetation and to correlate this analysis with the postglacial vegetational periods or zones. The postglacial vegetational history of northern Europe has been well dated by Carbon 14 dates:

Pre-Boreal (zone IV):	c. 8000–6800 B.C.
Early Boreal (zone V):	c. 6800–6500 B.C.
Late Boreal (zone VI):	c. 6500–5500 B.C.
Atlantic (zone VII or VIIa):	c. 5500–3000 B.C.

Outside northern Europe, on the basis of palaeobotanical evidence such as pollen remains and carbonised wood and gastropodal evidence, it is possible to a certain extent to correlate increased aridity with the Boreal vegetational period and increased humidity

Fig. 5

Mesolithic houses at Lepenski Vir (after Srejović, 1969).

a Ground-plan of House 37. Shaded area denotes the limestone plaster floor covered with red burnished surface.

b Reconstruction of a house at Lepenski Vir.

c Stone slab, possibly used as a club with incised designs (after Srejović, 1969).

d Stone head with human-fish characteristics (after Renfrew, 1969).

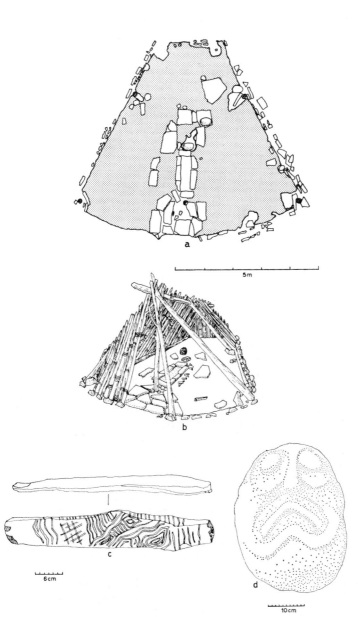

Fig. 5

with the Atlantic period. However, some of the attributions of climatic-vegetational conditions to particular north European vegetational periods should be regarded with extreme caution, since they may not be related to the general climatic development of northern Europe, but rather may be due to local conditions.[15] These sources do provide at least valuable evidence for the micro-environments of the mesolithic settlements of central and south-east Europe.

Upper Elbe basin

The mesolithic settlements of west Czechoslovakia located on sandy river terraces and limestone foothills have all been assigned to the 'early mesolithic' period. It is clear, however, from the vegetational evidence as well as the chipped stone industries that there is more than one period of mesolithic settlement represented in this region.[16] At some sites, similar assemblages to those of the Late Upper Palaeolithic Magdalenian and Epimagdalenian industries of this region have been excavated but with evidence for a local environment of mixed pine-hazel forest.[17] At other sites evidence for greater forest development with mixed pine-beech forest is associated with a stone industry consisting of 'geometric' microliths as well as long retouched blades.[18] It has been suggested that most of the meso-lithic settlements in west Czechoslovakia were contemporary with the Boreal, or perhaps Pre-Boreal, periods. In north-west Czecho-slovakia, however, near the Elbe–Vltava confluence, there is a group of three settlements, the best documented of which is the cave of Zatýni.[19] The palaeobotanical evidence indicates a mixed pine-hazel-oak forest during the period of mesolithic settlement, and the mollusca indicate a very damp but relatively warm climate without any extremes of temperature or precipitation. It has been suggested, therefore, that this settlement should be assigned to the Atlantic vegetational period, or later mesolithic phase. None of the stone implements at Zatýni is more than 3 cm long, but they comprise narrow microblades rather than 'geometric' microlithic blades. There are no bone implements from the site, but among the animal bone remains there is evidence for mixed hunting of woodland animals such as roe-deer and wild pig, pine marten and rabbit, as well as various birds, turtles, and for fishing, in particular carp.

In the limestone foothills north of the Ore mountains in the southern part of East Germany a series of mesolithic settlements of various phases has been discovered.[20] Most are unexcavated and none has provided any evidence for environment or chronology. As with those of west Czechoslovakia, some of the sites have a stone tool assemblage which is identical to that of the Epimagdalenian sites, others have 'geometric' microlithic blades as well as macro-lithic blades.

The Pannonian plain

Settlements with a predominantly 'geometric' microlithic industry have been discovered on the sandy dune-like mounds which provide dry ground in the seasonally waterlogged flood plains of the Danube and its tributaries. Surface collections of trapezes, triangles and lunates have been made sporadically in N. Yugoslavia, W. Hungary, N.E. Austria and S.C. Czechoslovakia.[21] One or two of the sites have been excavated, for example Sered' in S. Czechoslovakia.[22] It has been assumed that all these assemblages date to the later part of the mesolithic, that is the period immediately before or contemporary with the first appearance of food-producing groups in the same area.[23] This assumption is based on stylistic analogies with west European mesolithic sites where the assemblages of the later habitation layers of stratified sites show a predominance of 'geometric' microlithic blades. Support for this assumption has been sought in the palaeobotanical evidence from Sered' which indicates the presence of a mixed pine-oak forested environment during the mesolithic settlement. This may correlate with the moistening of the climate and thickening of the forest during the early Atlantic vegetational period, that is *c.* 5500–4500 B.C. An analysis of the animal bone material at Sered' produced the controversial evidence of domesticated cattle and pig in association with a mesolithic stone assemblage. The bones have since been tested for fluorine content, however, and many of them, including all those of the domesticated animals, clearly belong to the Halstatt Iron Age settlement on the same site.[24] The majority of wild animal bones are of large forest animals such as red-deer and wild cattle (aurochs). Part of the economy of the mesolithic settlements at Sered' must therefore have been based on hunting, and part on shell collecting. Although the settlement is very close to running water there is no evidence for fishing.

On the river terraces above these sites there are scattered settle-ments with a stone tool assemblage consisting predominantly of long narrow blunted blades and very few 'geometric' microlithic blades.[25] Although they have been termed Early Mesolithic they could as easily be dated to the Late Palaeolithic Epigravettian industry.

Great Hungarian plain

In the north-eastern corner of the plain is an area of alluvial sands blown into dunes, known as the Nyirseg. The stone tool assemblages of the sites on the dunes consist almost exclusively of 'geometric' microlithic blades. The assemblages are very similar to those of the Pannonian plain except that more implements are made of obsidian. This material produces a sharper edge than flint, but is not so strong. It was obtained from sources in the Bükk and Matra mountains about 180 km away in N.E. Hungary. It is interesting to note that at Ciumeşti in N.W. Rumania, half the blades from one such mesolithic site of Păsune were made of obsidian, whereas almost all the chipped stone artefacts from the nearby early neolithic site of Beria were made of obsidian.[26] In the Bükk and Matra mountains themselves obsidian was used relatively infrequently in the manufacture of the blades in the mesolithic settlements.[27]

Today the Nyirseg is covered by thick pine forests. The animal bone material from Ciumeşti (Păsune) indicates that animals which prefer a mixed deciduous forested environment such as roe-deer, aurochs, and wild pig provided an important part of the food supply. It is therefore presumed that this settlement existed at a time when the climate was relatively humid and the forest well developed, probably coinciding with the Atlantic period.

Central and south Poland

Sites whose assemblages consist predominantly of 'geometric' microlithic blades have been discovered north of the Carpathian mountains on the alluvial sands of the Vistula and its tributaries, and, to a lesser extent, the Oder river. In the past, the different assemblages have been assigned *en masse* to the 'Tardenoisian'.[28] Recently, however, a typological classification of the internal evolution of 'geometric' microlithic industries in Poland has been constructed on the basis of morphological comparison with the west European Tardenoisian industries, and several 'cultures' such as Komornica, Janislawice, and Czerwony Borek or Majdan have been distinguished. There is very little definite chronological evidence for the microlithic blade industries of Poland. Apart from the radiocarbon date from Witow referred to above, at Ostrowo on the lower Vistula microlithic blades were found in a fossil humus layer which, for geological reasons, has been dated to the humid Atlantic period. In addition the mesolithic site of Konin near Poznan yielded pollen evidence which dated it to the Atlantic period. The industries from the two latter sites have been identified on morphological grounds as 'late Tardenoisian'.[29] Thus there were clearly settlements of hunters and gatherers in existence in this area with a 'geometric' microlithic stone industry at least at the end of the Boreal period and beginning of the Atlantic period, and possibly before. It is clear, however, that the relevant criteria for distinguishing 'cultures' or any finer categories than 'industries' are lacking in the Polish evidence. It is also impossible to tell whether or not they represent a local evolution from the epipalaeolithic Swiderian industry.

The only evidence of a burial and artefacts made from organic materials in a mesolithic settlement in central Europe comes from the site of Janislawice near Warsaw.[30] The skeleton was buried in what seems to be a sitting position in a grave-pit which cut through the alluvial sand. The burial was accompanied by microlithic blades, long blades and cores. There were also several implements such as points, knife-like tools, and chisel-like tools made of aurochs and red-deer bones, and boars' tusks, as well as a small bone needle, perforated red-deer incisor teeth, and a beaver jaw-bone. On the basis of geological evidence and similarities of the chipped stone industry to the Danish Svaerdborg assemblage, the burial has been dated to the Late Boreal period. Apart from the unlikelihood of there being any connection between the Danish and Polish assemblages, the presence of bones of forest animals such as aurochs, red-deer, and wild pig could indicate either Boreal or Atlantic vegetational conditions.

Moldavia

Rather more positive evidence for chronology and economy comes from a group of settlements near Soroki in the middle Dniester valley. The sites are located on the narrow bank between the river and the steep slope of the lowest terrace. The chalk cliffs which rise above the river in this region provide a local source of flint. Two of the sites which have been excavated contain habitation layers representing settlements of hunters and gatherers stratified below layers containing a very similar chipped stone industry but with pottery and evidence for a fully developed food-producing economy based on stock-breeding and agriculture.[31] The mesolithic layers are only about 20 cm thick. At one of the sites (Soroki II) two mesolithic layers (3 and 2) were separated by a sterile layer which, as the Carbon 14 dates show, probably represents not more than 100 years (p. 221). On both sites there are shallow ovaloid pits which have been interpreted as semi-subterranean dwellings. It is assumed that they had a light wooden or skin superstructure although there is no positive evidence for this in the form of post-holes. The interiors of the pits contain one or more hearths, and often a stone-working area. Hearths also occur on the old land surface of the habitation layers. These latter have been interpreted as summer dwellings in the form of light surface structures of which no trace has survived. In support of this hypothesis, the surface hearths contain or are

surrounded by thick layers of freshwater mollusca shells and bones
of carp and roach whose exploitation is most profitable in the
summer. The semi-subterranean dwellings are interpreted as winter
or autumn habitations since the hearths inside them either did not
contain any mollusca (site II, layer 3), or were stratified with layers
containing mollusca shells alternating with layers without shells.
In the autumn certain mollusca are inedible.

Apart from collecting freshwater mollusca, the animal bone
evidence shows that hunting and fishing were both very important
sources of food and raw material. Forest animals such as red-deer,
roe-deer, aurochs, wild pig, fox, wolf, and rabbit were hunted, as
well as beaver. It is possible that some of the microlithic blades were
used as heads and barbs for projectiles such as spears and arrows,
or that some of the small bone points were used as projectile heads.
The presence of bones of domesticated dog may indicate that this
animal was used in hunting. There is no direct evidence, however,
for the methods of hunting the forest animals. Nor is there any
evidence of the methods of catching the large numbers of fish which
are found in these settlements. The majority of the fish belong to the
carp family, in particular the roach (*rutilus frisii*). This is a small
species of carp containing much less meat than most of the carp
family and being much more gregarious in nature. In modern times
they are extensively angled, but on the mesolithic sites there is no
evidence for the use of fish-hooks. It is more likely that the postglacial hunters took advantage of the shallow fast-flowing water
of the Bug and Dniester to construct traps such as weirs, or to use
nets.

Although there is no evidence for the methods of acquiring food,
there is direct evidence for the methods of processing it. The chipped
stone implements of the Soroki sites have been analysed for traces of
wear in the form of scars and scratches on their surface. By this
method, blades used as knives for cutting soft material, perhaps meat
or skins or even fish, have been identified. One of these knives was
found hafted in an antler handle. Other flint blades were used to
scrape meat or skins. Other blades were used to work on hard
material such as wood or bone, by cutting and scraping, as well as
sawing, boring and grooving. Evidence for the bone implements in
whose manufacture the stone tools were possibly used includes
antler picks and axes, some of which were perforated to hold a
handle, as well as knives made of boars' tusks and the bone points
mentioned above. The majority of chipped stone blades at Soroki
are macrolithic, and their shape has been modified by deliberate
retouch, especially by blunting or flattening of the distal end, a
technique used frequently in the Upper and Late Palaeolithic

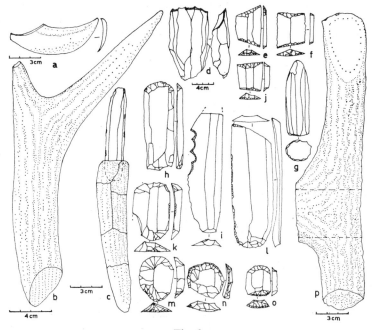

Fig. 6

Bone, antler and stone implements from the Bug–Dniester mesolithic
and neolithic cultures. Soroki, Moldavian SSR, USSR (Institute of
Archaeology, Kišinev).

a Knife made of split pig's tusk. Soroki II, layer 2 (mesolithic).
b Pick of red-deer antler. Soroki II, layer 2 (mesolithic).
c Flint knife blade inserted in antler handle. Soroki II, layer 3 (mesolithic).
d Blade core. Soroki I, layer 1b (neolithic–early phase) (after Markyevič,
1965).
e Trapeze-shaped microlithic blade. Soroki I, layer 1b (neolithic–early
phase).
f Trapeze-shaped microlithic blade. Soroki II, layer 3 (mesolithic).
g Pencil-shaped micro-core. Soroki II, layer 3 (mesolithic).
h Blade used as a scraper. Soroki I, layer 1b (neolithic–early phase).
i Blade used as a whittler. Soroki II, layer 3 (mesolithic).
j Trapeze-shaped microlithic blade. Soroki II, layer 2 (mesolithic).
k Blade used as a scraper. Soroki II, layer 3 (mesolithic).
l Blade used as a knife. Soroki II, layer 3 (mesolithic).
m–n Small scrapers. Soroki II, layer 3 (mesolithic).
o Small scraper. Soroki I, layer 1b (neolithic–early phase).
p Perforated antler 'axe'. Soroki II, layer 2 (mesolithic).
Unless otherwise stated, all the objects are drawn to scale 2:1.

D

industries of this region. There are relatively few microlithic blades. 'Geometric' microliths which predominate in the industries of the lower Dniester valley are very rare in these middle Dniester settlements, and in this respect the stone assemblage is closer to the upper Dniester assemblages.[32]

The pollen and carbonised remains of plants of the mesolithic settlements at Soroki indicate a very similar vegetation to the present-day deciduous light woodland of birch, maple, ash, and poplar. Gastropodal evidence also indicates the same environment with a possibly slightly higher rainfall than at present. These indications and the Carbon 14 dates of *c.* 5500–5400 B.C. would synchronise the mesolithic settlement of the middle Dniester valley with the beginning of the Atlantic vegetational period of northern Europe. It has been claimed that already in the mesolithic layers of the Soroki settlements there were domesticated dog, pig, and cattle. From the radiocarbon evidence these settlements could have been contemporary with the early food-producing settlements of the Danube basin and south-east Europe (Figs. 8, 39), but there is no indication from their material culture that there was any form of contact. It also seems unlikely that the settlements of early food-producing groups which do occur west of the Dniester in N.E. Rumania should be dated as early as 5500 B.C. The possibility of local domestication cannot be excluded. Domesticated dog appears as early as the pre-Boreal period in the hunting and gathering settlements of northern Europe, as well as in the mesolithic settlements of the Danube gorges at a period contemporary with the Soroki mesolithic settlements. Domesticated pigs have been claimed in the mesolithic cave settlements of Zamil Koba and Taš Ayir in the Crimean peninsula. They are associated with a chipped stone industry referred to as the 'Crimean Tardenoisian' which shows close affinities in its 'geometric' microlithic assemblage with the lower Dniester mesolithic sites, and certain similarities with the mesolithic sites of the middle Dniester.[33] There is no proof, however, that the aceramic layers at Taš Ayir and Zamil Koba are not much later than is claimed, nor that they did not exist at a time when the techniques of animal domestication had long been familiar on the mainland of the Ukraine. It was pointed out, in this context, that with encouragement, pigs like dogs will attach themselves relatively easily to a human group as scavengers, and may be bred quickly in captivity, but that they revert as easily to the wild state.[34] It should be noted that it is often very difficult to distinguish osteologically between young wild pigs and domesticated adults. A similar claim for very early independent development of animal domestication was made with reference to the cattle discovered in the site of Kamennaya Mogila, N.W. of the Sea of

Azov. These were also associated with a 'geometric' microlithic stone industry, the dating of which is as dubious as that of the 'Crimean Tardenoisian'. At Soroki, however, the chronological position of the bones identified as domesticated pigs and cattle has been established. The possibility cannot be excluded that there was some form of contact between the middle Dniester mesolithic sites and the early neolithic settlements further west which has no reflection in the archaeological material apart from the technique, or at least the idea, of domesticating animals.

Between the middle Dniester and the earliest neolithic groups in south-east Europe are mesolithic settlements which have quite a different topographical location. They are situated on the upper terraces of river valleys or the edge of high plateaus.[35] The chipped stone industries of these sites are predominantly microlithic, including 'geometric' microliths as well as microblades struck from conical microcores. They therefore show a greater resemblance to the assemblages of the lower Dniester sites, and the Crimean 'Tardenoisian' sites, than to the nearby sites of the middle Dniester valley. Evidence for the vegetation at Erbiceni indicates a mixed pine-oak-lime forest, and the relatively high frequency of wild horse among the animal bones may indicate drier, more open environmental conditions than in the middle Dniester valley, possibly due to the higher altitude of the sites. From the animal bone material, it is clear that hunting forest animals such as red-deer, roe-deer, aurochs, wild pig, and wolf played an important part in the economy, as at Soroki. Although they are situated some distance from the rivers, some of the higher settlements have large numbers of freshwater mollusca shells in their habitation debris. There is no evidence of fish-bones or of any fishing equipment from any of these sites, unless some of the microlithic blades could have acted as inserts on fish-spears, as was suggested for Soroki.

The mesolithic settlements of the lower Dniester valley are represented predominantly by assemblages consisting of large numbers of 'geometric' microlithic blades.[36] The sites are also distributed on the upper terraces of river valleys. The predominance of wild horse and aurochs among the animal bones would suggest that, as at Erbiceni, the environment consisted of lighter woodland than in the middle Dniester valley.[37] The vegetation of this area at present consists of steppe grassland. There is evidence in the Late Palaeolithic settlements of the lower Dniester area, for example at Bolšaya Akkarža, that there had been a specialised hunting of aurochs. In connection with this latter site, where a large number of animal bones were excavated but no bone implements, it was suggested that bone implements, being more difficult to make, were carefully carried with the user. Stone implements, on the other hand, were thrown away after very little use, particularly in areas like the Dniester valley, where there was an abundant supply of local flint. This hypothesis could possibly be applied to mesolithic sites of the Dniester and Prut valleys, where there is abundant evidence of animal bones but no bone implements.

Lower Danube valley

West of the lower Dniester sites towards the delta of the Danube, the mesolithic settlements are situated on the lower terraces of river valleys or in the flood plains themselves.[38] The chipped stone assemblages contain microlithic blades, but there is an absence of the trapezoid-shaped blades which characterise the lower Dniester sites. The microblades are unretouched or retouched into a segment shape. Unfortunately, there is no evidence of the economy of these settlements, but it seems likely that their chipped stone industry reflects a different emphasis in the sources of food and raw materials and different methods of exploiting these from the methods used in the lower Dniester valley.

South of the Danube delta a similar chipped stone assemblage has been excavated in the cave of La Adam, S.E. Rumania, stratified between a late glacial habitation layer and a late neolithic layer (p. 151). The stone implements are associated with a large number of bones of wild sheep or goats. These latter were formerly thought to provide proof that this site was a very early centre of sheep domestication, but there is no evidence to suggest that any of them were domesticated.[39]

In N.E. Bulgaria a site with an assemblage consisting of 'geometric' microlithic blades as well as macrolithic blades has been excavated in the sandstone hills known as Pobiti Kamani, associated with the bones of wild horse, wild sheep or goats, and red-deer.[40] Already in the Late Palaeolithic settlements of Bulgaria there is evidence for the diminution of stone implements, so that it is unnecessary to speculate on any long-range migrations of mesolithic hunters from the Ukraine.

Sites with a predominantly 'geometric' microlithic stone assemblage are scattered along the terraces of the Danube tributaries of southern Rumania, but without any evidence of environment, economy, or chronology.[41] They also are likely to represent local development from the Late Palaeolithic industries.

N.E. Hungarian mountains

The limestone Matra and Bükk mountains contain a number of settlements, both open sites and caves, which, on the basis of their palaeobotanical evidence, represent various later postglacial periods. Two sites in the west of these mountains, for example, have been assigned to the Boreal vegetational period of northern Europe, but the evidence is far from consistent, ranging from mixed oak forest to mixed pine-hazel forest.[42] The relative chronological framework for the mesolithic sites in these mountains has been constructed on the basis of a morphological typology of their stone assemblages, which consist predominantly of macrolithic implements including large flakes used as heavy scrapers, large leaf-shaped points, and possible flake axes. There is no evidence for the economy associated with these assemblages or what the purpose of these heavy tools and projectiles was. 'Geometric' microlithic blades occur on a few of the sites.

A similar stone industry consisting of large flakes and chipped stone axes has been found in other parts of eastern Europe, and has been referred to as 'Campignian', for example in central Rumania (Transylvania), and S.E. Rumania.[43] At Lapoș a so-called 'Campignian' assemblage was stratified below a layer which contained 'geometric' microlithic blades. Generally, chronological and environmental evidence for these assemblages is entirely lacking, so that it is impossible to tell whether the macrolithic industry referred to as 'Campignian' is a few hundred or a few thousand years earlier than the microlithic industry, and whether or not the two were associated with a different environment and economy. In northern Europe, the presence of large stone axes has been interpreted as large-scale wood-working and forest clearance.

The Danube gorges (*Iron Gates*)

In the limestone mountains of S.W. Rumania above the gorge cut through by the Danube, there are several caves with traces of prehistoric habitation from various periods.[44] The postglacial habitation layers of the caves of Băile Herculane, Veterani, and Cuina Turcului, which represent settlements of hunters and gatherers, have been dated to a slightly later period than Climente II (p. 64) on the basis of a morphological typology of their chipped stone assemblages. Palaeobotanical evidence from these early mesolithic caves indicates an Alpine forest-steppe environment at that time with juniper and willow predominating among the trees. The economy was based on hunting forest animals such as red-deer, fox and, to a certain extent, bison and bear, as well as open woodland and scrubland animals, such as ibex, and riverine mammals, such as beavers. Fish-bones also occur. The chipped stone industry shows strong ties with the preceding Late Palaeolithic Epigravettian industry of this region. The assemblage at Băile Herculane has often mistakenly been referred to

as 'Azilian' because of a superficial resemblance between the small
blunted blades of the Rumanian site and those of the French Azilian
industry.[45] The assemblage also includes small denticulated blades
and scrapers and a very few microlithic blades.

At the bottom of the gorges, on the banks of the Danube itself,
a series of open sites of settlements of food-gatherers has recently
been excavated. Thanks to a number of radiocarbon dates, their
chronological position is much clearer than is that of the mountain
sites. At least seven sites have produced evidence for homogenous
settlements, house types, burial rites, economies as well as artefacts
of stone, bone and antler.[46] The best-documented so far and the most
thoroughly excavated is Lepenski Vir which lies on the narrow sloping
southern bank of the Danube, between the river and the steep
limestone sides of the gorge (Pl. 1). Eight habitation levels have been
distinguished representing three distinct culture layers, two of which
(I and II) are virtually 'aceramic' and have evidence of a hunting-
fishing economy. They are referred to by the excavator as the
Lepen culture. Above them is a culture layer (III) with an assemblage which is typical of the early neolithic Starčevo culture with
evidence of a food-producing economy. Below these three culture
layers there is evidence for a possible habitation level which pre-
cedes the main mesolithic settlement of I and II. So far, however, it is
apparent only in isolated hearths and may not represent a separate
culture layer. The two mesolithic culture layers are separated by a
thin sterile layer of sand. Although this represents a break in
occupation of the settlement, there is little evidence for a break in
the evolution of the 'Lepen culture'.

The houses of layers I and II were built on terraces which were cut
into the sloping bank of the Danube in order to obtain a horizontal
foundation. They were aligned in rows along the terraces, with their
entrances pointing towards the river, each successive habitation
level utilising the same terraces. The culture layer I at Lepenski Vir
comprises five habitation levels each of which consisted of about
twenty dwellings. All the houses are trapezoidal in plan, varying
in size from 5·5–30 m² but with uniform proportions and internal
arrangements, and all with their wide ends towards the river. The
house floors were of hard limestone plaster covered by a thin red
or white burnished surface (Fig. 5). They were surrounded by post-
holes which were reinforced by stones, as the basis of a relatively
solid wooden structure. In the later culture layer (II) which consists of
one habitation level only, the houses were placed further apart,
were not of such a regular design and were without a plastered floor.
Inside the houses of both periods, hearths consisted of elongated pits
lined with limestone blocks and were often surrounded by a pattern

of thin red blocks of sandstone. Near the hearth at the opposite end to the entrance in almost every house there was placed a block of limestone, rounded by river action, often very large and sometimes carved with features such as eyes and a mouth, and even scales; these have been interpreted as representations of humans or fish. Their significance is naturally open to great speculation, but so far they are a unique phenomenon among the postglacial food-gathering settlements of Europe. In a number of houses, burials were placed near to the hearths. The bodies were inhumed in a shallow pit lying on their backs in an extended position (Fig. 15), occasionally more than one in the same grave. The grave-goods were few in number, but always included a red-deer antler (the main hunted animal) and occasionally beads, amulets or pieces of rock. It is interesting to note that all the skeletons from the mesolithic burials at Lepenski Vir have been identified as representing a tall, robust physical type, very similar to the eastern Upper Palaeolithic 'Cro-Magnon' men.

The settlement of Lepenski Vir is situated near a very large and deep whirlpool which is in close proximity to the river bank. It is assumed that the whirlpool existed during this mesolithic period and helped to churn up the small organisms on which the fish of the Danube fed. It is therefore further assumed that the whirlpool would have been an attractive place for the many species of fish which inhabited the Danube, and no doubt the area just below the whirlpool would have provided very lucrative fishing. From the bone material found in the mesolithic layers it is clear that fishing, especially for the larger carp species, was a very important source of food. No fish-hooks have been found among the bone implements of the mesolithic layers, although they do occur in the neolithic layer (III). There are a large number of long sandstone and schist blocks, 25–50 cm long, sometimes with designs scratched on them, which could have served to club carp during the mating season when, contrary to their normal behaviour, they float motionless near the surface of the water. Or they could have been used to club fish brought out of the water alive. If so, this would suggest the use of nets, possibly weighted by the stones found on the site which have runnels for attaching ropes. This method is still used in the Danube gorge in modern times. Other possible methods which would not leave any trace in the archaeological record are the use of fish-weirs, traps and even wooden hooks. It has been suggested that the long hearths in the houses might have been specially constructed for the process of drying and smoking the large quantities of fish.

Pollen and charcoal remains at Lepenski Vir show that the slopes and bottom of the gorge were covered in mixed pine-juniper-birch forest, with a wet and relatively cool climate. Juniper and hackberry,

which is also found at Lepenski Vir, are typical of present-day inland upland areas which have a Mediterranean climate. From the
bone remains it is clear that hunting animals in these forests, in
particular red-deer and aurochs as well as wild pig and roe-deer,
provided the mesolithic inhabitants of Lepenski Vir with a substantial part of their diet. As with Soroki, there is no direct evidence
for the methods of hunting these animals. Some of the bone points
may have been used as projectile heads, but there are very few chipped
stone blades which could have served as heads or barbs for projectiles. The chipped stone industry used poor quality local pebble
flint, chert and frequently quartz. The blades are struck off and
normally used without any subsequent modification of their shape
by deliberate retouch. There are no 'geometric' microliths and very
few of the blades could be termed microlithic. It is assumed that the
domesticated dog whose bones also occur in the mesolithic layers at
Lepenski Vir was used in hunting forest animals, and that traps, pits
and nooses, etc., were used but have left no surviving trace. Apart
from food, many of the animals provided a valuable source of raw
material as may be seen in the rich bone and antler industry. Many
of the points are very small and fine, and some are decorated by
engraving. The function of most of the bone and antler implements
is very difficult to assess without a careful examination of their
working edges. The series of implements referred to as 'shovel-
shaped objects' and 'chisels' may even have been used for digging in
the earth.

As will be seen in the following chapter, the material culture,
economy and population of the mesolithic settlement at Lepenski
Vir presents a complete contrast to that of the succeeding early
neolithic assemblage from this site. The radiocarbon dates which
range from 5410–4610 B.C. show the mesolithic settlement to have
been contemporary with the early part of the Atlantic vegetation
period of northern Europe, and therefore contemporary with the
initial expansion of a food-producing early neolithic population into
the plains and loess basins of south-east and central Europe (Fig. 39),
but there is no indication in the archaeological material of the mesolithic settlement of Lepenski Vir, for instance in the form of domesticated animals or cultivated grain, that there was any contact between
the two populations (Fig. 8). Pottery does occur in some of the mesolithic houses but this has been assumed to be contamination from
the upper Starčevo layer at Lepenski Vir, although it may be imported or manufactured locally in the 'mesolithic' settlements.

On the northern side of the gorge on the banks of the Danube in
S.W. Rumania, a series of settlements, similar to but not so well
preserved as Lepenski Vir I–II, has recently been excavated.[47]

Several of the sites have more than one mesolithic habitation level and, like Lepenski Vir, are stratified below early neolithic habitation layers. There are no floors of houses but square or rectangular hearths surrounded by a border of stones, and in one case set on a platform of polished clay and sand, occur at three sites. At two of these sites burials have been excavated near the hearths. As at Lepenski Vir they consisted of extended inhumations lying on their backs with very few grave-goods. At Schela Cladovei there were twenty burials all with their feet pointing towards one hearth. The assemblages and evidence of the economy found in these sites are also similar to that of Lepenski Vir I–II.

Inland Yugoslav mountains
Evidence for habitation layers of late postglacial food-gatherers comes from caves in the limestone mountains of S.W. Yugoslavia.[48] The mesolithic levels are stratified between Late Palaeolithic levels and levels with Impressed Ware which may be contemporary with the earliest introduction of agriculture to the plains of south-eastern Europe (p. 102). The chipped stone industry shows very little change in form during the period of development from the Late Palaeolithic to the early pottery-producing layers. The stone implements consist of long blades modified by deliberate retouch on the lateral edges to form knives and scrapers. There are small flake scrapers, but there are no 'geometric' microliths or any microblades. Nor are there any stone blades which could have acted as heads or barbs of projectiles. The faunal remains on the settlements include bones of red-deer as well as wild pig, roe-deer, and aurochs, all of which would indicate that the limestone mountains were rather more thickly forested than they are today. At Crvena Stijena the bones of wild goat occur in the habitation level immediately below that containing the earliest pottery. As at La Adam, these were interpreted as indications of an early domestication of ovicaprids in S.E. Europe, but this suggestion has since been withdrawn.

Adriatic coast
Along the Adriatic coast there are further cave settlements with habitation levels of hunters and gatherers dating to the later postglacial period. The chipped stone assemblages of these coastal sites is rather different from those inland in that they contain a larger proportion of microlithic blades, including those of geometric shape. A local evolution can be seen in the morphological types of these industries from the Late Palaeolithic settlements through later mesolithic levels and continuing until the layers in which pottery decorated by impressions of Cardium shell occurs.[49]

Well-documented evidence for this local evolution and associated economy comes from the Azzura cave near Trieste where a number of postglacial levels have been divided into two main mesolithic culture layers.[50] The chipped stone industry consists of coarse round flakes and long blades with their lateral edges retouched, sometimes so that they are narrowed in the middle as at Crvena Stijena. There are also a large number of small, round scrapers and narrow micro-blades with one edge blunted by retouch in a manner which character-ises the Late Palaeolithic Romanellian industry of the Italian Adriatic coast. In the later mesolithic habitation levels, these were supplemented by wider 'geometric' microlithic blades including trapezes and segments. The hunting of larger forest animals, in particular red-deer, but also roe-deer, wild pig, ibex and wolf, formed the basis of subsistence throughout the duration of the mesolithic settlement. In the later mesolithic habitation levels, however, there is a marked increase in marine mollusca, although the cave is at present several miles from the sea.

'Baltic forest culture'

Sites with assemblages which belong to the techno-complex referred to as the 'Baltic forest culture' are located predominantly by rivers or on former lake-shores, many of which have since been covered by peat. Under these waterlogged conditions, the evidence of stone artefacts is supplemented by rich evidence of artefacts made in organic materials such as wood, bone, and antler. The relative and absolute chronology of the settlements within the north European postglacial vegetational periods has been well established and checked by Carbon 14 evidence. The settlements date to the Boreal and early Atlantic periods, and continue with a similar economy

---

Fig. 7

The heads of thrusting and projected weapons from the E. Baltic (Kunda culture) hunting and gathering settlements.
a Blades inserted in wooden spearhead. Tarvastu, Estonia (after Indreko, 1948).
b Barbed antler harpoon head. Kunda, Estonia (after Indreko, 1948).
c Barbed antler harpoon head. Kunda, Estonia (after Indreko, 1948).
d Single-barbed antler spearhead. Gniewino, N.E. Poland (after S. Kozlowski, 1965).
e Barbed antler blade of fish-spear (leister). Kunda, Estonia (after Indreko, 1948).
f Barbed antler harpoon head with a slot for the insertion of flint blades. Kunda, Estonia (after Indreko, 1948).
g Bone dagger fragment with incised decoration. River Užava, Latvia (after Loze, 1968).
h Bone dagger with incised decoration. Lake Luban, Latvia (after Loze, 1968).

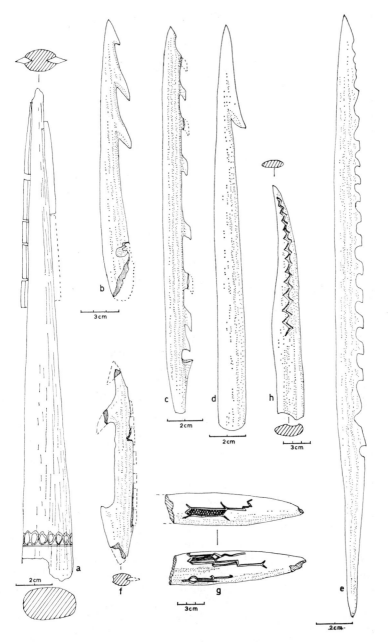

Fig. 7

and material culture, but with the addition of pottery, into the later part of the Atlantic period. The mesolithic settlements of the eastern Baltic Kunda culture were probably not inhabited until the end of the Boreal period.[51] Throughout these periods, the mixed deciduous and coniferous forest extended north of its modern limits as far as Finland and Karelia. It seems probable that animal life favoured the marginal zones of the forests such as rivers, lakes and marshes rather than the interior, because of the greater variety of food sources and comparative ease of movement. This may have been as important a factor in the siting of mesolithic settlements by rivers and lakes as the potential source of food from freshwater fish and mammals. This hypothesis is supported by the faunal remains of the Maglemose and Kunda culture settlements, where the bones of forest mammals such as red-deer, elk, aurochs, wild pig, and roe-deer are very numerous. Unlike the settlements of the Maglemose[52] culture, the faunal material from the settlements of the Kunda culture indicate a consistent degree of specialisation in hunting one animal—the elk—which was unusual in mesolithic settlements.[53] It is impossible to tell from the existing analysis of animal bones from these sites whether the elks were hunted only in the summer when they come down to the lakes to eat water-lilies. At this time of year they only move in very small groups. In winter, however, when they form larger bands, they move away from the lakes to drier, higher ground. In all seasons the elk, by its great speed of movement and excessive shyness, is a very difficult animal to hunt. The methods used by mesolithic hunters may have included such traps as pitfalls and nooses, none of which have left any trace in the archaeological record. They very probably made use of the domesticated dog, the bones of which occur on all sites of the Kunda culture as in the west Baltic Maglemose sites. There is a large variety of barbed bone and antler points found in the Kunda assemblages which may have been used as the heads of thrusting or projected spears, but there is no evidence for the use of the bow and arrow in the east Baltic sites. Chipped stone implements, including possible inserts for bone and antler hafts in the form of microlithic blades, occur much less frequently than in the west Baltic Maglemose assemblages. The chipped stone artefacts of the Kunda culture are made from small river and moraine pebbles. The only source of flint is in Estonia and this of very poor quality. The decrease in the importance of elk in the economy of the settlements during the Atlantic period, and its virtual disappearance in the west Baltic during this period, must be associated with the drastic decrease of pine, whose bark is essential to the diet of the elk.

Some of the barbed bone and antler points were perforated at the base. They have been interpreted as 'harpoons', or spears whose heads are attached to a long line in order to retain contact with the victim. They may be used on land, although this is difficult in a thickly forested environment. They are especially effective in hunting animals, whether mammals or fish, moving through water, such as beavers which were an important source of food in the Kunda settlements, or seals which were also hunted at this time. The seals were hunted in the east Baltic in the spring and autumn, and possibly even winter. The methods of hunting them would have varied depending on the season and the species of seal.[54] During the breeding season they may have been clubbed while on the ice; during the season when the sea was frozen they may have been harpooned while surfacing at their breathing holes. Among the bone implements there are thick segments of long bones which have been sharpened at one end and interpreted as 'ice-picks', and may possibly have been used to widen existing breathing holes or make artificial ones. Other possible evidence for winter habitation of the settlements is the presence of a ski for use in soft seasonal snow. It is also possible that seals were hunted from boats but no evidence for these has yet been found in the east Baltic. Seals, however, did not become important in the economy until the subsequent Sub-Boreal vegetational period in association with the Narva culture.[55]

Fish-bones, particularly those of pike, have been found on the settlements whose bone material has been analysed. Pike bones were found at the site of Kunda itself in close association with unperforated bone points, which were armed down their whole lengths by small barbs.[56] It is very likely that these barbed points were hafted doubly or trebly in the manner of modern leisters, in order to have a better chance of spearing a fish. They are especially effective in shallow water, and when used in conjunction with fish-weirs. The presence of barbless bone hooks in the settlements of the east Baltic coast indicate that other methods were used in fishing. Fragments of nets have survived at Kunda and Narva, as well as net-weights of stone or gravel wrapped in bark, and floats of pine-bark. Many other methods of fishing including traps were probably used, but there is no evidence of them in the east Baltic mesolithic sites.

Evidence of other activities include polished greenstone, granite, or diabase axes and adzes. They are trapezoid in shape and oval or plano-convex in cross-section and were probably used for similar functions to those assumed of the chipped flint axes of the Maglemose culture, such as wood-working, tree-felling, and bark-stripping. Antler sleeves for these axes and perforated antler axes closely resembling those of the Maglemose culture have also been found.

Many of the bone and antler objects of the Kunda culture settlements were decorated with incised designs which consist exclusively of chevrons, cross-hatching, and other geometric patterns (Fig. 7). On the other hand, incised decoration of the antler and bone objects of the Maglemose assemblages often takes the form of human and animal representations as well. There is no evidence for amber pendants in the Kunda settlements of Boreal and Atlantic periods, although they occur in the west Baltic Maglemose settlements. There are no traces of houses in the east Baltic from this period, except possibly the evidence for a rough flooring of wood and bark at Menturiai bog in former east Prussia. Similar flooring of brushwood and bark has been found in some sites of the Maglemose culture, and it has been suggested that these represent seasonal summer habitations. It is possible that more permanent habitations, or those inhabited during winter as at Kunda, may have been lifted off the ground and supported on corner-stones or corner pillars, in which case they would leave very little trace.

Conclusion

As far as it is possible to tell from the rather sporadic nature of the palaeontological evidence from the mesolithic settlements of eastern Europe, there was no specialisation in the exploitation of any one animal species for food or raw materials apart from the Kunda culture; a variety of animals was eaten, including a large number of mammals, fish, birds and mollusca. It is presumed, although there is no proof apart from sporadic finds of hazel-nut shells, that a similarly large variety of plant species was exploited. There may have been a greater concentration on the exploitation of fish at some settlements, for example those on the banks of rivers, or on large forest animals at others, but in no case to the exclusion of other resources at their disposal.

The mesolithic settlements of eastern Europe were located by lakes and along rivers, either on the sandy alluvial and flood plains, or on the banks of the rivers, or on terraces and the edges of high plateaus overlooking the rivers. A small number were situated in mountain areas, but only in the foothills. As far as it is possible to tell from the available evidence, no mesolithic settlements were located on loess deposits in eastern Europe. During the Boreal vegetation period, the loess deposits were very probably covered by open steppe-like grassland with very few trees, in which case they would have been avoided by mesolithic hunters and gatherers because of their lack of game. During the period equivalent to the north European Atlantic zone, however, the loess areas were certainly covered by a light mixed oak woodland with a rich undergrowth, which would have been highly suitable for the mammals hunted by mesolithic groups, such as red-deer, aurochs, roe-deer, and wild pig. There are two factors which may account for the continued lack of mesolithic settlement on loess areas during the Atlantic period. First, it is possible that the growth of the deciduous forest and spread of large mammals on the loess may have been a relatively slow process and may only have reached its climax during the middle of the Atlantic period. By this time the loess deposits would have been settled by early neolithic food-producing groups (Fig. 8). Secondly, the location of settlements by rivers and lakes may not have been so much to facilitate fishing or even mobility, as to exploit the rich sources of food which tended to congregate in the convergence areas of various micro-ecological zones. Such convergence areas occurred most frequently by rivers and lakes. A characteristic of loess regions is the lack of large expanses of surface water and of streams and rivers with definite valleys, the majority of which would be insufficient to break up the large homogenous ecological zones provided by the loess basins. There are a few large rivers which run through the loess basins, such as the Danube and its tributaries, and mesolithic settlements do occur along these. But in each case the settlements are strictly limited to the alluvial or flood-plain sand, although the loess plains may have been used to a certain extent as hunting territory.

1. For general discussion of the epipalaeolithic and mesolithic industries of eastern Europe: Boriskovski, P. I., 'Očerky po paleolitu Centralnoi i Yugo-Vostočnoi Evropi', Pt. I, *SA*, XXVII (1957), 29–70; ibid., Pt. II, *SA*, XXIX (1959), 5–41; Valoch, K. (1968); Vertes, L. (1960); Waterbolk, T. (1968).
2. e.g. at Hendelhammer, Chocovice and Třeben on the S. edge of the Ore Mts. (Klima, B., 'Epipaläolithikum im oberen Egertal', *Quartär*, XVII, 1966, 91–116) and at Pfortener Berg and Döbritz on the N. edge of the Ore Mts. (Feustel, R., 'Das Mesolithikum in Thuringen', *Alt-Thüringen*, V, 1961, 18–75).
3. e.g. Szekszard, C 14 (H 408) 8350 ± 500 B.C. and dated by palaeobotanical evidence to the transition between the Allerød and Younger Dryas periods: Vertes, L., et al, 'Die Ausgrabungen in Szekszard-Palank und die archaeologischen Funde', *Swiatowit*, 24 (1962), 182. Also Witow, C 14 8855 ± 160 B.C. and palaeobotanical dating to the Younger Dryas period (Valoch, K., 1968; Hont: Gabori, M., *Arch. Ert.*, 83, 1956; Kůlna cave: Valoch, K., et al., 'Die Erforschung der Kůlna-Höhle bei Sloup in Mährische Karst', *Quartär*, XX, 1969; Bolšaya Akkarža and Borševo: Valoch, K., 1968 and Boriskovski, P. I., 'Problemele paleoliticului superior şi ale mesoliticului de pe coasta de nord-vest a Marii Negre', *SCIV*, XV: 1, 1964, 5–15; Ostroměř: Vencl, Sl., 'Ostroměřska skupina', *Arch. Rozh.*, XVIII; 3 Prague, 1966, 309–40).
4. For the widespread diffusion of 'Swiderian' points: Gimbutas, M. (1956), 28; Sulimirski, T. (1970), 31–2.

5. Kylešovice in N. Czechoslovakia: Boriskovski, P. I., 'Voprosi mezolita Čekhoslovakii i Rumuni', MIA, 126 (1966), 136; Klima, B., 'Mesoliticka industrie na Kylešovskem kopci v Opavě', Časopis Zemskeho Musea, I, Opava (1948). Ceahlău (La Scăune) in N.E. Rumania: Boriskovski, P. I., op. cit. (1966), 132; Nicolaescu-Plopşor, C. S., 'Şantierul arheologic Bicaz', Materiale, VI (1960), 57–63.

6. e.g. Devetaki, C. Bulgaria: Mikov, V., & Džambazov, N., Devetaškata Peštera, Sofia, (1960); Loveč, C. Bulgaria: Džambazov, N., 'Loveškite Pešteri', IAI, XXVI (1963), 195–241; Climente II, S.W. Rumania: Boroneanţ, V. (in press); Crvena Stijena, S.W. Yugoslavia: Benac, A., & Brodar, M., 'Crvena Stijena', Glasnik Z.M. Sar., 13 (1958) 43–61.

7. Clarke, D. (1968), 357.

8. Clarke, D. (1968), 324; Clark, J. G. D. (1958); Zotz, L. (1932).

9. Clark, J. G. D. (1969), 91–123; id. (1958).

10. Bordaz, J. (1970), 88–93.

11. e.g. Soroki, Moldavia SSR: Markyevič, V. I., Neolit Moldavii, unpublished thesis for Kandidat Istoričeskikh Nauk degree in Inst. of Archaeology, ANSSSR, Moscow (1968); Icoana and Schela Cladovei, S.W. Rumania: Boroneanţ, V. (in press).

12. e.g. Mikhailovka, nr. Odessa, USSR: Boriskovski, P. I., & Kraskovskii, V., Pamyatniki drevneišei čelovyečeskoi kulturi severo-zapadnovo Pričernomorye, Odessa (1961), 31.

13. e.g. Smolin, C. Czechoslovakia: Valoch, K., 'Ein mittelsteinzeitlicher Wohnplatz bei Smolin in Südmähren', Quartär, XIV (1962), 105–14, fig. 1; Tašovice, Czechoslovakia: Prošek, F., 'Mesolitická chata v Tašovicich', Arch. Rozh., III: 1, (1951), 12–15, fig. 4; Ražice (Putim I), S.W. Czechoslovakia: Mazalek, M., 'Mesoliticka chata z Pisečniku u Ražice (Putim I)', Anthropozoikum, II, Prague (1952), 161–72, fig. 2; Fiera (Cleanov), S.W. Rumania: Nicolaescu-Plopşor, C. S., 'Industries microlithiques en Oltènie', Dacia OS, VII-VIII (1937–40), 3–8; Soroki, Moldavia, SSR: Markyevič, V. I., op. cit. (1968).

14. East Baltic Carbon 14 dates: Radiocarbon, VIII (1966). Witow: Radiocarbon, VIII (1966); Chmielewska, M., 'Badania stanowiska mezolitycznego w Witowie, Leczyckim pow.' Spraw. Arch., 3 (1957), 11–23. Soroki: Carbon 14 dates in Quitta, H., & Kohl, G. 'Neue Radiocarbondaten zum Neolithikum und zu frühen Bronzezeit Südosteuropas und der Sowjetunion', Zeitsch. für Arch., 3, Berlin (1969), 249–51; Soroki II, layer 3—5565 ± 120 B.C. (Bln 588); Soroki II, layer 2—5470 ± 80 B.C. (Bln 587): Lepenski Vir: Quitta, H., in Srejović, D. (1969), 229–38.

15. For example, at Lepenski Vir in N.E. Yugoslavia, layer I was attributed to the pre-Boreal period and layer II to the Boreal. The same two layers have been dated by a reliable series of Carbon 14 dates to a period which coincides with the north European Boreal/Atlantic transition.

16. Mesolithic of W. Czechoslovakia: Boriskovski, P. I., op. cit. (1966); Klima, B., op. cit. (1966); Neustupny, J., 'Zum Tschechoslowakischen Mesolithikum', MAGW, XCII (1962), 239–46; Prošek, F., & Ložek, V., 'Stratigraficke otazky československeho paleolitu', Pam. Arch., XLV (1954), 35–74; Skutil, J., 'Přehled českeho paleolitika a mesolitika', Sbornik NM., VI, Prague (1952); Vencl, Sl., 'Mladopaleoliticka a mesoliticka stanice v Libine na Jičinsku', Arch. Rozh., XVI: 1 (1964), 3–10; Žebera, K., 'Nova paleoliticka a mesoliticka sidlište v ceskych zemich', Pam. Arch., XLII (1946); Zotz, L., & Freund, G., 'Die paläolithische und mesolithische Kulturentwicklung in Böhmen und Mähren', Quartär, V (1951), 7–40.

17. e.g. Souš and Tři Volů cave: Klima, B., op. cit. (1966).

18. e.g. Tašovice and Ražice (Putim I): Beneš, A., & Vencl, Sl., 'Prispěvek k poznani mesolitickeho osidleni Jižnich Čech', *Arch. Rozh.,* XVIII: 1 (1966), 67–71; Klima, B., op. cit. (1966); Vencl, Sl. 'Pokus o klasifikaciji posdě glacialnih a staroholocennich osidleni okoli Režabnice', *Pam. Arch.,* LVL 2 (1964), 233–45.
19. Prošek, F., & V. Ložek, 'Mesoliticke sidliště v Zatyni u Dubé', *Anthropozoikum,* II (1952), 93–172.
20. Feustel, R., 'Zum Problem des Uberganges Mesolithikum-Neolithikum', *Alt-Thuringen,* II, Weimar (1957), 27–47; id., op. cit. (1961).
21. Mesolithic settlements of the Pannonian Plain: Boriskovski, P. I., op. cit. (1966), 134; Neustupny, J., op. cit. (1962); Klima, B., 'Nove mesolitické nalezy na jižni Moravě', *Arch. Rozh.,* V: 3 (1953), 297–302; id., 'Ubersucht über die jüngsten paläolithischen Forschungen in Mähren', *Quartär,* XIX (1957), 85–130; Dobosi, V., 'Mesolithische Fundorte in Ungarn', *Alba Regia* (in press); Barta, J., 'Tomašikovo, mezoliticka stanica na Slovensku', *Arch. Rozh.,* VII: 4 (1955), 433–6; id., 'Mezoliticka industria z Mostovej pri Galante', *Arch. Rozh.,* XII: 6 (1960), 787–90; Brukner, B., 'Die Tardenoisischen Funde von "Pereš" bei Hajdukovo und aus Bačka Palanka, und das Problem der Beziehungen in Donaugebiet', *Arch. Iug.,* VII (1966), 1–12; Mazalek, M., 'Mesoliticke nalezy ze Slovenska', *Arch. Rozh.,* VI: 1 (1954), 7–12; Gulder, A., 'Beiträge zur Kenntnis des niederösterreichischen Mesolithikums', *Arch. Aust.,* 12 (1953), 5–33; Zotz, L., & Freund, G., op. cit. (1951); Lichardus, J., & Pavuk, J., (1966); Vencl, Sl. (1968).
22. Barta, J., 'Pleistocenné piesocné duny pri Seredi a ich paleolitické a mezolitické osidlenie', *Slov. Arch.,* V: 1 (1957), 5–72.
23. For discussion of the possible mesolithic-neolithic relationships on the Pannonian Plain: Brukner, B., op. cit. (1966); Lichardus, J., & Pavuk, J. (1966); Mazalek, M., 'Zur Frage der Beziehungen zwischen Mesolithikum und Neolithikum', *Anthropozoikum,* III, Prague (1953), 203–34; Zotz, L., (1941); Tringham, R. (1968); Vencl, Sl. (1968).
24. Vencl, Sl. (1968).
25. e.g. Smolin: Valoch, K., op. cit. (1962); Šakvice: Klima, B., op. cit. (1953).
26. Păunescu, Al., 'Perežitki Tardenuazkoi kulturi v drevnei neolite v Ciumeşti (Beria)', *Dacia NS.,* VII (1963), 467–75; id., 'A propos de la période finale et quelques persistences de l'epipaleolithique dans le néolithique ancien au Nord-Ouest et Nord-est de la Roumanie', *SCIV,* XV: 3 (1964), 321–35; id. (1970), 31–2, 148; Nicolaescu-Plopşor, C. S., 'Date noi cu privire la cunoaşterea inceptului şi sfirşitului Paleoliticului Romînei,' *SCIV,* XV: 3 (1964), 314–15. Also see Barca, E. Czechoslovakia: Boriskovski, P. I., op. cit. (1966), 135; Prošek, F., 'Mesoliticka obsidianová industrie ze stanice Barca I', *Arch. Rozh.,* XI: 1 (1959), 145. Also see Valea lui Mihai (Galospetrei), N.W. Rumania: Nicolaescu-Plopşor, C. S., & Kovacs, E., 'Cercetările paleolitice din regiunea Baia Mare', *Materiale,* VI (1959), 40.
27. Gabori, N., 'Quelques problèmes du commerce de l'obsidienne à l'age préhistorique', *Arch. Ert.,* 77 (1950), 50–3.
28. Chmielewska, M., op. cit. (1957); Gimbutas, M. (1956), 35–7: Ginter, B., 'Niektóre zagadnienia mezolitu w Polsce', *Arch. Polski,* XII: 1 (1967), 7–19; Kozlowski, L., 'L'époque mesolithique en Pologne', *L'Anthropologie,* XXXVII, Paris (1926), 47–61; Jażdżewski, K. (1965), 52–5; Kozlowski, S. K., 'Z problematygi polskiego mezolitu', *Arch. Polski,* X: 1 (1965), 151–77. Polish–Byelorussian connections in the mesolithic: Gurina, N. N., 'Noviye mezolitičeskiye pamyatniki lesnoi polosi evropeiskoi časti SSSR', *SA,* 1, Moscow (1960), 125–36; id., 'K voprosu o pozdnepaleolitičeskikh i mezolitičeskikh pamyatnikakh Polši i vozmožnosti sopostavlyeniya s nimi

E

pamyatnikov severo-zapadnoi Byelorussii', *MIA*, 126 (1966), 14–34; Formosov, A. A., 'O vremeni i istoričeskikh usloviyakh složeniya plemennoi organizatsii', *SA*, 1 (1957), 13–21; id., 'Periodizatsiya mezolitičeskikh stoyanok Evropeiskoi časti SSSR', *SA*, XXI (1954), 38–51.
29. Gimbutas, M. (1956), 36.
30. Chmielewska, M., 'Grob kultury tardenuaskiej w Janislawicach pow. Skierniewice', *Wiad. Arch.*, 20 (1954), 23–48; Gimbutas, M. (1956), 36–7.
31. Soroki (Trifautski Les I and II): Markyevič, V. I., 'Issledovaniya neolita na Srednem Dnestre', *KSIA*, 105 (1965), 85–90; id., op. cit. (1968).
32. e.g. Ataki and Osilevka: private communication from Markyevič, V. I., Kišinev (August 1968).
33. Bibikov, S. N., 'Pozdnepaleolitičeskoye poseleniye v navese Šan-Koba i v grote Murzak-Koba v Krimu', *KSIIMK*, 13 (1946), 130; id., 'Raskopki v navese Fatma-Koba i nekotoriye voprosi izučeniya mezolita Krima', *MIA*, 136 (1966), 138–43; Danilenko, V. N. (1969), 19–24, fig. 2; Krainov, D. A., 'Peščernaya stoyanka Taš-Ayir I', *MIA*, 91 (1960); Vencl, Sl., review of Krainov (1960) in *Arch. Rozh.*, XIII (1961), 594–5; Formosov, A. A., op. cit. (1954).
34. Stolyar, A. D., 'Ob odnom centre odomašnivaniya svinyi', *SA*, 3 (1959), 3–18; Tringham, R. (1969), 384.
35. e.g. Florešti, Varvarovka and Kostešti in Moldavia, SSR: unpublished information from Markyevič, V.; Spinoasa and Erbiceni in N.E. Rumania: Zaharia, N., 'Palaeolithic discoveries in Moldavia 1952 and 1957', *Arch. Moldovei*, I (1962), 28–30. General discussion of the mesolithic in Moldova, N.E. Rumania, and Moldavia, SSR: Boriskovski, P. I., op. cit. (1964); id., op. cit. (1966); Nicolaescu-Plopşor, C. S., 'Descoperiri tardenoasien în R.S.S., Moldovanească', *SCIV*, XI: 1 (1960); id., op. cit. (1964); Păunescu, Al., op. cit. (1964); id., op. cit (1970).
36. e.g. Grebeniki, Ghirževo: Boriskovski, P. I., op. cit. (1964), 15–17; Korobkova, G. F., 'Tardenuazkaya stoyanka Grebeniki na Nižnem Dnestre', *KSIIMK*, 63 (1957), 59–62; Stanko, V. N., 'Nekotoriye voprosi pozdnevo mezolita Severo-zapadnovo Pričernomorye', *Zapiski Odesskovo Arkheologičeskovo Obščestva*, II, Odessa (1967), 155–67.
37. Analysis of animal bones from Ghirževo: Stanko, V. N., op. cit. (1967).
38. e.g. Mirnopolye, Mikhailovka, S.W. Ukraine, SSR: Boriskovski, P. I., & Kraskovski, V., op. cit. (1961), 31; Stanko, V. N., op. cit. (1967), 165.
39. Berciu, D. (1966), 25–31; Radulesco, C., & Samson, P., 'Sur un centre de domestication du mouton dans le mesolithique de la grotte "la Adam" en Dobrogea', *Zeitschrift fur Tierzuchtung und Zuchtungsbiologie*, 76, Hamburg (1962), 282–320; Piggott, S. (1965), 40.
40. Džambazov, N., 'Proučvaniya na paleolitnata i mezolitnata kultura v Bulgarija', *Arkheologiya*, VI: 3 (1964), 74; Stanko, V. N., op. cit. (1967), 165.
41. e.g. Fiera (Cleanov): Berciu, D., 'Şantierul archeologic Verbicioara-Dolj', *SCIV*, II: 1 (1951), 229–48; Nicolaescu-Plopşor, C. S., op. cit. (1937–40); Vertes, L. (1960), 94.
42. Evidence from Remete cave, near Budapest, and Koporostétö, near Eger: Vertes, L. (1960), 93; id., *Az őskőkor és az átmeneti kőkor emléki Magyarországon* (the palaeolithic and mesolithic sites of Hungary), Budapest (1965), 214–21; Dobosi, V., op. cit. (in press).
43. e.g. at Giurgiu (Malul Roşu) and Lapoş: Roska, M., 'Le Campignien en Transilvanie', *Buletinul Societaţii de Şţiinţce din Cluj*, 4, Cluj (1929); Mogoşanu, Fl., 'Probleme noi în aşezarea de la Lapoş', *SCIV*, XV: 3 (1964), 337–50; Mogoşanu, Fl., & Bitiri, M., 'Asupra prozenţei Campignianului în Romîna,' *SCIV*, XII: 2 (1961), 215–26; Nicolaescu-Plopşor, C. S., 'Le

paleolithique dans la Republique Populaire Romaine à la lumière des dernières recherches', *Dacia NS*, I (1957), 40–60 (Giurgiu); Vertes, L. (1960), 94; Păunescu, Al. (1970), 25.
44. Boroneanţ, V. (in press); Păunescu, Al. (1970), 29–30.
45. Nicolaescu-Plopşor, C. S., & Păunescu, Al., 'Azilianul de la Băile Herculane în lumina noilor cercetări', *SCIV*, XII: 2 (1961), 203–10; Nicolaescu-Plopşor, C. S., op. cit. (1964), 316.
46. Icoana, Ostrovul Banului, Răzvrata and Schela Cladovei in S.W. Rumania: Boroneanţ, V. (in press); Padina in. N.E. Yugoslavia: unpublished excavation (1970), Jovanovič, B., Institute of Archaeology, SAN, Belgrade; Vlassac, N.E. Yugoslavia: unpublished, private communication from Srejović, D., University of Belgrade; Lepenski Vir, N.E. Yugoslavia: Srejović, D., (1966); id. (1969); Nandris, J. (1968); Bökönyi, S. (1970).
47. Boroneanţ, V. (in press), see n. 46 above.
48. Crvena Stijena, S.W. Yugoslavia: Benac, A., & M. Brodar, op. cit. (1958); Velika Pećina and Vindija Pećina, N.W. Yugoslavia: Malez, M., 'Paleolit Velike Pećine na Ravnoj Gori u sjeverozapadnaj Hrvatskoj', *Arh. Rad. i Raspr.*, IV–V (1967), 7–68.
49. e.g. Gudnja cave: unpublished in Dubrovnik Museum; Jamina Sredi, Is. of Cres: Miroslavljević, V., ' "Jamina Sredi" prilog prethistorijskoj kulturi na Otoku Cresu', *Arh. Rad. i Raspr.*, I (1959), 131–69.
50. Cannarella, O., & Cremenosi, G., 'Gli scava nella Grotta Azzura di Samatorca nel Corso triestino', *Rivista di Scienze Preistoriche*, XXII: 2, Firenze (1967), 1–50.
51. Dolukhanov, P. M., 'Paleogeografija mezolita severnoi Evropi', *MIA*, 126 (1966), 64–74; Gaerte, W., *Urgeschichte Ostpreussens*, Königsberg (1929); Gimbutas, M. (1956), 28–35; Jannits, L. Ju., 'Noviye danniye po mezolitu Estonii,' *MIA*, 126 (1966), 114–23; Kozlowski, S. K., 'O mezolice Polski polnocno-wschodniej i terenów sąsiednich', *Arch. Polski*, XII: 2 (1967), 219–56; Loze, I., 'Nekotoriye mezolitičeskiye nakhodki na territorii Latvii', *MIA*, 126 (1966), 108–13; Sulimirski, T. (1970), 49–51.
52. Clark, J. G. D. (1968), 94–108.
53. Paaver, K. L., *Formirovaniye teriofauni i izmenčivost mlekopitayušikh Pribaltiki v golocene*, Tartu (1965), 33.
54. Clark, J. G. D. (1952), 72–83; Nelson, R., *Hunters of the Northern Ice*, Chicago (1969), 220–349.
55. Paaver, K. L., op. cit. (1965), 34; Gurina, N. N., 'Iz Istorii drevnikh plemen zapadnikh oblastei SSSR', *MIA*, 144 (1967).
56. Clark, J. G. D. (1952), 47.

3

THE EARLIEST FOOD-PRODUCERS

5500–3800 B.C.

The preceding chapter consisted of an examination of the settlements and assemblages of food-gatherers in Eastern Europe roughly
7000–4500 B.C. On the basis of the present evidence, the hunters and
gatherers during this period avoided settling in the fertile loess basins
and plateaus of Europe north of the Danube and large alluvial
plains of the southern tributaries of the Danube. Settlements of the
earliest food-producing groups in Europe occur in a period contemporary with the latest of these food-gatherers and with the early
part of the north European Atlantic vegetational period. They are
distributed, however, in exactly those areas which were avoided by
the hunters and gatherers. They occur on the brown forest soils and
alluvial deposits of the rivers of south Bulgaria, south Yugoslavia and
Greece which drain into the Aegean Sea. North of this they are
located on the loess deposits of the widespread Danube basin and
the upper reaches of rivers in Poland and Germany which flow into
the Baltic Sea and the North Sea. Carbon 14 evidence (Fig. 39)
shows that the earliest of these settlements are on the south-east
edge of Europe, in Bulgaria, Yugoslavia and Greece where they are
dated to 5600–4500 B.C.[1] Settlements at the north-western limits of
the initial expansion of agriculture and stockbreeding (in Holland
and Germany) are dated to 4500 B.C. at the earliest. It is accepted
that the expansion of the earliest agriculturalists into Europe was
from the Near East on the basis of evidence of the presence of the
initial stages in the cultivation of plants and the domestication of
animals in this region. Thence they spread westwards and northwards via south-east Europe into temperate Europe. But whether

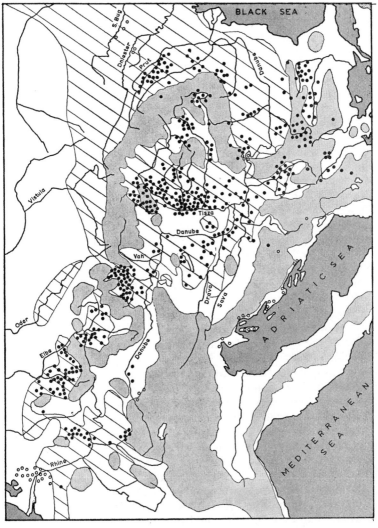

Earliest
agricultural
settlements

Settlements with
a predomi-
nantly hunter-
gatherer
economy

Over 500 m.a.s.l

Loess deposits

Fig. 8
Map of the spread of
the earliest agricultural
settlements in relation
to the distribution of
loess deposits and the
contemporary hunter-
gatherer settlements.

this was an expansion of actual human groups or a diffusion of the techniques and equipment relating to agriculture and stockbreeding is still open to question. The hypothesis that the majority of the early food-producing or neolithic settlements of south-east and central Europe represent an intrusive population is based partly on the lack of any European mesolithic elements such as microlithic blades in their assemblages, and the lack of evidence of continuity or contact with the preceding and contemporary food-gathering mesolithic population.[2] It is also based very much on the close similarities in the form and content of the early neolithic assemblages of south-east Europe to the contemporary and immediately preceding assemblages in Greece and the Near East, particularly Anatolia.[3]

The break between the mesolithic and early neolithic assemblages in eastern Europe is emphasised by their mutually exclusive distribution. It may also be seen very clearly in the few cases where a mesolithic habitation level is stratified below an early neolithic habitation level. Such evidence occurs at several open sites at the bottom of the Danube gorges in N.E. Yugoslavia and S.W. Rumania.[4] The Carbon 14 evidence from Lepenski Vir (I–II) shows that the site was occupied by hunters and gatherers at a time when the area south of the Danube gorge was already settled by food-producers, *c.* 5500–4500 B.C. (Fig. 39). Yet there is no trace in the material culture of these layers that the hunters and gatherers had any knowledge of the existence of their food-producing neighbours, or had any relationship with them. The upper layer (III) at Lepenski Vir whose assemblage belongs to the early neolithic shows a completely different basis of economy, method of house construction, form and function of stone, bone and antler implements, burial rites and (although the evidence is rather too sparse to make such broad generalisations) physical type from that of the preceding mesolithic layers. There are no Carbon 14 dates from the early neolithic layer at Lepenski Vir or the other stratified sites. Carbon 14 evidence (Fig. 39) from sites in N. Yugoslavia and S.E. Hungary, however, which have identical assemblages, have been dated *c.* 4800–4400 B.C. Thus the lapse in time between the mesolithic and early neolithic occupation of Lepenski Vir would seem to have been no longer than 2–300 years.

On the periphery of the early neolithic culture area of eastern Europe sites occur at which habitation levels of late mesolithic hunters and gatherers are stratified below levels with evidence of pottery and a partially food-producing economy, for example, in the mountains of W. Yugoslavia, on the banks of the Dniester in Moldavia SSR, or in the C. Rumania Carpathian mountains.[5] Apart from the presence of pottery and food-production, the assemblages in the neolithic habitation levels of these sites are identical to the preceding mesolithic layers. It is very probable, therefore, that they represent a continuation and partial acculturation of the original mesolithic hunters and gatherers, who adopted some of the characteristics of their early neolithic neighbours and rejected others.

The similarities of the early neolithic assemblages of eastern Europe to contemporary or immediately preceding assemblages in Greece and the Near East include rather shaky evidence from the skeletal material of a common predominant physical type in the population (dolichocephalic 'gracile Mediterranean' type), but this should perhaps be treated with caution.[6] In both areas the skeletons were buried in a contracted position lying on their sides. The major factor in interpreting the early neolithic cultures of eastern Europe in terms of an intrusive population is the economy itself which is based to a large extent on the domestication of sheep and goats and the cultivation of wheat and barley. Although the wild ancestors of wheat occur on the southern edge of the Balkan peninsula in S. Bulgaria, Greece and S. Yugoslavia, and in some cases the occurrence of einkorn wheat in these areas might indicate domestication of local grasses, it is very unlikely that emmer wheat, which occurs in large quantities in early neolithic sites in south-east Europe, was locally domesticated.[7] Similarly, although there is evidence of wild goats on some mesolithic sites in south-east Europe, there are no animals in a semi-domesticated form. The sheep, goats, pigs and cattle on the early neolithic sites of central and south-east Europe were already completely domesticated. On the other hand the early processes of the domestication of these animals and plants have been traced in considerable detail in the Near East.[8] It seems very likely, therefore, that the actual domesticated animals and plants were brought into south-east and central Europe from the Near East. Supporting, but less conclusive, evidence of an intrusive population includes evidence in the Near East and south-east Europe of settlements of long duration with thick culture layers frequently consisting of a number of stratified habitation levels. The material culture shows many similarities in its content including pottery with painted decoration (Fig. 12), clay figurines (Fig. 13), clay 'stamp-seals', spinning and weaving equipment, a macrolithic chipped stone industry, polished stone artefacts, bone spatulae, etc. (Fig. 11).

Modifications in environmental conditions and associated cultural adaptations in the material culture and economy occurred very gradually as a more temperate and less Mediterranean climate was reached. Even in the southern part of the Balkan peninsula, however, an important feature of the Near Eastern neolithic–early chalcolithic assemblages was modified. This consisted of a change in the form and method of construction of *houses*.[9] The use of mud-bricks, which had been the predominant building material in the Near East, was abandoned in favour of walls constructed of clay and straw or of wattle daubed with clay, in both cases on a framework of wooden posts of varying solidity (Fig. 9). It has been suggested that this was an adaptation to an environment of increasingly heavier rainfall and denser woodland. Other factors may also have been responsible, such as the relative stability or instability of settlements, the absence of sufficient hours of the right kind of sunshine for drying clay bricks, and the presence of a different kind of clay. The houses of the Near East were square multi-roomed structures with flat roofs, joined to each other by a common wall to form

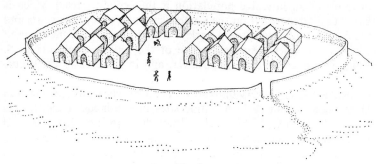

Fig. 9

Reconstruction of the neolithic settlement at Karanovo, Bulgaria (after a model in the National Archaeological Museum, Sofia).

'agglomerated' villages. Those of south-east Europe, including neolithic Greece, were square or rectangular one-roomed structures. On the basis of evidence from house-models the roofs were gabled. The houses were arranged in close proximity to each other but completely detached. The causes of the change to a sloping gabled roof may have included protection of the house, particularly the wall foundations, from rain and dripping water. Others factors were undoubtedly the use of different roofing materials from those used in the Near East, particularly deciduous trees. It is impossible to tell whether the change in building materials and roofing method were responsible for the change from agglomerated to detached houses, or whether the change in village type, caused by a modification of the social structure, necessitated a different roofing method.

Evidence for the vegetation and climate of the areas of Europe into which the primary agriculturalists were moving is still very scarce.

To a great extent it is based on the Carbon 14 evidence for dating the early neolithic settlements and synchronising them with the north European vegetational zone system. The dates which range roughly from 5600–3800 B.C. all fall into a period contemporary with the early part of the Atlantic vegetational period. This period was characterised by generally increased humidity which is reflected by an overall increase in vegetation particularly of mixed oak forest both in temperate central and south-east Europe. The processes involved in the expansion of agriculturalists from the Near East into Europe were presumably not associated with any conscious organised movement to a new land mass. It was more a continuous process associated with the movements of semi-shifting agriculturalists and stockbreeders who took advantage of the increase in extent and density of vegetation on the fertile soils of their northern edge. It would seem that, at least as far as the whole Danube valley, the upper Elbe, Vistula and Rhine rivers, there was a spread of an agricultural population, but that beyond those areas the presence of early neolithic cultures indicates a diffusion of the techniques and equipment associated with agriculture rather than of the agriculturalists themselves.

Throughout the whole area of the initial expansion of the agriculturalists from the south Balkans to temperate Europe there is a large variety of micro-environments, but a general increase in humidity and a decrease in annual hours of sunshine is apparent from south to north, with a transitional zone in the middle Danube valley in E. Hungary and N.E. Yugoslavia. Variation and innovation in the economy and material culture of the early neolithic settlements of eastern Europe reflects the response to these qualitative changes in the natural environment. It would seem that the evolution of the early and middle neolithic cultures of this area from 5500–3800 B.C. was largely internal with little diffusion of innovations from outside central and south-east Europe. The variations in the assemblages and settlements of the earliest food-producers of eastern Europe have been divided into two main groups: those of south-east Europe or the lower Danube basin, which have no single name but are referred to as the Karanovo I–Kremikovci–Starčevo–Körös–Criş culture group; and those of temperate central Europe, which were formerly known collectively as Danubian I, following V. Gordon Childe's terminology,[10] but since they are not confined to the Danube drainage area have now been more correctly grouped under the name of the distinctive decoration of their pottery—the Linear Pottery cultures or culture group.

In both the culture groups the economy was based on agriculture and stockbreeding. In the settlements of each area, however, rather

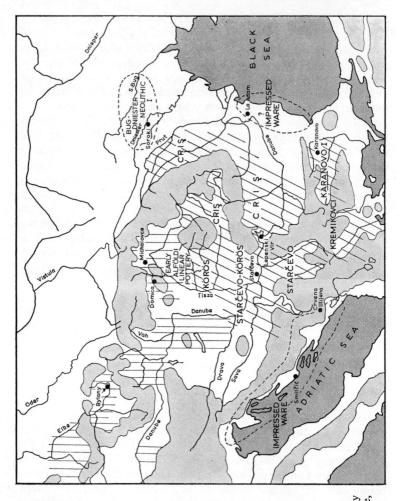

Early Linear Pottery
cultures

Early painted pottery
cultures

Land over 500 m.a.s.l.

Fig. 10
Map of the distribution of early
neolithic cultures in E. Europe,
c. 5500–4300 B.C.

different emphasis was placed in the economy on domesticated sources in relation to other sources, such as wild animals. In addition the stockbreeders of each area concentrated on rearing different domesticated animals. The pottery of central Europe includes forms and fabric similar to certain categories of early neolithic south-east European pottery, but there is an absence of painted decoration and a predominance of incised decoration. The chipped and polished stone industries of the two culture groups were very similar. Flat trapezoid *polished stone* implements (Fig. 11) occur in both areas.[11] They have identical forms and presumably were used in very similar ways. (The function of these implements, however, is pure speculation without a detailed examination of their surfaces for traces of wear.) They have been interpreted as axes or adzes for use in woodworking such as cutting down trees and preparing wood for the construction of houses. They may also have been used in the manufacture of wooden artefacts. After the initial expansion of the agriculturalists, in the so-called 'middle-neolithic' settlements in both areas, the flat 'axe-adzes' were supplemented and in many cases superseded by polished stone implements of a narrower more rectangular shape with a high plano-convex cross-section. From their shape they could only have been used with a transverse edge, that is as an adze, and it is likely that they performed different tasks from the flat axe-adzes, possibly digging earth or even in the preparation of skins in addition to woodworking. It has been suggested that, because of their large quantity on neolithic sites, polished stone implements were the principal implements of production. It is possible, however, that wooden implements which have not survived were of equal importance.

Chipped stone implements (Fig. 11) are a constant feature of neo-lithic assemblages, but occur in relatively small quantities.[12] This, however, may be an accident of excavation. There are no examples, in the settlements of the primary area of expansion, of blades made deliberately of microlithic size or shape apart from S. Rumania. The blades are generally not longer than 6 cm, as in the contemporary settlements of the Near East and Greece, with little or no modification of their shape by deliberate retouch. From traces of wear on their surfaces it is possible to see that the blades were used to saw, cut, scrape, shave and bore both hard materials such as bone or wood and soft materials such as meat and skin. There is very little evidence of the way in which they were hafted, whether singly or compositely. At Karanovo and Azmak in S. Bulgaria, and at Valea Răii in S.W. Rumania, antlers were excavated in which flint blades had been slotted and fixed with resin. From the high gloss on the surface of the blades, these composite implements had been used as 'sickles' to cut grass, reeds, or cultivated wheat.[13] The blades were inserted diagonally in order to form as continuous an edge as possible folowing the curve of the red-deer antler. From the distribution of gloss across one corner of the blades on other early neolithic sites of eastern Europe, it would seem that this was the usual method of constructing sickles in eastern Europe in this and later periods. It is possible that wooden as well as antler handles were used, but these would not have survived. The Near Eastern sickles were constructed rather differently with the blades inserted with their edges parallel to the handle. The flint blades were made in the same way and in the same shape as the European sickle blades, but it is clear that the handles were of different material. The Near Eastern examples were made of straight or only slightly curved wood such as those from Fayum in Egypt or Jarmo and Hassuna in Iraq, or they were made of straight horns of ibex or gazelle as with the Natufian knife-sickle from Jericho. It would seem that the early neolithic European method of constructing sickles was determined to a certain extent by the more

---

Fig. 11

Bone, stone and baked clay artefacts of the early neolithic settlements of E. Europe.

a Bone 'spatula'. Azmak, Bulgaria. Karanovo culture (Stara Zagora Museum).

b Bone 'spatula'. Kopancs-Zsoldos, S.E. Hungary. Körös culture (after Kutzian, 1947).

c Clay spindle-whorl. Agyai Erdö, S.E. Hungary. Körös culture (after Kutzian, 1947).

d Clay 'tomato-shaped' weight. Sövenyhaza, S.E. Hungary. Körös culture (after Kutzian, 1947).

e–f Polished stone axes. Azmak, Bulgaria. Karanovo culture (Stara Zagora Museum).

g Polished stone 'shoelast' adze (middle neolithic). Bylany, Czechoslovakia. Linear Pottery culture (Kutna Hora Museum).

h Reconstruction of the method of hafting prehistoric stone axes (after Bordaz, 1970).

i Reconstruction of the method of hafting prehistoric stone adzes (after Bordaz, 1970).

j Polished stone adze. Bikovo, Bulgaria. Karanovo culture (after Detev, 1960).

k Bone awls. Maroslele-Pana, S.E. Hungary. Körös culture (after Trogmayer, 1964).

l Clay conical weight. Tiszaug-Topart, S.E. Hungary. Körös culture (after Kutzian, 1947).

m Clay lamp. Hatched areas denote decoration by excising filled with white encrusted paint. Azmak, Bulgaria. Karanovo culture (Stara Zagora Museum).

n Clay lamp. Maroslele-Pana, S.E. Hungary. Körös culture (after Trogmayer, 1964).

o Clay 'stamp-seal' (pintadera). S.E. Hungary. Körös culture (after Kutzian, 1947).

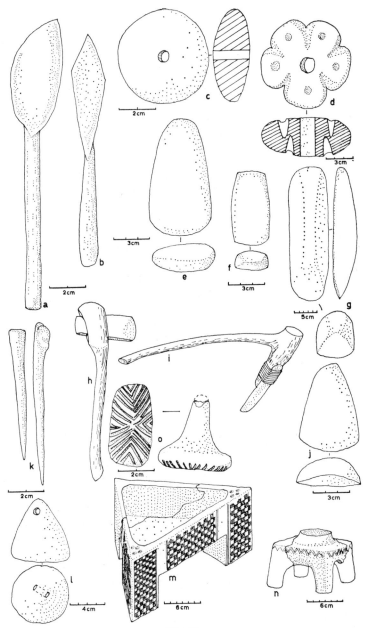

Fig. 11

deciduous forested environment and the shape of red-deer antler. These antlers incorporate a straight lower part near the head which was used as a handle, and a comparatively tightly curved point which was used as the cutting end.

In general there was a scarcity of *bone and antler* tools (Fig.11) excavated on early neolithic sites of eastern Europe. This may be explained partly by the poor preservative qualities of loess and related soils, but it is possible, as was speculated with the food-gathering settlements, that bone tools were carried with the settlers with each move of occupation site, whereas stone tools which have a shorter working life were made afresh at each new site. The implements which do occur in the Linear Pottery settlements, such as small bone points, have their counterparts in the early neolithic settlements of south-east Europe. These may have been used for piercing leather or even as heads of projectiles. The bone spatulae which are a common feature of early neolithic assemblages of south-east Europe are absent from temperate central Europe. In S.E. Europe these were often excavated in association with saddle querns and may have been employed in grinding activities. It has also been suggested that they were used in burnishing pottery.

Other features which are common to the assemblages of both areas include the custom of burying the dead lying on their side, in a contracted position among the houses without any specific grave area, and the form and construction of the houses.

KARANOVO I–KREMIKOVCI–STARČEVO–KÖRÖS– CRIŞ CULTURE GROUP

The early neolithic settlements of south-east Europe are divided in the literature into five or six cultures or sub-cultures (Fig.10, p. 74): Karanovo I in S. Bulgaria, Kremikovci in W. Bulgaria and S. Yugoslavia (Macedonia), Starčevo in E. Yugoslavia (Serbia and Bosnia), Körös in S.E. Hungary, a transitional form Starčevo-Körös in N.E. Yugoslavia (Vojvodina) and S.W. Rumania, and Criş in the rest of Rumania. Generally these cultural names correspond to a variation in settlement type and location and basis of economy. Much less variety is apparent in the material culture. First of all, the features which these 'cultures' share in common with each other will be examined, including pottery, figurines, houses and burials.

Pottery

The pottery may be divided into three categories:

1. Thick, coarse chaff-tempered pottery (Fig. 12), poorly fired to a buff or orange colour. The surface is often roughened all over by patterns of reed-, finger-, and nail-impressions, or by patterns made by running the fingers over the surface while it was still wet, or by the application of strips of clay sometimes in the form of animals and humans, especially in the Körös culture. In the Körös culture the unslipped surface was occasionally painted with vertical black stripes in addition to the rustication.[14] This coarse ware comprised the main domestic pottery, including large storage vessels. It was made predominantly into bomb-shaped or globular pots, up to 50 cm high, with short, flaring, or cylindrical necks and low disc or flat bases. This category of pottery is found on every site and in many cases, especially further north, it is almost the only category of pottery.

2. Finer pottery tempered (Fig. 12) with less organic material, better fired to a grey or buff colour. The surface was often covered with a slip of the same clay (self-slip) or a wash which was then polished or burnished. The pots of this category were generally undecorated. The most characteristic forms are hemispherical or three-quarter spherical bowls, with a flat or disc base, or standing on a low hollow pedestal or on four cylindrical legs. There are also globular pots with cylindrical necks and ribbon or perforated lugs. The pottery of this category occurs on the majority of settlements.

3. Fine, hard well-fired pottery (Fig. 12) without any organic admixture. This was made into the same forms as the preceding category, especially pedestalled bowls. In the Karanovo I culture the bowls were tall and tulip-shaped. The surface of this pottery was covered by a thick red or white slip which was painted before firing in red, black or white patterns or a combination of these. After firing the whole surface was polished. The finer painted ware has been found much more rarely and in smaller quantities than the other categories. Only in Bulgaria and S. Yugoslavia does it occur on every site about which information is available, whereas in a large number of the more northern sites of the Körös and Criş cultures it has not been found at all. Cultural variation occurs to a certain extent in the various combinations of colour of slip and painted patterns in the different areas. For example, in the Karanovo I culture with very few exceptions decoration was by white-painted patterns on a red ground.[15] This combination (and light on dark designs in general) occur very rarely in south-east Europe outside S. Bulgaria, and apart from the Thessalian Sesklo culture and the early neolithic culture (Nea Nikomedea) of Greek Macedonia it is rare in the Near East and Greece. In the Kremikovci culture, white-

on-red decoration occurs only in association with pottery decorated by black painted designs on a red slip.[16] Black-on-red decoration predominates in the painted pottery of the Starčevo and Körös cultures, and it is this type of painted pottery which was diffused furthest north to occur in the southernmost Linear Pottery assemblages of N.E. Hungary.[17] Black-on-red painted pottery has no prototypes in the preceding early Chalcolithic culture of Anatolia or middle neolithic cultures of Greece where red painted patterns on a white slip predominated. The red-on-white painted pottery occurs only very rarely north of Greece. It seems possible, therefore, that the black-on-red decoration was the north Balkan adaptation to the same principle of painting dark patterns on a light ground as was seen in the red-on-white painted patterns of the south Balkans. The patterns themselves consist of bands of thick parallel lines filled with thin parallel stripes, or cross-hatching, as well as running spirals, etc. Although elements of these patterns occur in the contemporary middle neolithic assemblages of Greece, they are combined into quite different patterns, in the same way that the Greek middle neolithic patterns differed from the late neolithic and early Chalcolithic patterns of W. Anatolia.

Fig. 12

Pottery of the early neolithic cultures of S.E. Europe.

a Painted white-on-red pottery. Kapitan Dimitrievo (Banjata), Bulgaria. Karanovo culture (after Georgiev, 1961).

b Fine unpainted ware. Azmak, Bulgaria. Karanovo culture (Stara Zagora Museum).

c Coarse-tempered ware decorated by anthropomorphic relief. Azmak, Bulgaria. Karanovo culture (after Georgiev, 1961).

d Painted black-on-red pottery. Tečić, E. Yugoslavia. Starčevo culture (after Galović, 1962–3).

e Fine-tempered unpainted ware. Endröd, S.E. Hungary. Körös culture (after Kutzian, 1947).

f Coarse-tempered ware decorated by 'barbotine' relief. Starčevo, E. Yugoslavia. Starčevo culture (after Grbić, 1968).

g Painted black-on-red pottery. Valea Raii, S.W. Rumania. Criş culture (after Berciu, 1965).

h Fine-tempered unpainted ware. Valea Lupului, N.E. Rumania. Criş culture (after Berciu, 1961).

i Painted black-on-red ware. Obrež-Baštinte, N.E. Yugoslavia. Starčevo–Körös culture (after Brukner, 1968).

j Coarse-tempered ware decorated by finger-nail impressions. Ludaš-Biserna Obala, N.E. Yugoslavia. Starčevo-Körös culture (Subotica Museum).

k Coarse-tempered ware. Large storage pot decorated by zoomorphic and possible anthropomorphic relief designs. Kotacpart-Vata, S.E. Hungary. Körös culture (after Kutzian, 1947).

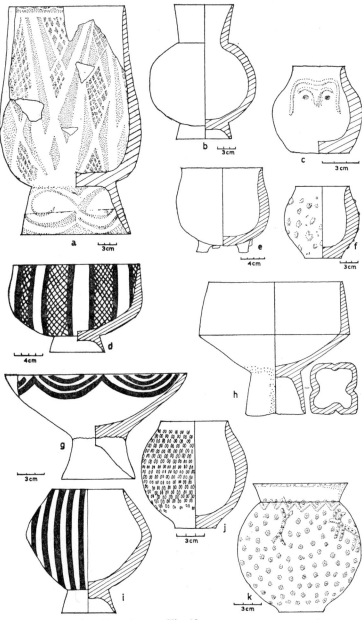

Fig. 12

F

Clay anthropomorphic figurines (Fig. 13) were a constant feature
of the neolithic and chalcolithic assemblages of the Near East and
Greece.[18] They also occur in the neolithic and eneolithic assemblages
of south-east Europe.[19] In the early neolithic assemblages they do not
occur in more than 20 per cent of the sites and in some areas such
as the Karanovo and Criş cultures they only occur sporadically on
one or two sites. Any resemblance between the figurines of Anatolia
and Greece and those of the north Balkans is unrecognisable, although the Near Eastern figurines undoubtedly provided the prototypes for those of south-east Europe. Generally the south-east
European figurines have been found in a broken state in rubbish
pits, or as surface finds. A complete figurine from Nea Nikomedia

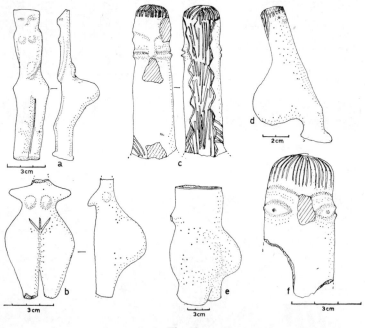

Fig. 13

Anthropomorphic figurines of the early neolithic settlements of S.E.
Europe.
a Clay figurine from Karanovo, Bulgaria (after Georgiev, 1961).
b Clay figurine from Slatina, W. Bulgaria (Sofia City Museum).
c Clay head of figurine. Obrež-Beletinci, N.E. Yugoslavia (after
    Galović, 1968).
d Clay figurine from Vinča, N.E. Yugoslavia (after Vasić, 1932–6).
e Anthropomorphic pot. Gorzsa, S.E. Hungary (after Kalicz, 1970).
f Clay figurine head. Gladnice, E. Yugoslavia (after Galović, 1968).

in Greek Macedonia, and one from Ludvár in S.E. Hungary (Pl. 2), show the range of the early neolithic figurines of S.E. Europe.[20] The figurines consisted of a tall cylindrical or conical head, a flat upper part of the torso on which the arms were rarely more than stumps. Those further south had more carefully portrayed arms.[21] The lower part of the body consisted of fat buttocks with the feet unportrayed. The figurines were in standing position, especially in the south, or a semi-reclining position. Facial features such as eyes, nose, and hair, but very rarely the mouth, were incised or modelled in relief. The majority of the figurines had only small pointed breasts, although those on a few were more substantial. From the fact that breasts are present, however, and buttocks are exaggerated, it has been assumed, perhaps dangerously, that all the figurines of this type represent females. In addition there were clay cylinders on which facial features were portrayed as well as sporadic anthropomorphic pots.[22] The anthropomorphic pot from Gorzsa contained burnt remains of a human skull. It is more than likely that these various kinds of human representations had different functions and significance. What these functions were is very much open to speculation. They have frequently been associated indiscriminately in the literature with hypotheses of prehistoric fertility rites and a belief in the Great Mother Earth Goddess, but so far there is no contextual evidence in the early neolithic settlements to support these hypotheses. Zoomorphic representations, apart from relief decoration on pottery, are very rare in the early neolithic assemblages of south-east Europe.

While on the subject of 'cult objects', it is interesting to note the presence of small triangular clay vessels with straight sides and a foot at each angle (Fig. 11). They are decorated over their whole surface by excised and incised patterns filled with white encrusted paint. The patterns and form of decoration are quite unknown in the pottery of the early neolithic assemblages of S.E. Europe, and it has been suggested that they were copied from patterns carved on wooden prototypes. They also occur in the preceding and contemporary assemblages of Anatolia and Greece. There is no evidence of their function. They have been excavated predominantly in a broken state from rubbish pits, and have been interpreted as 'altars' and as 'lamps'.

Clay *stamp-seals* or pintadera (Fig. 11) are a common feature of the neolithic assemblages of the Balkans and the Near East. They consist of a flat, concave or convex stamping surface and a short, roughly conical handle. The stamping surface is provided with excised patterns including spirals and meanders, again of a type which never occurs on the pottery. From the available evidence it is impossible to tell what material, if any, the seals were used for stamping, whether bone, skin, clay or wax.

Small round perforated clay objects have been found on almost every neolithic site in the Balkan peninsula and the Near East. They have been interpreted as *spindle-whorls* (Fig. 11) designed to rotate at the end of a long spindle (which was probably made of wood) in order to spin fibres or the wool or hair of sheep and goats. The bone material indicates that sheep and goats played an important part in the economy of the early neolithic sites. In addition to spindle-whorls, there were larger perforated clay objects for which various interpretations have been suggested. The cylindrical, conical or pear-shaped objects with longitudinal or small transverse perforations have frequently been interpreted as *loom-weights* (Fig. 11) designed to weigh down the warp threads which were suspended from the roof of a house. Recently, at Tiszajenő (Fig. 14) in S.E. Hungary, two small post-holes were excavated inside a house.[23] One of these was close to a side-wall, the other was 185 cm away towards the centre of the house. It was suggested that these could not be structural elements of the house. It was further suggested that they may represent the upright posts of a loom inside the house, particularly since a pile of so-called 'loom-weights' lay near the posts and did not occur elsewhere in the house. The bone analysis from this site showed a predominance of sheep and goats.

The other large clay objects are the 'tomato-shaped weights' (Fig. 11) which are rounded, up to 10 cm in diameter with a large perforation in the middle, from which radiate indentations which may have been for attaching further ropes in addition to the perforation. These have been interpreted as weights for fish-nets.

Houses

The habitations of the early neolithic settlements of south-east Europe have been divided in much of the literature into surface and semi-subterranean dwellings. It has been suggested on the basis of certain stratified sites, where only pits occur in the lower habitation

---

Fig. 14

Early neolithic house construction in S.E. Europe.

a–b House from Karanovo, Bulgaria. Karanovo culture (after Georgiev, 1961, and Piggott, 1965). a Isometric reconstruction. b Ground-plan of the house.

c–d House excavated at Tiszajenő, S.E. Hungary. Körös culture (after Selmeczi, 1969). c Isometric reconstruction. d Ground-plan of the house: (i) hearth, (ii) storage pot, (iii) post-holes possibly for weaving-loom, (iv) conical clay weights possibly from loom.

e Fragment of clay house-model with reconstruction. Röszke-Ludvar, S.E. Hungary. Körös culture (after Trogmayer, 1969).

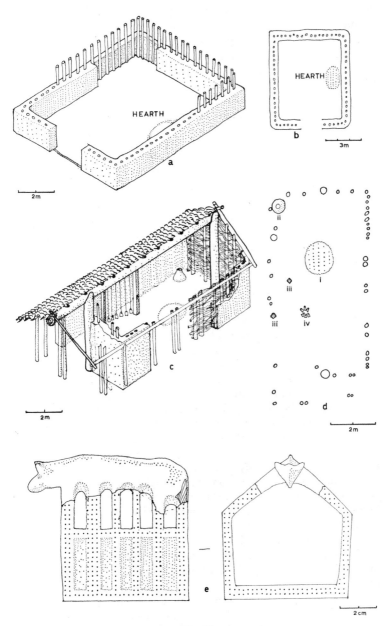

HEARTH

HEARTH

a

b

3m

2m

c

i

ii

iii

iii   iv

d

2m

2m

e

2cm

Fig. 14

level and surface houses in the upper level, that there was an evolution from the semi-subterranean to the surface form of habitation.[24] There is no positive evidence to support this theory. From the absence of any traces of a superstructure over the pits or habitation floor within them, it seems very unlikely that any of the pits were lived in. The absence of any traces of surface habitations on a site may be explained either by poor local conditions of preservation, the fact that in most cases, if the houses were not accidentally fired, the clay comprising the walls would not be preserved, or lack of recognition of the traces. The evidence from the foundations of houses which have survived show that they were small rectangular one-roomed structures on average 8 m long and 4 m wide.[25] None of the houses show any traces of internal divisions.

There seem to have been two main methods of house construction.[26] The first was to construct a framework of thin vertical wooden posts on which were built thick walls of clay and chaff (Fig. 14). At Azmak the clay walls have been preserved up to a height of 30 cm.[27] The small, densely packed post-holes of the framework are visible in the thickness of the clay wall. The second method was to build a framework of a few heavy upright posts, visible in the large widely-spaced post-holes, as at Tiszajenő (Fig. 14). On this framework the walls were constructed of plaited branches or wattling which were daubed on both sides with clay. Evidence of the wattling is seen in impressions of branches in the daub which has survived. There is evidence (e.g. at Karanovo) that the plaster walls were painted red and white, and the house-model from Ludvár in S.E. Hungary showed the addition of an animal's head at the gable end of the roof (Fig. 14). The clay for the walls and roof of the houses was obtained from pits alongside or nearby the houses. These were frequently used secondarily as rubbish pits, or for storage, hearths, ovens or even burials. It seems that the two methods of construction are distributed arbitrarily in the settlements of south-east Europe, some sites having houses constructed by both methods. The advantage of the first method with heavy clay walls is that, although it takes longer to build, it lasts longer. It has therefore frequently been assumed to indicate a greater permanence of settlement. Permanence of settlement, however, is not the only factor to affect methods of house construction. Social factors and available raw materials may be of equal importance.[28] It is true, though, that the first method of construction with the clay and chaff walls was favoured more, as far as one can tell from the present state of evidence, in the southern settlements of Bulgaria and S. Yugoslavia in those settlements whose stratigraphy shows continuous habitation over a considerable period of time. Further north, on the other hand, where occupation layers were thinner, houses were built predominantly with walls made of wattle daubed with clay. The distribution of the two methods, however, is by no means mutually exclusive.

Evidence of the interior furniture of the houses of the early neo-lithic settlements of south-east Europe is a rare feature. In many houses the original floor, beaten hard, has been preserved and often contains traces of hearths, especially at the end opposite the entrance. There is never more than one hearth to each house. They are generally round and up to one metre in diameter. The more solid examples built of clay and chaff on a foundation of stones are more likely to have been the remains of ovens for drying grain and re-moving the clinging hull of emmer wheat. Both hearths and ovens are also found outside the houses. Querns and rubbers of sandstone for grinding grain, fibres and other plants were a universal feature in the houses. Many houses also have facilities for storing grain and presumably other vegetable commodities inside the houses in the form of large storage pots. In the house at Tiszajenő, the pot was 70 cm in diameter and was dug 60 cm into the ground below the floor of the house (Fig. 14). At other sites, clay-lined storage pits were dug outside the houses.[29] They were about 1 metre in diameter, not more than 60 cm deep and were used to store forest products as well as cultivated grain (Pl. 1).

Evidence of any specific arrangement of the houses in the early neolithic settlements of south-east Europe is severely limited by the lack of large-scale excavations in this area. Generally, only one house or a very small group of houses has been excavated. At Karanovo (Fig. 9), however, it was possible to see that the houses were arranged very close to each other in rows separated by a street which may have been covered by logs.[30] At Varoš in N.W. Yugoslavia, situated on a mound rising above swampy ground, the houses were arranged in a semi-circle.[31] Along rivers, houses were arranged in a long row with their entrances facing the river[32] or in an irregular cluster.[33]

Burials

Of the large number of early neolithic sites of south-east Europe, burials have been excavated at only twenty-eight.[34] The majority were buried in refuse pits, to one side of the pit or in a slightly deepened grave. In several sites, one particular refuse pit was used for burying the dead, while the other pits were not used for this purpose. In some cases the dead were buried in specific shallow grave-pits among the houses. The dead were always buried in a contracted position lying on their side but without any consistent orientation. The very few grave-goods which occur generally consist of a pot placed near the head, or ornaments such as a *Tridachna* shell arm-ring or shell necklace. Apart from grave-goods, other indications of definite rites associated with the burial in the early neolithic period include red ochre scattered round a woman's head at Szarvas and the skull covered by red paint at Endröd in S.E. Hungary.

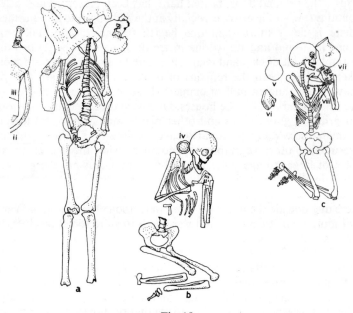

Fig. 15

Burial practices of the mesolithic and early neolithic settlements of E. Europe.
a Lepenski Vir, mesolithic burial 7 (after Srejović, 1969): (i) auroch's skull, (ii) red-deer antler, (iii) hearth stones.
b Deszk, S.E. Hungary. Early neolithic burial (after Trogmayer, 1969): (iv) pot.
c Sonnenhausen, S.E. Germany. Linear Pottery culture burial (after Kahlke, 1954: (v) pot, (vi) grindstone and rubbing-stone, (vii) pot, (viii) polished stone axe.

The means of subsistence of the early agriculturalists in southeast Europe, the localities of their settlements, and the duration of these settlements show rather greater regional variation.[35] Unfortunately, the evaluation of the differences in the economy is not as reliable as it could be, since analyses of the faunal and floral evidence has rarely been carried out. The analyses which have been made are not of uniform accuracy or detail.

North Greece

Animal bones have been analysed from sites contemporary with or immediately preceding the earliest food-producing settlements of S.E. Europe in the Proto-Sesklo cultural layers of 'tell' settlements in early neolithic levels in Macedonia.[36] There was an almost complete absence of wild animal bones and an overwhelming predominance of the exploitation of domesticated animals, in particular sheep or goats, and to a much lesser extent cattle and pigs. Domesticated dogs occur in very small numbers; it is possible that these were used in sporadic hunting expeditions. The wild animals which do occur are the same large forest mammals which were hunted in the mesolithic settlements of S.E. Europe: red-deer, aurochs, and wild pig. Evidence for domesticated wheat, both einkorn and emmer wheat, as well as barley and lentils, comes from the same sites.[37] Analyses of flora and fauna from the preceding preceramic neolithic settlements of Thessaly, for example at Argissa, indicates a very similar basic economy to that of the ceramic neolithic sites.

These analyses of faunal material from the north Greek sites may be used, to a certain extent, as analogies for the economy of the Bulgarian and south Yugoslav settlements, where the examination of animal bones has so far been based only on the roughest calculations. On the other hand, there are some detailed analyses of the cultivated grain from the Bulgarian and S. Yugoslav sites.

Karanovo I

In the form of its pottery and its preference for white-on-red painted decoration, the Karanovo I culture of the Maritsa valley in S. Bulgaria[38] is an exception to the general north Balkan pattern. This is further emphasised by the form of its settlements. Several of the settlements of the earliest agriculturalists occur as habitation levels at the base of large stratified mounds referred to as 'tells' following the Near Eastern terminology. These are the only instances of genuine 'tell' settlements of the early neolithic period outside Greece and the Near East. They comprise steep-sided mounds, sometimes as high as 12 metres, which were formed, as far as it is possible to assess from the present state of research, by the accumulated occupation debris of continuous habitation of the same spot over many generations.[39] The occupation may have lasted several millenia and have involved several successive cultures. The process of 'tell' formation is extremely complex, involving factors of natural environment, of economy in the stability and permanence of settlement, and of choice of building materials, especially those which are not easily destroyed, such as clay. The stratigraphical evidence of the largest south Bulgarian 'tells', Karanovo, Azmak, Kapitan Dimitrievo, Imrančevo and Kazanlak has formed the basis, in recent years, of the chronological framework for the neolithic cultures of south-east Europe.[40] It is particularly valuable since at Karanovo and Azmak each cultural layer is supported by a consistent series of Carbon 14 dates.[41]

The early neolithic habitation levels at the base of the 'tells' are thin in comparison to the later neolithic and eneolithic levels (see Chapter 4). At Karanovo, for example, the early neolithic layer with painted pottery (layer I) is 1 m thick and contains three habitation levels. This, however, is much thicker than the majority of the more northern early neolithic sites. The evidence of continuous habitation for a long period of time would suggest a considerable degree of permanence of settlement. Evidence that this stability of settlement was made possible by an economy based largely on food-production, as in the Near East and Greece in this period, comes from only two sources. First, cultivated grain has been found on all sites in the form of grain impressions on pottery and fired wall plaster and carbonised grain, and has been identified as wheat, of einkorn and especially emmer varieties.[42] The absence of barley may be explained by the fact that wild barley only grows east of this region. Secondly, although, unfortunately, there are no analyses of faunal material available, the choice of location of the settlements in S. Bulgaria away from rivers in the middle of the fertile plain or at the spring-line may indicate a lack of importance of hunting activities. As was pointed out in Chapter 2, the margins and not the centres of micro-ecological zones are the most profitable for settlements with an economy based on hunting and gathering, whereas the reverse would seem to be the case for settlements with an economy based on agriculture and stockbreeding. It should be noted, however, that a spring-line may also be a convergence area of several micro-ecological zones.

In the Stara Planina mountains several cave settlements have been discovered whose assemblages are identical to the lowland sites of the Karanovo I culture, even in the painted decoration of the pottery.[43] Analyses of their faunal evidence shows an equal importance of domesticated animals, especially ovicaprids and wild animals, in particular red-deer. It is possible that these were summer settlements of herders from the plains who practised a form of trans-humance.

Kremikovci culture

Early neolithic 'tell' settlements occur only occasionally in west Bulgaria (for example at Čelopeč),[44] south Yugoslavia and, apparently, Greek Macedonia. The settlements form much shallower mounds with a more widespread distribution of habitation debris, which may reflect a partial horizontal displacement of the settlement after each break in habitation. Many of the sites have stratified layers of several cultures as in south Bulgaria, but there is much less continuous occupation of the sites. The early neolithic culture layers of these sites are relatively thick, all thicker than 1 metre; the culture layer at Vršnik in S. Yugoslavia is 3·7m thick. At many sites the early neolithic culture layer consists of one thick habitation level, at others there are 2–5 habitation levels.[45] The habitation levels on these sites, unlike those of S. Bulgaria, are frequently separated by a thin sterile layer of mud, gravel or humus representing a temporary abandonment of the site. In many cases it has been suggested that the break in occupation is of a long duration. On some sites, such as Slatina and Vršnik, there is a difference in the assemblages of the various levels in the presence or absence of pottery decoration by white-painted patterns along with the constant black painting. Whether this difference represents a vital stage in the evolution of the Kremikovci culture is questionable.

The settlements are located on the spring-line and on the banks or lower terraces of rivers. From their thick habitation layers, and with the help of the evidence from north Greece, it seems probable that the economy of the settlements was based on the products of domesticated animals and cultivated grain. The analysis of grain remains at Vršnik showed that, as in Bulgaria, only wheat was cultivated, predominantly emmer and einkorn.[46]

Starčevo culture

The settlements of the earliest agriculturalists in central and east Yugoslavia are generally situated on the upper terraces of river valleys or on the edges of plateaus.[47] In many cases the early neolithic culture layers are stratified below later neolithic and eneolithic layers but the layers rarely form mounds and never form 'tells'. This would suggest that occupation of the site was less continuous than further south, with longer and more frequent breaks. The early neolithic culture layer is generally c. 1 metre thick, rarely comprising more than one habitation level. Gornja Tuzla and Pavlovac are exceptions in this respect.[48] What this reflects in terms of basic economy is impossible to tell until the faunal and floral evidence of at least one site has been analysed.

Starčevo–Körös and Körös culture

Further north the settlements were located on the banks or low terraces of rivers or on mounds of alluvial sand which rise above

the waterlogged or marshy flood plain.[49] They are therefore unusual
in following the favoured location of the settlements of the mesolithic hunters and gatherers (Chapter 2). There are a number of sites
in N.E. Yugoslavia and S.E. Hungary whose bone material has been
analysed in detail, thanks to the efforts of Dr S. Bökönyi.[50] Although the bones of domesticated animals form up to three-quarters
of the total bones, they are generally not such an overwhelming
majority as in the south Balkan sites. Domesticated sheep and goats
are consistently more important than cattle and pigs. Bökönyi has
pointed out the illogicality of the dependence on domesticated
sheep and goats in these settlements, which were generally situated
very close to water or in waterlogged surroundings. Such conditions
were unfavourable for the growth and breeding of these animals. It
is interesting to note that the sheep and goats of these settlements are
of a considerably reduced size in comparison with those further south.
This may be due either to the unfavourable conditions or to the
necessity of breeding from a limited stock owing to the complete
absence of wild sheep and goats in this area. By necessity, or by
cultural choice, the resources available from domesticated animals
were supplemented by the exploitation of wildlife. In waterlogged
sites, for example Ludvár and Maroslele (Pana), this comprised
predominantly water mammals such as turtle, and fish, freshwater
shellfish and water-birds, as well as forest mammals such as roe-
deer and aurochs. The fish include specially the large wels or catfish which sometimes weighed up to 200 kg. There is no evidence
of the use of hooks or fish-spears which is the method used to catch
fish in this area at the present time. There are large numbers of the
tomato-shaped clay objects described above (p. 84) which have been
interpreted as net-weights, and it is likely that the net was an important method of catching fish. It has also been suggested that, for
example, in the spring when floods were frequent, the fish were collected as they lay stranded on the land after the flood-water had
receded. It is interesting to note in this context that at the site of
Ludvár a pit was excavated in which fish bones were concentrated
at a certain depth, below which was a layer in which were concentrated the bones of forest mammals. Below this was a 30 cm thick
layer of freshwater mussel shells.[51] It has been suggested that this
stratification of the bones represents the seasonal exploitation of the
resources, fish in summer, forest animals in autumn or winter and
shell-fish in spring. It is likely that the pit, therefore, contains the
debris of one year's occupation of the site. The birds from the waterlogged sites were all fish-eaters, and all lake or marsh-birds. At the
present time most of these, such as the grebes, grey heron, mallard,
herring-gull, are resident in this area all the year round. Only the

crane no longer occurs in central Europe, but at that time may have been a summer visitor.

On the sites located on the banks and lower terraces of rivers, such as Ludaš (Budžak) (which is now situated in the river's flood plain), there was less exploitation of water resources and a greater concentration on the hunting of land mammals. The animals included especially aurochs, roe-deer and species such as wild ass (*asinus hydruntinus*) which are more familiar in parkland vegetation. It seems likely from the fauna that the forest in this area was considerably thinner than further north or south. There is a marked decrease in hunting red-deer and wild pig which are animals of the thicker deciduous forests. There is a lack of any tools in the Starčevo–Körös assemblages which could be interpreted as projectile armatures. As was pointed out in the previous chapter, however, this need not be the only method of hunting, nor are projectiles necessarily manufactured in a durable material. There are a small number of domesticated dogs represented among the bones which may have been used for hunting as well as for rounding up the wild or domesticated animals. Along with frequent occurrence of aurochs' bones in the early neolithic assemblages of this area, it is interesting to note the presence, for example at Maroslele, of individuals which appear to be of a transitional form between the wild *Bos Primigenius* and the domesticated *Bos Taurus*. This might indicate either a deliberate, or at least encouraged, interbreeding between the local wild stock and the imported domesticated stock as the initial stages in the domestication of the local wild cattle.

It is difficult to assess to what extent the animal resources were supplemented by vegetable resources in these settlements. Direct evidence for the cultivation of einkorn and emmer wheat comes from the remains and impressions of grains. It is probable that grain cultivation was not so important on the sites located in the flood plains. On some of the sites such as Ludaš (Budžak) and Nosa (Biserna Obala) which were formerly on the drier banks of the river there is evidence, in the form of shallow storage pits containing millet, acorns and beechnuts, of intensive collection and probably cultivation of plants (p. 87). As in central Yugoslavia the thickness of the culture layer of the Starčevo–Körös settlements varies from half to one metre, and rarely consists of more than one habitation level.[52]

In the Danube gorges, in particular the *Iron Gates gorge*, settlements with assemblages whose pottery and many other features are identical to those described above, were frequently stratified above mesolithic habitation layers (e.g. Lepenski Vir and Schela Cladovei). They are situated on the banks of the Danube or its terraces, or on the edge of the mountains on top of the gorge. The analyses of the

bone material from these sites show that the basis of their economy
was rather different from that of the Starčevo–Körös settlements.[53]
The percentage of wild animal bones was often greater than those of
domesticated animals. There is palaeobotanical evidence that the
settlements of this area were surrounded by thick deciduous forest
and that large forest mammals, in particular red-deer, were the
most important quarry for the hunters, as they had been for the
preceding mesolithic hunters in this region. Wild pig and roe-deer
were also hunted, and, to a lesser extent, aurochs, bear and lynx.
Dogs were more numerous than on other early neolithic settlements
and were probably used predominantly for hunting. The chipped
stone industry of these settlements differs from that of the mesolithic settlements of this area and from those of other early neolithic
settlements in S.E. Europe in that good-quality flint from a mined
source was used, whereas in the mesolithic assemblages the stone
artefacts were made of quartzite and pebble flint. It is interesting to
note the presence in the early neolithic assemblage at Lepenski Vir
of two blades of obsidian, which must have been acquired from the
mountains of N.E. Hungary (p. 46). In addition to the use of different
raw materials, the early neolithic blades were larger, more numerous
and of a more standard shape which was frequently modified by
the use of deliberate retouch. It is possible that some of these
chipped stone implements were used for hunting weapons, but it is
more likely that some of the large bone points were used for this
purpose and that, as in the mesolithic, various forms of trap were
used. Bird- and fish-bones also occur in large quantities at these sites.
Although 365 of the 400 fish-bones at Lepenski Vir (layer III) cannot
be identified, it would seem that there and at Cuina Turcului, as in
the Starčevo–Körös waterbound sites, the early food-producers
preferred to fish for the huge voracious wels and the barbel, a large
member of the carp family. Like the carp, which was the fish predominantly exploited in the mesolithic settlements of this region,
these fish are not only difficult to catch, but they are also difficult to
kill. Both these species, however, produce a large amount of meat.
The fish may have been caught in nets, weirs, or clubbed to death
as they lay stranded on the land after inundation water had receded.
In the neolithic settlement of Lepenski Vir there is evidence of
barbless bone fish-hooks which do not occur in the mesolithic
assemblages of eastern Europe and are very rare in the early neolithic
assemblages.[54]

Among the domesticated animals, unlike the Starčevo–Körös and
south Balkan settlements, cattle were more important than sheep
and goats. As in some of the Körös settlements, some of the cattle
appear to be the result of interbreeding between the imported

domesticated stock and local wild cattle. There is no direct evidence of grain cultivation on any of the settlements in this area. The settlements of the Iron Gates area tend to form thicker layers of occupation debris than those elsewhere along the Danube valley, in some cases as thick as 2·5m. It is possible that this accumulation reflects a greater degree of permanency of settlement due to the exploitation of all the rich resources of the surrounding forests and river.

Criş culture of Rumania[55]

The Criş culture can be subdivided into three regional variations. West of the curve of the Carpathian mountains in *Transilvania* the settlements are situated on the lower terraces of river valleys, and comprise a thin culture layer, less than half a metre thick, consisting of a single habitation level.[56] The site of Let in S.E. Transilvania is an exception to the general pattern in that it is located on a high terrace and comprises three early neolithic habitation levels stratified below later neolithic and eneolithic culture layers (see Chapter 4). In general, however, it would seem that the Criş settlements of this region were occupied for only short periods. The little evidence for the economy shows that here too there was a greater importance attached to cattle breeding than sheep or goats. It is interesting to note that in the Carpathian mountains themselves there are cave settlements whose assemblages are identical to those of the lowland sites.[57] Unfortunately, there is no evidence to indicate the basis of economy, but it is possible that, as with the Bulgarian cave settlements such as Devetaki (p. 90), these may represent the summer settlements of herders practising a form of transhumance.

The majority of early neolithic settlements in Rumania south of the Carpathians (*Oltenia and Muntenia*) are also located on the lower terraces of river valleys and also consist of a thin culture layer, less than half a metre thick.[58] The Criş culture layers of these settlements, however, frequently consist of more than one habitation level. This would suggest a different economic basis from that of the settlements described above. From the animal bone material at Verbiţa (although this is a very small sample) it is clear that domesticated animals were more important in the economy than wild animals. As in the Iron Gates and Transilvanian settlements cattle predominated among the domesticated animals whereas sheep and goats were relatively unimportant and pigs were almost absent. The cattle are of a small variety and were unlikely to be locally domesticated animals. Among the wild animals hunted on the site, however, aurochs were the most numerous and, as in the Körös sites, this may indicate the initial stages in the domestication of, or interbreeding with, the local wild cattle, rather than merely a concentration on hunting aurochs for food. At the drier, more elevated site of Valea Răii in N. Oltenia there is evidence of a greater importance of sheep- and goat-breeding. At the same site clay figurines of rams have been excavated. These represent some of the rare occurrences of solid animal figurines on early neolithic sites of south-east Europe. There is evidence at these sites of fishing in the form of fish-bones, but there are no fish-hooks. It is interesting to note that on several sites in S.W. Rumania 'geometric' microlithic blades occur among the chipped stone implements of the early neolithic assemblages. Their size and form is identical to that of the microliths of the preceding mesolithic settlements of this area. From the evidence of the main content of the early neolithic assemblages, any cultural contact between the mesolithic and neolithic populations of this region seems unlikely. It is possible that the microlithic blades were used to arm fish-spears or as insets in antler handles to act as sickle blades. Apart from the blades with 'sickle-gloss' on their surface, there is no evidence of grain cultivation on these sites.

East of the Carpathians in *Moldova* occurred the northernmost expansion of the sites with a Criş culture assemblage including painted pottery.[59] As in the rest of Rumania, the sites were located on the lower terraces of river valleys and comprise predominantly a thin culture layer, less than half a metre thick, consisting of a single habitation level. Evidence for the economy shows that domesticated animals, in particular cattle, predominated over wild animals. Domesticated sheep or goats were of less importance and there were very few pigs. The bone sample is very small, but it is interesting to note that, unlike S. Rumania, the main hunted quarry was red-deer rather than aurochs. Grains of einkorn wheat have been excavated on sites of N.E. Rumania, but there are no traces of emmer wheat.

Contact between the early agriculturalists and food-gatherers in Moldavia

The north-eastern limit of the diffusion of the Karanovo I–Starčevo–Körös–Criş culture group with painted pottery, etc., and of the agriculturalists themselves, was the Prut river basin of N.E. Rumania (Figs. 8, 10). East of this area, in particular along the Dniester and southern Bug rivers, assemblages with a category of pottery, which is very similar in fabric and shape to the fine undecorated ware of the Criş culture, and with evidence of a partially food-producing economy, occur in habitation levels stratified above mesolithic levels (Chapter 2). Apart from the presence of pottery and food-production, the assemblages of this so-called Bug–Dniester (previously called southern Bug) culture and those of the preceding mesolithic are identical (Fig. 6). The settlements are located on the banks and the

1. The hunter-fisher settlement of Lepenski Vir in the Danube Iron Gates gorge, N.E. Yugoslavia, c. 5500 B.C.

2. Clay anthropomorphic figurine from Ludvár-Röszke, S.E. Hungary. Körös culture. About 15 cm high. (Szeged Museum)

3. Clay anthropomorphic figurine from Karanovo, layer III, S. Bulgaria. Veselinovo culture. 13·4 cm high. (Reproduced by courtesy of G.Georgiev from *Le Fin de l'âge de Pierre*, 1961)

lowest terraces of rivers. A settlement consists of thin stratified layers of occupation debris, each 10–50 cm thick, which represent successive stages in the evolution of the Bug–Dniester culture.[60] These are frequently overlain by layers containing assemblages of the eneolithic Tripolye culture (Chapter 4). From the stratigraphy of these sites, for example at Soroki on the Dniester, and at Basikov Ostrov, Sokoletz and Zankivtse on the S. Bug, three distinct phases of the culture are visible:

Early Bug–Dniester (Petčora–Skibenitz–Sokoletz variants)
Middle Bug–Dniester (Samtčin)
Late Bug–Dniester (Savran–Khmelnik–Haivoran sub-phases)

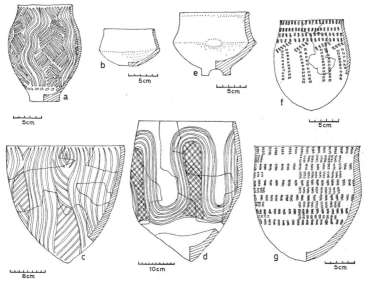

Fig. 16

Pottery of the Bug–Dniester culture. Early and middle (Samtčin) phases.
a Coarse-tempered pot decorated by wide deep channels. Soroki II, layer 1. Early Bug–Dniester (after Markyevič, 1965).
b Fine-tempered undecorated ware. Soroki I, layer 1b. Early Bug–Dniester (after Markyevič, 1965).
c Coarse-tempered ware decorated by wide deep channels. Sokoltse II, S. Bug river. Early Bug–Dniester (after Danilenko, 1969).
d Coarse-tempered ware decorated by wide incised lines. Basikov Ostrov, S. Bug river. Early Bug–Dniester (after Danilenko, 1969).
e Fine-tempered undecorated bowl. Glinskoye, S. Bug river. Early Bug–Dniester (after Danilenko, 1969).
f Coarse ware decorated by comb-stamped designs. Soroki I, layer 1a. Middle Bug–Dniester (after Markyevič, 1965).
g Coarse ware decorated by comb-stamped designs. Glinskoya S. Bug river. Middle Bug–Dniester (after Danilenko, 1969).

G

The early phase of the Bug–Dniester culture is contemporary with the Criş culture of Rumania as is shown not only by the occurrence of identical pottery but by the Carbon 14 dates of c. 4800 B.C. from the early Bug–Dniester level at the site of Soroki 2.[61] No surface houses have been found in these sites, but there are shallow pits in which, as in the mesolithic levels, occupation floors have been excavated. The pits may have been lived in or they may have provided material for building surface huts. However, since there are no traces of fired clay from the walls of such houses, it seems probable that the mesolithic form of dwelling construction was continued.

The food-producing economy was not on such an established basis as it is on the Criş settlements. Only a small percentage of bones were of domesticated animals. Among these, as in the Rumanian Criş culture, cattle predominate. Sheep and goats, however, are entirely absent from the bone material of all phases of the Bug–Dniester culture, although they form an integral, if sometimes small, part of the economy of the early neolithic sites of south-east Europe. Domesticated pigs, on the other hand, are more important than in the Criş culture. Large forest animals, in particular red-deer and aurochs, and to a lesser extent roe-deer and wild pig, continued to be the main hunted quarry, as in the preceding mesolithic, along with birds, fish and mollusca. The fish include predominantly roach, as in the mesolithic, as well as a small number of larger, meatier fish such as wels and pike. The evidence of the bird bones shows that two species of birds of prey (sparrow hawk and honey buzzard), two species of duck (mallard and teal) and wood pigeon were caught, presumably for food, although it is possible that their feathers were used. At present these birds breed and live all year round in the Dniester and S. Bug valleys except for the teal, which only lives there in the winter. This and the fact that roach hibernate from November to March would indicate that the settlements of the Bug–Dniester culture at this time were occupied at all seasons of the year, perhaps only for a few years. The techniques and equipment with which these animals were caught and processed are identical, as far as the evidence can indicate, to those used in the mesolithic, and remain the same in the later phases of the Bug–Dniester culture. Apart from a single example of a possible fish-hook made from a boar's tusk found in the S. Bug valley, there is no direct evidence of fishing equipment. However, there is a type of bone point which occurred for the first time in the Bug–Dniester area in this period but continued to be used in later phases of the culture; this is a short bone point, perforated at one end, which may have acted as a harpoon, possibly against the large wels and pike.

Grain impressions of einkorn wheat have been identified, for example at Soroki. There is no trace, however, of the cultivation of emmer wheat in any phase of the Bug–Dniester culture, although this species commonly occurred in the early agricultural settlements of central and south-east Europe. From the small number of sickle blades found on sites of the Bug–Dniester culture, it has been suggested that the einkorn wheat was harvested by plucking off the heads with fingers. The lack of saddle querns and grindstones of S.E. European type would suggest that there was also a difference in the method of processing the cultivated grain and other vegetable products. In the evidence of impressions of leaves and seeds, it would seem that a variety of plants was deliberately collected for food and fibres, in particular various grasses, not all of which occurred as weeds of cultivated wheat. It is even possible that the large numbers of perforated antler 'axes' (Fig. 6), which occur in all phases of the culture, may have been used for these activities, since their wide cutting edges would hardly be strong enough to cut wood. They could have been used to chop small branches, roots, fibres, etc., or even for digging in the ground, as was suggested for the implements of the same form from mesolithic levels.[62] There are very few polished stone artefacts of the type which occur in large numbers on the neolithic sites of S.E. and C. Europe, and it has been suggested that the antler perforated axes of the Bug–Dniester culture may have acted as substitutes for many of the functions performed by the polished stone implements.

It would seem, therefore, that the techniques and equipment of agriculture and stockbreeding were only partially taken over by the population of the Dniester and S. Bug valleys, whose economy was still based predominantly on hunting, fishing and gathering. They only partially accepted the innovations in the techniques and equipments of the Criş culture. To a large extent they adapted these to methods and activities which were already familiar. In this way their cultural equilibrium and identity was not vastly upset and was enriched by the presence of agricultural communities on their western border.

The main innovation which was accepted from the Criş culture was the technique of manufacturing pottery. In the early phase of the Bug–Dniester culture, there were two categories of pottery:

1. Fine, hard, grey or buff ware (Fig. 16), slightly tempered with vegetable material, with the surface covered in a self-slip and polished after firing. The most frequent form of this category was the hemispherical, three-quarter spherical or sharply biconical bowl, frequently with a beaded rim, with a flat, disc, ring or low pedestal base. The pots are generally undecorated and are identical in form and

fabric to the category of fine, undecorated pottery of the Criş culture
in N.E. Rumania.

2. The coarse rusticated ware of the Criş culture does not occur.
The second category of pottery (Fig. 16) consists of pots which are
unique in form and decoration to this early phase of the Bug–
Dniester culture. The pottery is tempered by a high proportion of
organic material including straw and leaves, as well as sand, grog
and shells. It is generally poorly fired to a dark grey colour on the
inside and light buff or orange on the outside. The characteristically
pock-marked surface was sometimes smoothed or even polished.
The basic methods of decoration are all known in the Criş coarse
rusticated ware, but the various elements are combined in a re-
markable diversity of styles, most of which have no recognisable
prototypes in the Criş culture. Thus reed-impressions are used in
zigzags; incised lines are used in volute patterns filled with cross-
hatching, or in stabs in combination with finger- and nail-impressions
and impressions of shells, small bones, etc.; fingers are drawn
across the wet surface of the pot in wavy lines. The forms into which
this category of pottery was made are also very different from those
of the early neolithic coarse ware of S.E. Europe, except for one
group with flat bases, globular bodies and low ring necks. The
majority of pots, however, were made in a truncated egg-shape with
rounded or pointed bottoms. It is interesting to note that identical
decoration frequently occurs on both flat- and pointed-based pots.
The important question is whether these pots are to be interpreted
as a local response to the manufacture of pottery by western neighbours and the conversion of basketry or leather prototypes to the
medium of fired clay, or whether they represent a more complex
diffusion of pottery, along with the technique of cattle-breeding,
from the east from the lower Dnieper valley. In this region are
assemblages with evidence of cattle-breeding, and pottery which
bears a superficial resemblance in its decoration by impressions and
pointed bases to that of the early Bug–Dniester culture.[63] The
problem is whether these assemblages are earlier or even contemporary with the early phase of the Bug–Dniester culture. There is no
definite evidence of their relative chronology, and it is possible that the
presence of these techniques in the lower Dnieper and Don valleys
may be the result of diffusion either eastwards from the Dniester
and Bug rivers, or westwards from Turkmenia and the north Caspian
Sea settlements.

On the basis of the form and decoration of the pottery, but without any relation to the stratigraphy of the sites, attempts have been
made to classify the early phase of the Bug–Dniester culture into

three divisions: Skibenitz, Sokoletz and Petčora. It was suggested that these were successive chronological sub-phases although there is no stratigraphical evidence for this. It seems more likely that they are regional variations. Generally, in the so-called Petčora assemblages there are closer resemblances to the Criş culture. In the so-called Skibenitz assemblages, which occur only on the Bug river, Criş elements are very rare.

Habitation levels of the middle (Samtčin) phase of the Bug–Dniester culture predominantly occur stratified over levels of the early phase, frequently with a thin sterile layer between the two levels. The assemblages show a sudden break in the pottery traditions but a strong continuity in the form and function of the stone, bone and antler implements, and in the basically hunting and fishing economy. It is interesting to note from the evidence of the fish-bones, which form a greater percentage even than in preceding periods, that there is a great increase in fishing activities. This coincides with an increase in fishing for carp and wels, both of which produce a large amount of meat. Roach continued to be important. There is a complete break in the pottery styles, indicated by a disappearance of any Criş culture elements such as flat-based pots. The pottery became uniform in fabric, form and decoration (Fig. 16). The fabric was coarse and tempered with sand and graphite giving the pottery a hard gritty texture and dark grey surface. The pots were exclusively of a truncated egg-shape with a pointed bottom and short cylindrical neck. Decoration was confined to the upper part of the pot and consisted of simple rows of comb or bone impressions or, very occasionally on the Bug, incised. It has been suggested that this pottery was diffused from further east where pottery of the same fabric and, to a superficial extent, of the same form and decoration, is characteristic of the middle phase of the Dnieper–Donetz culture. The economy of the Dnieper–Donetz culture, however, is quite different; unlike the Bug–Dniester fishing was unimportant, domesticated sheep and goats were present, and domesticated cattle were of great importance.[64] In addition, the middle phase of the Bug–Dniester culture has been synchronised with the middle and late phases of the Linear Pottery culture by the presence of sherds of the latter culture on Bug–Dniester sites, and Samtčin sherds at a Linear Pottery site in Moldavia SSR.[65] Settlements of the Linear Pottery culture occur to the north and west of the Bug–Dniester settlements, and have been dated in S. Poland and C. Europe to *c.* 4200 B.C. The Linear Pottery settlements of Moldavia and the Ukraine cannot be much later (p. 134). The middle phase of the Dnieper–Donetz culture, on the other hand, has been synchronised with the early phases of the Tripolye culture which did not develop until after the Linear Pottery

and Bug–Dniester cultures had ceased to exist. It is possible, therefore, that the Samtčin pottery should be interpreted in terms of the
result of local evolution after isolation from the neolithic cultures
of south-east and central Europe, rather than the result of diffusion
or 'influence' from the east. As will be seen below, there is very little
evidence of contact or interaction between the settlements of the
Linear Pottery culture in the west and north and the predominantly
hunting and fishing groups of the southern Bug and middle Dniester
valleys. In the later phases of the Bug–Dniester culture, however,
contact was again renewed with the agricultural communities in the
west, and the culture of the hunters and gatherers of the Bug and
Dniester valleys gradually became absorbed in the westwards
spread of the Cucuteni–Tripolye culture (Chapter 4).

Contact between the early agriculturalists and food-gatherers in west Yugoslavia

Settlements of early agriculturalists with an assemblage containing
painted pottery of the Starčevo culture and evidence of sheep and goat
breeding do not occur west of the Drina river in west Yugoslavia.[66]
West of this river, in the mountains, the narrow coastal plain and
the islands, assemblages have been excavated (in open sites such as
Smilčić and cave-sites such as Jamina Sredi and Crvena Stijena)
which consist of a chipped stone, bone and antler industry very
similar to that of the preceding mesolithic but with evidence possibly
of a partly food-producing economy and of the manufacture of
pottery.[67] The pottery, however, is quite unlike any found in the
early neolithic settlements on the inland plains of east Yugoslavia.
Its fabric is soft and poorly fired with large pebble and shell inclusions. It was characteristically decorated by patterns made by the
impressions of trimmed and untrimmed shells, in particular those
of the *Cardium* species. For this reason the pottery is often referred
to as Cardial Impressed Ware. The only resemblance it has to the
Starčevo pottery is in the forms into which it was manufactured,
which consist predominantly of hemispherical bowls with flat or
concave bases. More globular and shallow bowls also occur, some
of which have slightly flaring rims. This feature is absent from
Starčevo pottery.

In many cave-sites, habitation levels containing Impressed Ware
are stratified above settlements of mesolithic hunters and gatherers.
On both open and cave-sites they are frequently overlain by habitation
levels with later neolithic assemblages of the Danilo culture. The
occupation debris of the Impressed Ware settlements generally
formed a single habitation level, frequently more than one metre
thick.

The most extensively excavated and best documented open site is Smilčić, which is situated on the narrow sandstone plain of the Adriatic coast near Zadar, 6 km from the sea, near a spring. Fragments of baked clay with impressions of plaited branches have been found concentrated in and around two pits which were dug 10 m from each other. It is possible that the area between the pits was formerly occupied by a surface house constructed in the same way as the Starčevo houses. As in Moldavia, there is an absence of polished stone implements, but there are large numbers of artefacts made of bone, antler and chipped stone. The bone implements include those with flat, sharp transverse edges ('axes') and those with thick pointed ends. Many of the latter could have been used as projectile heads, as was suggested for the mesolithic bone points. None of the bone material has yet been systematically analysed, but sheep or goats, cattle and red-deer have been identified. Whether any of these species was domesticated is still open to doubt. Wild members of all these species were hunted during the late mesolithic period (Chapter 2), and it is possible that the economy continued unchanged in the Impressed Ware settlements. There is abundant evidence on all the sites for the collection of marine shellfish, including *Cardium*, *Spondylus*, etc., both as equipment for decorating pottery and probably for food. The plant remains have not yet been identified so that it is not known whether they are wild or domesticated species. There are a few saddle querns and rubbers, but, as mentioned above, these do not necessarily indicate the exploitation of cultivated grain. None of the flint blades have traces of 'sickle-gloss'. Thus, at present there is no positive evidence to suggest that the economy of the population with the Impressed Ware culture in Yugoslavia was based on anything but hunting and gathering.

Similar assemblages have been discovered inland in caves such as Crvena Stijena and Zelena Pećina. At neither of these sites is there evidence of agriculture or stockbreeding in the Impressed Ware levels. The site of Zelena Pećina is the only Impressed Ware settlement with polished stone artefacts.[68] In addition, at this site there are a few imported monochrome sherds of the Starčevo culture. This may be explained by the relatively close proximity of Zelena Pećina to Starčevo sites on the Drina river.[69] From the stratigraphical evidence of the cave-sites of Crvena Stijena and, on the coast, Jamina Sredi in the north and Gudnja in the south, a local evolution of the stone and bone industries is observable from the Late Palaeolithic to the Impressed Ware levels. However, it is still unclear what the significance is of the initial manufacture of pottery on these sites, whether it was a local response of the food-gatherers as a result of

contact with the pottery-producing agriculturalists on their eastern
border in east Yugoslavia, or whether it was the result of diffusion
from the south or west.[70] On the other side of the Adriatic in S.
Italy and further west, on the Ligurian coast of Italy and the coast of
France and Spain, similar assemblages with Cardial Impressed
Ware have been excavated predominantly in cave sites and dated by
Carbon 14 to 4600–4200 B.C. Assemblages with Cardial Impressed
Ware have also been excavated in N. Greece, for example at Otzaki
between the Proto-Sesklo and Sesklo cultural layers. In many of
these settlements, however, there is definite evidence of the domestication of plants and animals. It is also unclear what the relationship
was between the groups inhabiting the cave-sites in which there was
evidence of long occupation from the Late Palaeolithic period and
the groups occupying the open sites which were uninhabited before
the Impressed Ware culture.

On many of the sites of west Yugoslavia, an assemblage of the
Danilo culture is stratified above the Impressed Ware culture layer, in
almost every case with a sterile layer between the two.[71] Not only
is there evidence of a break in occupation of the settlements, but
there is also a change in the chipped stone industry and pottery
styles. The Danilo culture is distributed in the same area as the
Impressed Ware culture, but it also occurs further east, for example
on the Drina river where it bordered on the area of the Vinča–
Tordoš culture (p. 108). On many sites the Danilo culture layer was
overlain, without any evidence of an hiatus, by eneolithic layers
with assemblages of the Hvar and Lisičići cultures on the coast and
the Butmir culture inland. It is clear that these eneolithic cultures
developed on the basis of the Danilo culture. There is no such
evidence, however, to indicate cultural continuation from the
Impressed Ware culture to the Danilo culture. On many sites the
Danilo culture layer consists of several habitation levels. At Smilčić,
for example, 13 Danilo habitation levels are stratified above the
single Impressed Ware level. At Danilo itself, however, the culture
layer, which was only 20 cm thick, included evidence of repeated
occupation along the valley floor. The settlement at Smilčić was
surrounded by two ditches *c.* 1·5 m deep and 2 m wide at the top.
These are more likely to have been a delimitation barrier, an expres-
sion of the settlement's territorial identity and its association with
the valuable spring. Or they may have acted as a corral for domesticated animals, rather than a defensive barrier.

Although there is as yet no analysis of the animal and plant
remains from Danilo culture sites, it would seem from the evidence
of material culture and settlement type that the Danilo culture was
made up of a combination of elements resulting from the absorption

of the local hunters and gatherers by neighbouring agriculturalists from the east with the Vinča culture, and possibly also from the south from Albania and Greece and the west from Italy. Chipped stone blades with 'sickle-gloss' across one corner occur, as in the neolithic sites of the plains of south-east Europe. Other east Yugoslav elements include clay anthropomorphic figurines, polished stone implements, long chipped blades of flint, some of which were re-touched down one side or at one end. There are even sporadic blades of obsidian which it is assumed were obtained from the central European source in N.E. Hungary, as were those of the Vinča settlements. It is not impossible, however, that the obsidian was obtained from the Aegean or south Italy. There are also sporadic occurrences of triangular tanged arrowheads of chipped stone flakes, which were shaped by shallow retouch over their whole surface. The only other occurrence of such implements in S.E. Europe at this time was in the Linear Pottery settlements in N.W. Yugoslavia, for example at Donja Branjevina. Tanged arrowheads of this type need not necessarily have been used in hunting. They may also have been used by stock-breeders in drawing blood of domestic animals.[72]

The pottery of the Danilo culture comprises three categories:

1. Coarse ware with large stone inclusions decorated by finger- and nail-impressions.

2. Hard, slightly finer ware with gritty inclusions; this ware was polished and decorated by incised spirals, cross-hatching, herring-bone designs, filled with white or red paint after firing. Parallels for this pottery occur in the Vinča–Tordoš assemblages of E. Yugoslavia and the early Slavonian–Syrmian assemblages of N. Yugoslavia.

3. Thin ware with very fine mineralogical inclusions, fired to a light orange colour and covered with a white slip; the surface was painted with black and red patterns before firing and then burnished; the patterns were predominantly rectilinear. The closest parallels for this category of pottery occur in the Ripoli and Capri ware of southern Italy. Finally, in the Danilo culture assemblages there occur four-legged vessels with large mouths set obliquely and with massive ring handles, whose closest analogies are found in the middle neolithic of central Greece, for example Elateia, where they are referred to as 'cult vessels'.[73]

The middle neolithic of south-east Europe

At about 4200 B.C. (Fig. 39) in S.E. Europe, as early as *c.* 4400 B.C. in S. Bulgaria, contemporary with the middle and later phases of the central European Linear Pottery cultures, the early neolithic assemblages underwent a certain change.[73] Foremost among these was the disappearance of painted pottery and an increasing predominance of black-burnished pottery and decoration by channelling and incising. Assemblages with this type of pottery occur on a number of sites in habitation levels stratified above those with early neolithic assemblages; they also occur on newly established sites in the same area. It has been suggested that the appearance of this pottery signifies a break with the early neolithic traditions in this and many other aspects of the material culture as a result of stimuli or even further expansion of agriculturalists from Anatolia (late chalcolithic) and Greece (late neolithic).[74] However, there are many features of the latter assemblages, such as white painting on black pottery, which never occurred in the neolithic cultures of the northern Balkan peninsula. On many of the stratified sites, a sterile layer representing a break in occupation occurs before the full acceptance or appearance of the black-burnished and incised ware. This layer is frequently associated with a layer of burning, which has often been taken as an indication that the new pottery was brought by 'invaders'. The break in occupation, however, frequently does not correspond to the disappearance of painted decoration and the appearance of black-burnished ware. On many sites (for example Karanovo and Vinča) black-burnished pottery occurs in the same assemblage as the declining painted pottery *before* the break in occupation. Apart from this evidence, it should be noted that there are many factors besides the intrusion of a population which may cause a sudden change in pottery styles.

The recent evidence from the S. Bulgarian sites argues against any 'wave of new farmers' coming in from the Near East or the south Balkans and causing the development of the middle neolithic cultures of the northern Balkans. At Karanovo, for example, culture layer II is stratified directly above I and contains such a similar assemblage to I that they were formerly termed Ia and Ib. The fine pottery of II (Fig. 18) was made in the same shapes as those of I, in particular tulip-shaped pots on a low pedestal. Instead of the painted decoration on a coloured slip, however, the surface of the pot was covered with a self-slip which was decorated by fine channelling or fluting and was then burnished. Layer II at Karanovo was covered by a sterile layer, indicating a break in occupation. The succeeding culture layer (III) contains an assemblage of the south Bulgarian *Veselinovo* culture (Fig. 18), dated by Carbon 14 *c.* 4400 B.C. At the 'tell' settlement of Yasa Tepe, the lowest culture layer contains an assemblage identical to that of Karanovo II. Stratified above this, without any evidence of a break in occupation, is an assemblage of the Veselinovo culture.[75] Furthermore, at Kazanlak there is evidence

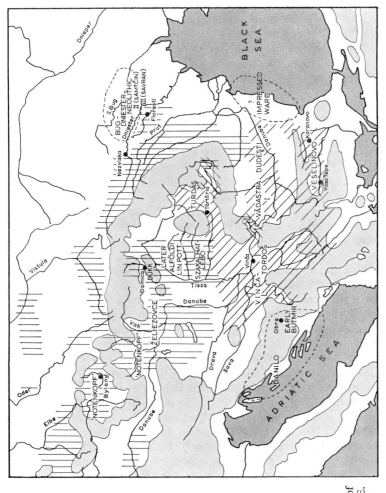

Fig. 17

Map of the distribution of middle neolithic cultures in E. Europe, c. 4300–3900 B.C.

Black-burnished pottery cultures

Middle and later Linear Pottery cultures

Land above 500 m.a.s.l.

Possible surviving painted pottery cultures

of continuous occupation of the 'tell' from the Karanovo I culture
to the Veselinovo culture and later. At this site a gradual transition is
visible to the pottery, houses, bone, antler and stone industries, etc.,
of the Veselinovo culture.[76]

In Yugoslavia, W. Bulgaria and S.W. Rumania, the middle neolithic assemblages comprise the early part of the Vinča culture,
referred to as the *Vinča–Tordoš* culture.[77] There is evidence of a
local evolution of the culture from the early neolithic cultures,
especially in the south in Macedonia where there is an analogous
situation to that in S. Bulgaria.[78] The internal chronology of the
Vinča culture is based on the excavations of the large stratified
site of Vinča on the banks of the Danube.[79] An assemblage of the
Starčevo culture has been recognised in the lowest levels of this site.
The early neolithic settlement was overlain by a layer containing a
transitional assemblage, referred to as Vinča–Tordoš A or Proto–
Vinča, in which an increase of black-burnished pottery was associated with a decrease of painted pottery. The transitional assemblage
was covered by a charcoal layer interpreted as a 'destruction level'
which has been dated by Carbon 14 4240 ± 60 B.C. Above this was
stratified the Vinča–Tordoš culture layer in which two main phases
of development have been recognised: Vinča B1 and B2. Later
neolithic and eneolithic Vinča–Pločnik levels overlay the Vinča–
Tordoš culture layer (Chapter 4).[80] Generally, the area occupied by
the Vinča–Tordoš culture is the same as that of the Starčevo culture
except that its westwards expansion was somewhat limited by the
development of the Danilo culture (p. 104) on its western borders as
far as the Drina river. In the north, in the area in which assemblages
of the Starčevo–Körös culture had previously occurred, the Vinča–
Tordoš assemblages were mixed with elements of the Linear Pottery
cultures. The latter, by this time, dominated the area formerly
occupied by the Körös culture (p. 132). Throughout the area of its
distribution, the Vinča–Tordoš culture is located in the same habitats
and frequently, in a stratified context, on the same sites as the early
neolithic settlements.

North of the Stara Planina mountains, in N. Bulgaria and S.
Rumania, similar 'middle neolithic' assemblages occur and are
referred to as the *Vădastra I* culture in the west (Oltenia) and the
Dudeşti culture in the east (Muntenia).[81] Although the locations of the
settlements with these assemblages are similar to those of the early
neolithic settlements, the 'middle neolithic' assemblages are never
stratified above Criş culture layers. There is, therefore, no evidence
yet of any local evolution of the Vădastra I or Dudeşti cultures and
no indication of the chronological and cultural relationship of the
Criş settlements and those of the Vădastra I and Dudeşti cultures.

A similar situation exists in C. Rumania (Transilvania). The middle neolithic assemblages which bear a close resemblance to those of the Vinča–Tordoš culture, and are referred to as the *Turdaş* culture, are never found stratified above those of the early neolithic Criş culture. Very frequently, however, they are excavated in the lowest habitation levels of large stratified sites.[82] The thin habitation level of the Turdaş culture was generally covered by thick later neolithic and eneolithic layers of the Petreşti culture (Chapter 4).

The most distinctive change in the material culture which marks the transition from early to middle neolithic cultures in south-east Europe was the *pottery*. The Veselinovo culture was rather distinct in having only two categories of pottery: coarse ware and thick finer ware. The latter category was almost always undecorated and was manufactured into piriform and cylindrical beakers with flat bases or standing on cylindrical legs; many of the pots were provided with the very characteristic curving handle with a round cross-section and frequently a knobbed terminal. In general, however, the middle neolithic settlements had three categories of pottery:

1. Coarse rusticated ware (Fig. 18) tempered by micaceous inclusions rather than organic material.

2. Thick, finer ware (Fig. 18), fired to a brown or grey colour, with the surface covered by a self-slip and frequently polished. The main forms manufactured in this ware were globular or biconical pots with flat bases and sometimes cylindrical collars. They were frequently provided with ribbon lugs. Decoration of this ware was by incised lines, in particular by bands filled with dots and stabs, referred to as 'winkleband' style. In S. Rumania, however, the incised decoration was characterised by incised bands filled with cross-hatching with white paint applied in the incisions after firing.

3. Fine, thin ware (Fig. 18) often fired under controlled reducing conditions to a black or dark grey colour. The surface was decorated by shallow fluting or channelling, especially on the upper part of the pot, and the whole surface was highly burnished. The fine pottery was also less frequently covered with a red slip which was burnished but otherwise undecorated. This technique was especially popular in the Transilvanian Turdaş culture. The fine ware was made predominantly into wide sharply-angled biconical bowls with a flat base or standing on a tall solid pedestral. Pedestalled bowls are absent from the S. Rumanian sites. It has been suggested that the highly burnished surface of the fine ware was produced by rubbing with bone spatulae, which are found on all the sites. It seems more likely, from their context, however, that the spatulae were associated with querns and grinding activities.

The 'middle neolithic' assemblages of S.E. Europe are distinguished by an increase in the quantity of artefacts made of durable materials such as *antler, bone and stone*.[83] In general, however, the same categories of implements were manufactured as in the early neolithic settlements. Polished stone artefacts were made in large quantities on all sites. The flat trapezoid 'axes' were supplemented, in particular in the Vinča–Tordoš settlements, by the high-backed rectangular 'shoelast' adze (p. 75). Chipped stone blades were also made in increasing quantities but were still predominantly unmodified by retouch. Blades of obsidian frequently occur in N. Yugoslavia and S.E. Hungary in the mixed assemblages with Vinča–Tordoš and Linear Pottery elements (p. 132). They must indicate contact and some form of exchange, direct or indirect, with the central European source of obsidian in N.E. Hungary. (On the other hand, the presence of Mediterranean shells such as *Spondylus, Cardium* and *Penctulus*, usually perforated as bracelets, amulets and beads in Vinča–Tordoš assemblages, indicates contact with the south and west.) It is interesting to note that in S. Rumania, as in the preceding Criş and mesolithic settlements, a few 'geometric' microlithic blades have been found among the chipped stone artefacts (p. 96). Many of the bone and antler implements such as the spatulae, flat bone points,

---

Fig. 18

Pottery of the middle neolithic cultures of S.E. Europe.
a Pot with fine channelled decoration. Karanovo, layer II, S. Bulgaria (after Georgiev, 1961).
b Pot with burnished surface. Ghedeme Mogila, nr. Kazanlak, C. Bulgaria. Karanovo II culture (after Georgiev, 1961).
c Pot with fine-channelled decoration. Karanovo, layer II, Bulgaria (after Georgiev, 1961).
d Burnished pot. Yasa Tepe I, S. Bulgaria. Veselinovo culture (after Georgiev, 1961).
e Yasa Tepe I. Veselinovo culture (after Renfrew, 1969b).
f Yasa Tepe I, S. Bulgaria. Veselinovo culture (after Georgiev, 1961).
g Coarse-tempered storage vessel. Vinča–Tordoš culture. Žarkovo, E. Yugoslavia (after Garašanin, M. & D., 1952–3).
h Fine-tempered pot with shallow channelled decoration. Vršnik II–III, S.E. Yugoslavia. Early Vinča–Tordoš culture (after Renfrew, 1969b).
i Pedestalled bowl with shallow channelled decoration. Žarkovo, E. Yugoslavia. Vinča–Tordoš culture (after Garašanin, M. & D., 1952–3).
j Pot with incised 'winkelband' design. Vinča, N.E. Yugoslavia. Vinča–Tordoš culture (Dept. of Arch., Univ. of Belgrade).
k Pot with incised and fine-channelled decoration. Magura Feţelor, S.C. Rumania. Vădastra I culture (after Berciu, 1939).
l Incised sherd. Dudeşti culture. Cernica, S.E. Rumania (after Cantacuzino and Morintz, 1963).
m Pot with fine-channelled decoration. Cernica, S.E. Rumania. Dudeşti culture (Inst. of Arch., Bucharest).

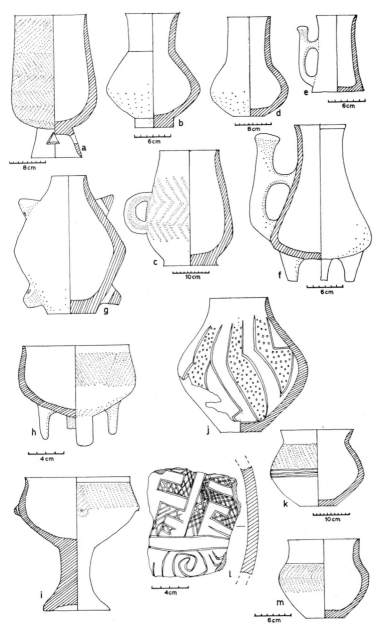

Fig. 18

awls, perforated needles were manufactured in the same forms, probably for the same functions as in the early neolithic settlements. Barbless bone fish-hooks were made slightly more frequently but only in the settlements of the Vinča–Tordoš culture along the Danube. For the first time in S.E. Europe, however, with the exception of the Bug and Dniester valleys, there were manufactured in this period large bone and antler artefacts, including perforated antlers with a wide cutting edge, which may have acted as 'hoes' for digging earth and roots; they may also have been used to crush and chop soft vegetable matter or even meat. In addition, it is interesting to note the perforated antlers with pointed ends which have been interpreted as 'picks' and the longbones with narrow sharp transverse edges which have been interpreted as 'chisels'.

As well as an apparent increase in the number of production implements manufactured in durable materials, there was an increase in the manufacture of *clay figurines*, both anthropomorphic and zoomorphic. All the figurines were small and solid, rarely taller than 15cm.[84] Although some of the anthropomorphic figurines retain the semi-reclining position which was popular in the early neolithic cultures, the majority were manufactured in a standing position (Pl. 3). At Yasa Tepe in S. Bulgaria, however, a large number of anthropomorphic figurines (Fig. 19) were manufactured with detached perforated limbs which could be articulated.[85] The anthropomorphic figurines of the eastern Balkans tended to retain the tall cylindrical head of those of the early neolithic settlements, whereas those of the Vinča–Tordoš culture were distinguished by heads with flat tops and triangular faces (Fig. 19). The facial features were incised but, as in the early neolithic cultures, the mouth was never portrayed. As in the early neolithic cultures, the figurines consist of a flat, upper part of the torso with small pointed arms and a lower part of the torso on which the buttocks were frequently sharply accentuated. When breasts are portrayed they consist exclusively of small pointed protrusions. Thus, even on the figurines with breasts and buttocks, there is no emphasis of the sexual features of the body. Many of the figurines are of indeterminate sex. Anthropomorphic or zoomorphic pots (Fig. 19) are a rare occurrence in the middle neolithic settlements, apart from the so-called 'face-lids' (Fig. 34) of the Vinča culture on which the eyes and nose (whether animal or human is still under discussion) were incised.

Little evolution in the size and shape of the *houses* is visible in the middle neolithic settlements of south-east Europe.[86] They were still the small rectangular one-roomed structures as in the early neolithic settlements. In the Veselinovo culture settlements of S. Bulgaria, however, there is evidence in some houses of internal division of the

4. The early agricultural settlement of Bylany, W. Czechoslovakia. Linear Pottery culture, c. 4400–3900 B.C. The letters refer to the three settlements in the 'cycle' (see p. 117)

5. Storage pit with clay lining. Early agricultural settlement of Ludaš-Budżak near Subotica, N.E. Yugoslavia. Starčevo-Körös culture, *c.* 5500 B.C. About 1 m diameter

6. Clay oven for parching grain. Early agricultural settlement of Bylany, W. Czechoslovakia. Linear Pottery culture, *c.* 4500–3900 B.C. About 1 m diameter

house into more than one room and of a specific area reserved for the oven, hearth and grinding quern.

Most of the evidence of the *economy* of the middle neolithic settlements of S.E. Europe comes from Rumania[87] where there is evidence of an overwhelming predominance of the exploitation of domesticated animals, in particular cattle, and to a much lesser extent sheep and goats and pig. These regions, however, had shown a preference for cattle-breeding rather than ovicaprid-breeding even in the early neolithic period. There is no evidence to show that the settlements

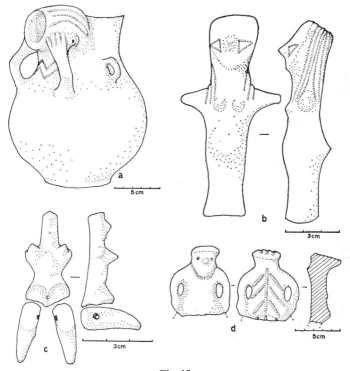

Fig. 19

Anthropomorphic figurines of the middle neolithic settlements of E. Europe.

a Anthropomorphic pot. Parţa, S.W. Rumania. Szakalhat–Lebö group (Timişoara Museum).

b Clay figurine. Vinča, N.E. Yugoslavia. Vinča–Tordoš culture (after Vassić, 1932-6).

c Clay figurine. Yasa Tepe, Bulgaria. Veselinovo culture (after Georgiev, 1961).

d Clay figurine. Boskovštejn, S.C. Czechoslovakia. Linear Pottery culture (after Vildomec, 1932).

H

south of the Danube which, in the early neolithic, had concentrated on ovicaprid-breeding did not continue with this activity. The small numbers of wild animal bones were of large forest mammals such as red-deer and wild pig, and of fish. An analysis of the grain from Lug in W. Yugoslavia indicates that both einkorn and emmer wheat, but not barley, were cultivated.

In connection with the relative and absolute chronology of the middle neolithic settlements of S.E. Europe it is worth noting the claims for a 'short chronology' made recently on the basis of the Tărtăria tablets (Pl. 10).[88] Three unbaked clay tablets were excavated at Tărtăria in C. Rumania (Transilvania) in a 'ritual pit' dug into the loess from the Turdaş culture layer. The pit also contained several clay (and one marble) anthropomorphic figurines. Designs had been impressed on the tablets which, it has been claimed, show more than a superficial resemblance to the signs on tablets from Uruk–Warka and Jemdet Nasr in Mesopotamia, from the Jemdet Nasr period which has been dated to c. 3000 B.C. On this basis, the Turdaş culture should be dated at least 1000 years later than the dates obtained for the Vinča–Tordoš culture by the Carbon 14 method, c. 4200–3900 B.C. There are several factors which might help to explain this inconsistency. It seems unlikely, as is suggested by some fanatics, that all the Carbon 14 dates obtained from archaeological sites are invalid or too early. Alternatively, it is quite possible that the similarity between the Transilvanian and the Mesopotamian tablets is no more than superficial and that they have no significant relationship. In addition, it is possible that the tablets are not from the Turdaş layer at all, but from one of the later habitation levels, and that the pit was not dug *from* the Turdaş layer but *near* it, i.e., from outside the area of the Turdaş settlement. The other contents need not be dated exclusively to the Turdaş culture. Signs similar to those on the tablets were incised on the bases of pots which have been excavated especially at the top of the Turdaş–Petreşti layer at Tărtăria, and in Yugoslavia in Vinča–Pločnik assemblages (for example, at Banjica and Vinča).

THE LINEAR POTTERY CULTURES

Unlike the early agricultural settlements of south-east Europe, the settlements of the Linear Pottery cultures (Figs. 10, 17) are distinguished by a uniformity of location and habitat.[89] Apart from those in the Bükk and Matra mountains, the settlements are situated exclusively on the loess deposits of central and western Europe (Fig. 8). During the early Atlantic vegetational period the loess deposits were covered by a light mixed oak forest, which varied in its composition and density according to the drainage from the dry east Hungarian plain to the wet Bohemian plain. In general, however, the forest was light and could be cleared easily at the same time as providing a rich foliage and undergrowth for cattle fodder. In addition, loess under these lightly forested conditions forms fertile, easily worked, well-drained soil which was highly suitable for the cultivation of wheat without the use of fertilisers.[90] From the evidence of the bone material, which shows an almost complete lack of hunting activities in the central European Linear Pottery settlements, it is clear that, as in S. Bulgaria, the settlers were interested in such factors as a large expanse of foliage and fertile soil rather than the presence of a variety of plant and animal resources. They, therefore, tended to settle in the centre of the ecological zones, that is in the middle of the gently undulating plains, and away from the marginal zones provided by rivers and lakes.

Because of their origin in very fine wind-blown deposits, loess soils are very quickly eroded once deprived of their vegetational covering. It seems that, in the case of many of the Linear Pottery settlements, up to 30cm of the deposits including the original house-floors have been removed. For this reason there is an apparent lack of a thick culture layer or superimposed habitation levels on the Linear Pottery sites. The habitation area of each of the Linear Pottery settlements is vast in comparison to the early agricultural settlements of south-east Europe. This does not necessarily mean, however, that the villages of the Linear Pottery cultures covered a much larger ex-panse. The greater area covered by occupation debris would appear to have been caused by a much greater horizontal displacement of the successive occupation phases. If the twenty-one habitation levels (or phases) at the Linear Pottery settlement of Bylany in W. Czecho-slovakia had been located on exactly the same spot, as in S. Bulgaria, they would have produced a considerable mound of occupation debris. As it is, however, the habitation phases are recognised only by a certain degree of horizontal stratigraphy as seen in the overlap and superimposition of successive pits and surface houses. The phases, and to a certain extent their duration and length of separation, are also distinguished on the basis of a statistical analysis of the morphological features and the technology of the fabric, forms and decoration of the pottery. A third criterion for distinguishing habita-tion phases was the orientation of the houses, assuming that all the houses of each phase faced the same direction. However, since the houses of all phases of the Linear Pottery cultures tended to be oriented in the general N.W.–S.E. direction, possibly against the prevailing wind, and since the difference in the orientation of the houses of two different phases could be as little as 5 degrees, this would seem a more doubtful criterion.[91]

The settlement of Bylany in each phase of its occupation contained approximately 5–6 houses, and rarely more than 10. Taking into account the fact that these houses were frequently longer than 30 m (Fig. 20) and very likely contained more than one nuclear family, it would seem that the Linear Pottery settlements of central Europe, even in the earliest phase, as at Novy Bydžov and Mohelnice in Czechoslovakia, comprised much larger populations than the Criş and Körös settlements. They may have been as large as the S. Bulgarian early agricultural settlements. It is clear from the faunal and floral remains from Linear Pottery settlements that the different settlement type in temperate Europe reflects a change in the basis of the *economy* of the earliest food-producers. The only evidence for the economy of the earliest Linear Pottery settlements comes from sites in E. Germany (Saxony and Thuringia), which show a predominance of domesticated animal bones, in particular those of ovicaprids.[92] This situation continued even in the later periods of the Linear Pottery culture in this region. This, however, would seem to have been a peculiar feature of the east German sites, although the material culture is identical to that of the other central European Linear Pottery settlements. In the analyses from other Linear Pottery sites of C. Europe, which are from the middle and later periods of the culture, there is an overwhelming predominance of bones of domesticated animals, in particular cattle.[93] This is a very different picture from the economy of the Starčevo and Körös culture settlements. The evidence of the Criş settlements of Rumania, however, shows a similar predominance of cattle among the domesticated animals, as do the Rumanian middle neolithic settlements. In the Linear Pottery settlements, pigs were the second most important domesticated animals and ovicaprids were almost absent. The few wild animals which were hunted included large forest mammals such as red-deer, roe-deer, wild pig and aurochs. There is no evidence of fishing in these settlements.

Direct evidence of grain cultivation occurs in the form of ovens for drying grain, and pits and storage pots in which grain identified as cultivated emmer and einkorn wheat has been excavated. The ovens (Pl. 6), generally found in pits alongside the houses, are a similar shape to those found in the early agricultural settlements of S.E. Europe. They were built of clay and chaff on a foundation of stone slabs, rarely to a height of more than 20 cm, in a rounded shape of *c.* 60 cm diameter. It has been suggested that baking was not only for drying the grain but also for removing the clinging hull, particularly of emmer wheat. Facilities for storing grain (and other vegetable products) included large storage pots and storage pits. The latter are steep-sided and up to 1 metre deep but, unlike those of the Körös settlements, they show very few traces of a thick clay lining. There is evidence, however, in the form of thin carbonised layers that they were regularly burnt out to prevent regermination of the grain. Indirect evidence of grain cultivation in the Linear Pottery settlements includes saddle-shaped querns and rubbers of sandstone (which need not only have been for grinding cultivated grain) and flint insets for sickles. At Bylany the sickle blades form 16 per cent of the used implements.[94] They consist predominantly of blades *c.* 4 cm long (Fig. 11) which were much more carefully prepared than the other chipped stone artefacts. Their bulbs of percussion were generally removed and their distal ends were carefully trimmed by deliberate retouch to facilitate insertion into an antler or wooden handle. It has been assumed from all this evidence that the economy of the Linear Pottery settlements was based on shifting agriculture in which the main factor causing the movement of the population was the loss of fertility of the soil. From the total evidence, however, it is clear that the economy could have been based to an equal extent on stockbreeding with the population shifting its habitation area and/or pasture area depending on the available supply of leaves and undergrowth for fodder.

On the basis of the evidence from Bylany (Pl. 4), the most extensively excavated of all the Linear Pottery settlements, it has been suggested that the early agriculturalists of temperate Europe shifted their settlements in deliberate patterns to allow the soil to regain its fertility and/or the forest to regenerate. In this way they could eventually move back and settle on the original site. It is suggested that there were several settlements, to which the group moved in rotation. At Bylany, for example, where 3–4 such steps in the cycle have been recognised by surface surveys and trial excavations, it was speculated that, if each site was occupied for an average of 10–15 years, the cycle would be completed and the site reinhabited every 30–50 years. Since the twenty-one habitation phases at Bylany represent all the main stages and periods in the evolution of the Linear Pottery culture of W. Czechoslovakia, it has been calculated that the culture lasted at least 700 years, *c.* 4500–3800 B.C. This duration of the Linear Pottery cultures of C. Europe is supported by Carbon 14 evidence and relative chronology of other neolithic cultures in eastern Europe.

The evidence of such a 'cycle' of Linear Pottery settlements having existed in the area of Bylany (apart from the discovery of other Linear Pottery sites nearby) is based on the statistical analysis of the fabric, forms and decoration of the pottery. On the basis of the proportion of the various components in it pottery content, each pit and associated house can, theoretically, be assigned to a particular habitation phase of the settlement. From the analysis of the pottery, it has been shown that there was not a continuous evolution of the pottery styles at the site of Bylany and that some styles must have been developed elsewhere. One of the main arguments against the hypothesis is that it is assumed that it was the same *group* of people who were evolving their pottery styles and sub-styles internally without any contact from other groups. On the basis of ethnographic parallels, however, it is clear that, even in the prehistoric period, people did not live in a vacuum and that such gaps in the evolution of pottery styles could as easily be the result of stimulus and contact with other groups with the same culture which, according to the evidence, could have been living nearby. The calculation of the duration of each habitation phase, and therefore of the whole Linear Pottery culture, is based on the evidence of the storage pits, in which stratified layers of burning and relining are visible. On the assumption that each relining was an annual event, it has been calculated that the pits (and therefore the associated houses) were used for 10–15 years. If, however, the pits were relined every two years or at irregular intervals, the whole calculation would be upset. From the super-imposition of the house complexes and from the pottery styles which date to different stages in the evolution of the Linear Pottery cultures, it is clear that several phases of occupation are represented at Bylany and other Linear Pottery settlements. It is still open to question, however, whether there was a gradual horizontal displacement of one settlement area (with or without abandonment and rehabitation of the settlement) or whether a cyclic movement was involved. It is also possible that a move in the cultivation and pasturing area need not have involved regular movement of the habitation area. Finally, until there are more extensive excavations on the scale of those carried out at Bylany, the concept of the 'micro-area inhabited by one population group moving in a cycle' should be applied only with great caution to other areas of the Linear Pottery culture.

The *houses* of the Linear Pottery cultures are distinguished by their large dimensions and the uniformity of their proportions and ground-plan.[95] In spite of the absence of the original occupation surface, the ground-plan of the houses is clearly indicated by post-holes and associated pits which are filled with the original neolithic black-earth (chernozem) soil and show up dark against the yellow loess sub-soil. The houses are rectangular in plan with a constant width of *c.* 6 m and length which varies from 8–45 m (average 20 m). The method of their construction seems to have been very similar to that of the majority of the more northern early neolithic settlements of southeast Europe, as for example Tiszajenő (Fig. 14). Heavy posts, probably mostly of oak, supported a framework of wattle walls which were covered or daubed with clay. Evidence from Hurbanovo in Slovakia shows that the plaster walls were painted in red and white, as in S. Bulgaria. The clay for the walls and possibly the roof was obtained from long irregular ovaloid pits which run along the outside walls of the houses.[96] The pits were subsequently used as rubbish pits and for hearths, ovens and even burials. Unlike the surface houses of S.E. Europe, those of the Linear Pottery culture had three internal rows of posts, which were needed to support the long gabled roof.

Elaborations of the house-plan with five rows of post-holes include a concentration of post-holes at the southern end of the house representing posts which may have supported a raised floor. This feature occurs particularly in houses of the early periods of the culture when there is no evidence of storage pits; it has therefore been suggested that such a raised floor may have been to act as a granary for storing grain. At the northern end of the house, or occasionally all round it, a trench (Fig. 20) was dug which could have held horizontal wooden beams into which the upright posts were inserted in order to retard the rotting processes. Alternatively the wall could have been embedded in the trench without the medium of a beam in order to strengthen the foundations and reduce draughts. In the early houses of the lower Rhine area, a characteristic feature was that the central part of the house was relatively free of post-holes, which frequently formed a Y-configuration (Fig. 20). On the basis of these houses the central part has been interpreted as the main habitation area with a single hearth. In this case the living space of the Linear Pottery 'long-houses' would have been little bigger than that of the small nuclear family houses of the early agricultural settlements of S.E. Europe. On the basis of the central European houses, however, where the central Y-configuration of post-holes is absent, another hypothesis has been proposed, according to which, even if part of the house was used as a granary, most of the space was occupied by several groups of people making up one extended family. Analogies have been drawn to support this hypothesis not only from the long-houses of the Iroquois Indians, but also from the late neolithic settlement of Postoloprty in W. Czechoslovakia, where three hearths were aligned down a long-house, and numerous houses of the Tripolye culture (Fig. 27) of the Ukraine, where the original floor surface was preserved (Chapter 4). In the latter, there is evidence not only of several hearths in the long-houses, but also of division of the houses into several rooms. In addition, at the Linear Pottery settlement of Nezviska in the Ukraine, the original floor of a house has been preserved.[97] The construction of the house included rather more clay and less interior post-holes than was usual in the C. European Linear Pottery houses, but its dimensions (12×7 m) and pro-

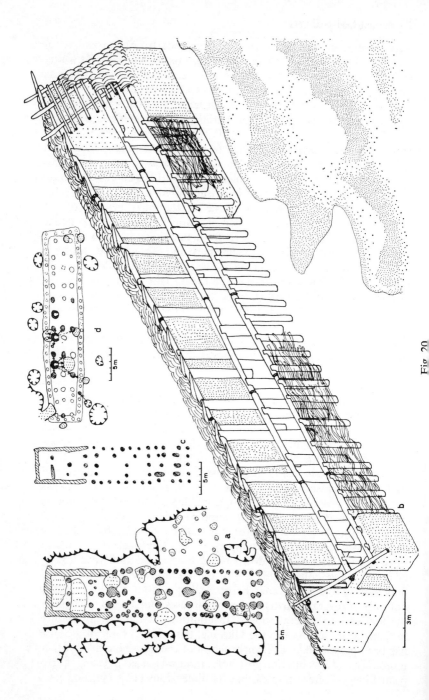

Fig. 20

portions were the same as many of those in C. Europe. Aligned down
the centre of the Nezviska house were at least three hearths. Unfortunately, neither of the above hypotheses can be tested since the
original floor surface of the houses of the Linear Pottery cultures of
C. and W. Europe has never been preserved. Although none of the
interior hearths has survived, it has been possible in certain cases to
reconstruct their approximate original position on the basis of the
distribution of the debris of charcoal and fired clay in post-holes inside the houses. At Bylany, for example, in house 1111 (Fig. 20) at
least three hearths have been reconstructed in this way. At Bylany
and many other Linear Pottery settlements, particularly of the later
periods of the culture, there were small rectangular houses in addition
to the long-houses. They have been interpreted on the one hand as
separate storage buildings, and on the other hand as houses for off-
shoots of the main extended family groups.

In many respects the material culture of the Linear Pottery cultures
represents an expansion of the traditions of the early agriculturalists
of S.E. Europe. The *pottery* of the earliest Linear Pottery settlements,
for example, consists of an organic-tempered fabric identical to that
of the Starčevo and Körös coarse ware.[98] There is a rough division
into very coarse ware with walls up to 8 cm thick, which was decorated by roughening the surface especially by finger-impressions, and
slightly thinner ware generally 1·5–2 cm thick, which was decorated
by wide incised lines. The two categories of fine pottery and painted
decoration of the early neolithic cultures of S.E. Europe are missing
in temperate Europe outside the transitional region of E. Hungary
and S.E. Slovakia. The early pot forms of the Linear Pottery culture
are similar to those of early neolithic pottery in S.E. Europe, including hemispherical bowls on low pedestals, bottles with cylindrical or
flaring necks and ribbon lugs, globular bowls with flat or ring bases,
etc. A similar continuity of tradition can also be seen in the forms
and presumably the functions of the chipped and polished stone
artefacts. As in S.E. Europe, there was a predominace of the flat

---

Fig. 20

Early neolithic house construction in temperate central Europe.
a Ground-plan of house 679 at Bylany, W. Czechoslovakia (after
Soudsky, 1966). Hatched features represent features of the house.
Dotted areas are earlier or later than the house.
b Isometric reconstruction of house 679 (after Soudsky, 1966, 1969).
c Ground-plan of house 2 at Sittard, S. Holland (after Waterbolk and
Modderman, 1958–9).
d Ground-plan of house 1111 at Bylany, Czechoslovakia (after Soudsky,
1966), showing reconstruction of three hearths (black 'horseshoes'):
hatched areas show concentration of charcoal; arrows show source
of charcoal; dotted features are earlier or later than house.

trapezoid polished stone axes in the earlier periods of the Linear
Pottery cultures, which were superseded by the high-backed narrow
'shoelast adzes' in the later periods, contemporary with the middle
neolithic cultures of S.E. Europe.

In spite of these similarities between the early neolithic cultures of
S.E. Europe and the central European Linear Pottery cultures there
are many aspects of the former's material culture which are missing
from the Linear Pottery assemblages. Apart from the absence of fine
pottery and painted decoration, there are almost no anthropomorphic or zoomorphic clay figurines or pots outside the transitional
region of east Hungary. The few anthropomorphic figurines (Fig. 19)
which do occur bear a strong resemblance to the figurines of the
Vinča–Tordoš culture of Yugoslavia in that they are small standing
figurines with clearly defined triangular faces. Along with figurines,
a number of other objects manufactured in fired clay in the south-
east European neolithic cultures do not occur in the Linear Pottery
assemblages, including ladles, 'lamps', 'stamp-seals', spindle whorls
and clay weights. The absence of the last two may be associated with
the lack of importance of sheep- or goat-breeding in the economy,

---

Fig. 21
Linear Pottery of the east Hungarian plain.
a Fragment of pedestal. Black-on-red painted decoration. Early phase.
  Tiszalok, E. Hungary (Nyiregyhaza Museum).
b Early phase. Incised bowl. Kiskanya, W.C. Hungary (after Csalog,
  1941).
c Sherd of black-on-red painted ware. Early phase. Domica, layer Ia,
  S.E. Czechoslovakia (after Lichardus, 1964).
d Incised sherd, Gemör group. Ardovo, S.E. Czechoslovakia (Inst. of
  Arch., Nitra).
e Black-on-red painted bowl. Esztar group. Nagykállö, N.E. Hungary
  (after Korek, 1957).
f Incised pottery, later Alföld Linear Pottery. Abadszalok, E.C.
  Hungary (Szolnok Museum).
g Incised pedestalled bowl, E. Carpathian Linear Pottery. Barca III,
  S.E. Czechoslovakia (after Hajek, 1956).
h Incised pot, Pre-Classical Bükk. Domica, S.E. Czechoslovakia (after
  Lichardus, 1968).
i Incised pot, Classical Bükk. Domica (after Lichardus, 1968).
j Painted brown-on-buff sherd. Michalovce-Hradok, S.E. Czechoslovakia. Szamos group (after Šiška, 1961).
k Incised sherd, Tiszadob group. Tiszadob-Okenez, N.E. Hungary
  (Nyiregyhaza Museum).
l Incised sherd, Szakalhát–Lebő group. Lebő C, S. E. Hungary (after
  Trogmayer, 1957). Dotted area denotes surface covered in red
  encrusted paint.
m Incised pot of Szakalhát–Lebő group. Parţa, S.W. Rumania
  (Timişoara Museum). Dotted area denotes surface covered with red
  encrusted paint.

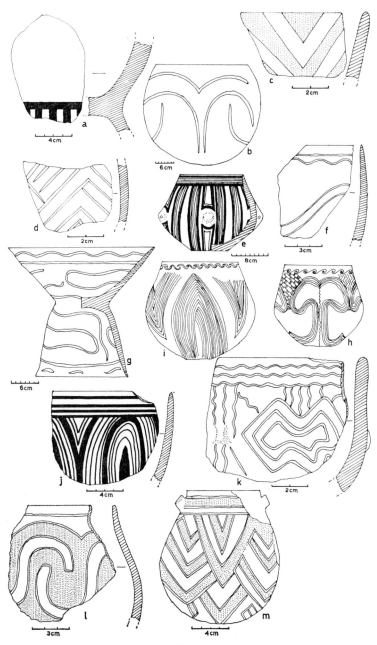

Fig. 21

and the lack of spinning and weaving. It has been argued, however, that many of the objects made in fired clay in S.E. Europe could have been reproduced in wood in the more forested environment of temperate central Europe. Since there is absolutely no positive evidence in this area for wooden artefacts from the neolithic period, this hypothesis should be treated with a certain amount of scepticism. Weights could quite naturally be reproduced less successfully in wood. On some of the rare Linear Pottery settlements which are located by rivers, however, and which may have practised fishing, there is evidence that net-weights, which were made of fired clay in S.E. Europe, were manufactured of stone.[99] Stone weights of this type were made of gneiss pebbles of elliptical shape with dents ground out on either side. These objects were formerly interpreted as stone figurines. It is possible that the general lack of fine pottery, painted decoration, and fired clay objects, in particular in the initial expansion of the agriculturalists into central Europe, may have been due to a lack of suitable clay or a lack of complex firing techniques. By the middle and later periods of the Linear Pottery cultures, a local form of fine ware which was well-fired and mica-tempered had been developed.

Burials of the Linear Pottery cultures generally occur in the settlement area, either in rubbish pits without any grave-goods, or in shallow grave-pits with a few grave-goods such as pots or *Spondylus* shells from the Mediterranean or the Black Sea which were perforated and made into necklaces.[100] The dead were always buried lying in a contracted position on their sides, as in the neolithic settlements of S.E. Europe (Fig. 15). In a few cases, particularly further west in East Germany (Thuringia), there were small groups of burials outside the settlements which have been dated to the early part of the culture.[101] Cemeteries do occasionally occur further east, for example in Slovakia at Nitra where twenty-four burials were excavated.[102] Each burial in these small cemeteries was accompanied by a pot, *Spondylus* shells and frequently a polished stone axe or adze. Further west still, in the Rhine valley, as at Flomborn and Elsloo, cemeteries were much larger and more frequent.

The study of the internal evolution and the *chronological classification* (Fig. 41) of the Linear Pottery cultures is based on the changes observed in the fabric, forms and decoration of the pottery.[103] These changes are reflected in very few other components of the assemblages. On the basis of the classification of the pottery (Figs. 21, 22), four or five main periods have been distinguished: earliest, early, middle, later and latest. In addition, the very large area embraced by the Linear Pottery cultures may be divided into three broad regions: eastern, central and western. In this book the western region, including especially the Rhine basin, will not be discussed. In the eastern region, there were strong ties with the Körös and, later, the Vinča–Tordoš culture. In the assemblages in the central and western regions there were very few south-eastern elements.

In the period of the *initial expansion* (Fig. 10) of agriculturalists into temperate Europe *c.* 4600 B.C. there was a marked uniformity of pottery fabric, forms and decoration throughout the whole area. The pottery is similar to the coarse ware of the Körös culture. Apart from roughening the surface, decoration consists of broad incised lines (3–6mm wide) in simple patterns of one to three parallel lines in curvilinear or rectilinear designs, especially two opposed spirals (Fig. 21), across the centre of the pot. The pottery was manufactured into similar forms to those of the Körös culture (p. 79).

In the *middle and later periods* (Fig. 17) of the Linear Pottery cultures, regional variation became apparent, in particular in the patterns of incised decoration. Certain tendencies, however, may be observed in all the assemblages. For example, organic material as a means of tempering the pottery was rejected in favour of mineralogical inclusions, such as the local mica in Bohemia, or graphite in Moravia. There is evidence that more advanced firing techniques were used with higher temperatures and more controlled reducing conditions. The pot form most characteristic of the middle period, apart from eastern Hungary, was the three-quarter spherical or bomb-shaped vessel with a rounded base. In the later periods, especially in the more western regions, the vessels tended to be made more piriform. In decoration, the elements most frequently used were parallel incised lines (Figs. 21, 22) which tended to increase in number and density in later periods of the culture. Other elements of the decoration, such as dots or stabs interrupting the lines, or filling in bands between two parallel lines, also tended to increase in number and density and to decrease in size until finally in the latest period of the culture the solid lines were dispensed with altogether and were superseded by bands of stabs and dots. In the eastern region, instead of the stabs and dots, the space between the parallel lines tended to be filled with paint after firing.

Thus, in the central region (Moravia, Austria, W. Slovakia, W. Hungary) on the *Pannonian plain*,[104] the decoration first consisted of the same patterns as in the early period with the addition of an indentation at the end of the line or, occasionally, interrupting it. Gradually the number of indentations increased to give the 'music-note' or 'notenkopf' effect (Fig. 22), and the patterns became more complex, including spirals, triangles, zigzags, etc. The rim of the pot was surrounded by one to three parallel lines. At the same time as the later evolution of the 'notenkopf' style was taking place, a style known as 'Želiezovce' (Figs. 21, 22) was developed in the later period of the Linear Pottery culture of the eastern part of the Pannonian plain. The assemblages with Želiezovce style pottery have many indications of close contact with the Linear Pottery settlements of the eastern region, for example in the application of red and yellow paint between the incised lines after firing.

Further west in settlements of the *Bohemian plain* and the *Elbe–Saale basin* the pottery decoration developed in a rather different direction in that the two or three parallel lines forming the patterns of the early period were not interrupted by indentations but were joined at the ends to make bands. The bands were filled with dots or stabs in patterns which resemble the 'winkelband' designs of the Vinča–Tordoš culture. In east Bohemia (e.g. Bylany) this form of decoration was generally replaced in the later periods of the Linear Pottery culture by the 'notenkopf' style whose popularity spread there from the Pannonian plain. Further west, however, and in the Rhineland, the 'notenkopf' style never became very popular and was generally used as a subsidiary element of designs which consisted

---

Fig. 22

Linear Pottery of the Pannonian and Bohemain plains and the Saale–Elbe basin.

a Early phase. Boskovštejn, S.C. Czechoslovakia (after Quitta, 1960).

b Early phase. Žopy, S.C. Czechoslovakia (after Quitta, 1960).

c Early phase 'Ačkovy style'. Praha-Veleslavin, W. Czechoslovakia (after Stocky, 1926).

d Early phase. Boskovštejn, S.C. Czechoslovakia (after Tichy, 1962).

e Early–middle phase (filled-in bands style). Praha-Bubeneč, W. Czechoslovakia (after Stocky, 1926).

f Middle phase (filled-in bands style). Leippen, S.E. Germany (after Hoffmann, 1963).

g Late phase (late 'notenkopf' style). Dresden-Nickern, S.E. Germany (after Hoffmann, 1963).

h Middle phase (early 'notenkopf' style). Bešeňova, S.C. Czechoslovakia (after Novotny, 1958).

i Late phase (late 'notenkopf' style). Ludanice, S.C. Czechoslovakia (after Novotny, 1958).

j Middle–late phase (later 'notenkopf' style). Gajara, S.C. Czechoslovakia (after Novotny, 1958).

k Late phase (Želiezovce style). Šturovo, S.C. Czechoslovakia (after Pavukova, 1966). Dotted area denotes yellow encrusted paint.

l Sherd with 'notenkopf' designs. Bienczyce, S. Poland (after Hachulska-Ledwos, 1963).

m Nezviska, W. Ukraine SSR (after Černyš, 1962).

n Florešti, Moldavia SSR (after Passek & Černyš, 1963).

o Glăvăneşti Vechi, N.E. Rumania (after Comşa, 1959).

p Pot decorated by shallow channelling and incised 'notenkopf' designs. Sudiţi, S.E. Rumania (Ploieşti Museum, Teodorescu, 1966).

q Pot of early Boian shape with incised 'notenkopf' designs. Sudiţi, S.E. Rumania (Ploieşti Museum, Teodorescu, 1966).

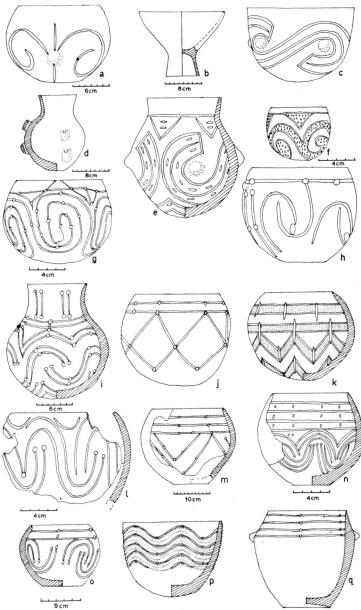

Fig. 22

basically of later developments of the filled-in bands (Fig. 22). The disappearance of the incised lines delimiting the bands of dots and stabs (Fig. 22) marks the transformation in central Europe of the Linear Pottery culture into the Stroke-ornamented Pottery culture (Stichbandkeramik) (Fig. 36) which according to Carbon 14 dates (Fig. 40) dominated the western part of central Europe c. 3800–3500 B.C. (Chapter 4).[105] In the western part of Bohemia, an individual style of pottery decoration developed in the latest period of the Linear Pottery culture in which the late 'noten-kopf' incised pots were painted, before firing, in black spirals on the buff ground.[106] It is still under discussion how this style known as 'Šarka' and the technique of painting pottery before firing evolved in Bohemia when it had been out of use in the rest of eastern Europe apart from a small area in east Hungary for several hundred years.

The classification of the Linear Pottery cultures has been checked to a certain extent by the only evidence of vertical stratigraphy in the culture, which occurs in caves in the limestone hills of *S.E. Slovakia and N.E. Hungary*.[107] In caves such as Domica, Aggtelek, Ardovo and Čertova Diera the Linear Pottery habitation levels form stratified deposits of considerable thickness. The stratigraphy in the caves has often provided the key to the complicated internal development of the Linear Pottery cultures of east Hungary and the assemblages form the link between the Linear Pottery cultures of the Pannonian plain and those of the Great Hungarian plain. Linear Pottery settlements in this area also occur in open sites in the mountains and valleys with identical assemblages to those in the caves. The evidence of the economy of one of the open sites in the mountains shows that, in spite of the apparently harsher environment, domesticated animals, especially cattle, predominated in the bone materials. Red-deer were hunted but did not play an important part in the economy. It is possible that, as was suggested for similar mountain sites in south-east Europe, these sites located in the mountains represent the summer habitation sites of herdsmen from the plains who were practising transhumance. It is also possible that the mountain sites were used by groups who settled there to obtain or mine obsidian. The northern mountains of Hungary and their extension in S.E. Slovakia are the main source of obsidian in continental Europe, which occurs as outcrops in the limestone. It was highly prized in the early neolithic settlements of the Near East and Europe as a raw material for chipped stone artefacts probably because of its very sharp cutting edge and was frequently obtained from very distant sources.[108] There is evidence that the central European obsidian found its way by some form of direct or indirect exchange to the neolithic settlements of south-east Europe, rarely south of the Danube, and to settlements north and east of the Carpathian mountains as far as the Dniester river. Its use was widespread in the Linear Pottery cultures of N.E. Hungary–S.E. Slovakia as well as the Great Hungarian plain (Alföld), and on many sites it was the only raw material used in the manufacture of chipped stone artefacts.

On a number of settlements representing the initial expansion of agriculturalists to temperate Europe, there occur sherds of fine, hard pottery with a red burnished slip and sherds of coarser ware which were painted before firing in a manner identical to that of the early neolithic cultures of south-east Europe. It is possible that the presence of this pottery may reflect an established trade-route in obsidian. The painted pottery does not occur on the Linear Pottery settlements immediately north of the Körös culture, but in those settlements on the northern edge of the E. Hungarian plain and in the N. Hungarian–S.E. Slovakian mountains. The painted ware (Fig. 21) occurs in particular on sites where large numbers of artefacts of obsidian have been excavated.[109] At the cave of *Domica* painted pottery of this type occurs with incised pottery of the early Linear Pottery culture in the lowest layer (Ia).[110] The succeeding layer at Domica (Ib) has no painted pottery, but the incised pottery is very similar to the early Linear Pottery of the E. Hungarian plain (Alföld Linear Pottery) and that of the valleys and plains of east Slovakia (east Slovak or east Carpathian Linear Pottery) (Fig. 21).[111] The pottery was chaff-tempered, covered by a self-slip and decorated by broad wavy incised lines which at Domica and northern Alföld sites were occasionally emphasised by black lines painted on the unslipped surface before firing.

The pottery of layer IIa at Domica shows the beginning of a certain amount of independence of the mountain area from the Hungarian plain in the development of the pottery decorated in the so-called Ardovo or Gemör style (Fig. 21). This is associated with the earliest stage in the development of the Bükk culture or variant of the Linear Pottery. This was an independent pottery style developed in the mountains of N. Hungary and S.E. Slovakia. The pottery was still tempered by organic material. It was decorated by parallel incised lines, in the Gemör pottery in rectilinear patterns including simple meanders, in the early Bükk pottery in curvilinear patterns such as spirals. The pottery of the upper layers at Domica and the later stages in the development of the Bükk variant is marked by an improvement of the fabric in mineralogical tempering, in firing at higher temperatures and in the quality of its surface which was frequently burnished. In decoration the incised lines became thinner, denser and more numerous. Thus, the same tendencies are visible in

I

the middle and later periods of the Linear Pottery culture of the eastern region as occurred further west.

The curvilinear patterns of the Bükk pottery evolved into rounded arches (Fig. 21) in the Pre-Classical (Bükk AB) phase and pointed arches in the Classical (Bükk B) phase (Fig. 21). At the caves of Ardovo and Čertova Diera the earlier Pre-Classical Bükk pottery was associated with another local style of Linear Pottery known as Tiszadob-Kapušany (Fig. 21) which was more characteristic of the lowland areas surrounding the Matra and Bükk mountains. The Tiszadob style was characterised by patterns of four or five parallel wavy lines. In the earlier Pre-Classical Bükk phase there is little evidence of regular contact between the N. Hungarian–S. Slovak mountains and the Pannonian plain. The direction of contact from the mountains, possibly as a result of the trade in obsidian, was all in a southwards direction. Slightly later, settlements with later Pre-Classical and Classical Bükk pottery spread to the foothills of the central Carpathains in N. Slovakia. Pottery of the same type frequently occurs in the eastern part of the Pannonian plain in settlements whose pottery was decorated predominantly in the Želiezovce style. The presence of Bükk pottery and obsidian in the Linear Pottery settlements of S. Poland, whose pottery was decorated predominantly in the later 'notenkopf' and Želiezovce styles, would indicate trade contacts across the Carpathian mountains (p. 133). Obsidian artefacts occur as far east of the Caparthians as the Linear Pottery settlements of the Upper Dniester valley (p. 134). Contact southwards, with the Great Hungarian plain, however, seems to have decreased, particularly at the end of the Classical phase and beginning of the Late phase of the Bükk variant, at a time when the Tisza culture or variant of the Linear Pottery cultures began to dominate most of the Tisza basin. This may be connected with a decrease in the popularity of obsidian long flint blades. The final or Late phase in the evolution of the Bükk pottery (Bükk C), as seen in layer IV at Domica, was characterised by incised lines which form a negative pattern and provide a base for white, yellow or red encrusted paint as in the contemporary late Želiezovce pottery and Tisza pottery of the Hungarian plain.

It is difficult to calculate to what extent the *Great Hungarian plain* (Alföld) was a transitional zone between the neolithic cultures of S.E. Europe and those of temperate central Europe because of the lack of any extensive excavations or systematic quantitative documentation of the finds. The early settlements of the Linear Pottery culture, contemporary with the Körös culture, tended to be located away from the rivers as in central Europe. Apart from this, however, there is no evidence from the early period of the means of subsistence.

There is no evidence of houses apart from the presence of pits. The pottery consists of coarse chaff-tempered ware decorated by broad incised lines. In certain of the more northern sites of the Hungarian plain this was associated with painted pottery which was possibly imported from the area of the Starčevo and Körös cultures (see above) and pottery decorated by combined incised and painted patterns.

In the middle and later periods of the Linear Pottery cultures, the technique of painting pottery before firing was practised only in settlements of the north-eastern part of the East Hungarian plain, where it was retained long after it had fallen into disuse in south-east Europe.[112] Two groups of Linear Pottery settlements of the Hungarian plain still painted their pottery before firing in the middle period of the culture. The first is referred to as the Esztar–Tócóvolgy group (Fig. 21), on the eastern part of the plain, in which the pottery was covered with a burnished brown self-slip or coloured bright red or occasionally white slip; the surface was decorated by black, or occasionally white or dark red, painted stripes similar to the patterns of the Körös culture. There was rarely any incised ware associated with the painted pottery, but that which does occur is identical to the later Alföld Linear Pottery incised ware of the Körös valley. The second group of painted ware occurs in the Szamos valley and the Potisia plain of the north-eastern corner of the Great Hungarian plain; in this the pottery was painted in the same combination of parallel broad and narrow stripes (Fig. 21) but in curvilinear patterns, in black or dark brown stripes on a buff self-slip.[113] The painted pottery occurs in the same assemblages as incised pottery of the later Tiszadob style, described above, which predominated to the west and north-west of the Szamos valley.

There is very little evidence that the relatively marshy western part of the East Hungarian plain and the adjoining middle course of the Tisza valley were occupied by Linear Pottery settlements until the latest (Tisza culture) period. It has been claimed that the Szilmeg group of settlements dates to the middle period of the Linear Pottery culture, but since the pottery rarely has incised decoration it is difficult to see the group as part of the Linear Pottery cultures. The pottery was decorated by the application of warts and strips of clay. The bones from Szilmeg and Polgar were analysed and indicate a similar basic economy to that of the Linear Pottery settlements of the Pannonian plain. Assemblages from settlements along the Körös river and in the area of the Tisza–Körös confluence contain pottery which was decorated by incised patterns evolved from the Alföld Linear Pottery, especially rectilinear patterns such as simple meanders. The pottery fabric of these settlements which are known as the

Szarvas-Erpart group was tempered by coarse mineralogical inclusions; it was unslipped so that its surface was generally rough and
gritty.

South of the Körös river after the initial period of expansion of the
early agriculturalists, the declining Körös culture of S.E. Hungary
was superseded by a culture which was the result of an amalgamation
of Linear Pottery, Vinča–Tordoš and surviving Körös elements, and
which is known as the Szakalhát–Lebő group (Fig. 21).[114] Further
south in N. Yugoslavia the Vinča elements gradually predominated
over the Linear Pottery elements[115] and Linear Pottery artefacts in
the Danube settlements are rare imports.[116] The settlements of the
Szakalhát–Lebő group are located in the same habitats as those of
the Körös culture, that is, in close proximity to water. Most of the
settlements consist of a thin culture layer with a single habitation
level. A few settlements (for example Csoka and Crna Bara) comprise thicker culture layers with several habitation levels. Fish-bones
and turtle-bones form an important percentage of the bone material,
and on many sites the fishing activities are also indicated by the presence of barbless bone fish-hooks and clay and stone weights which
may have acted as net-weights. As in the Körös settlements, approximately half the bones were of wild animals, including aurochs, wild
pig and red-deer. This is a sharp contrast to the evidence from the
other Linear Pottery settlements and Vinča–Tordoš settlements
which showed very few hunting activities. In contrast to the Körös
settlements, however, the most important domesticated animals were
cattle, with very few ovicaprids. This almost certainly involved the
domestication of local wild cattle, if only on a small scale. In spite of
the scarcity of sheep and goats among the bones, clay spindle whorls
and clay weights, which possibly acted as loom weights, continued
to be made in this period as in the contemporary Vinča–Tordoš
culture. It is possible that the material which was spun and woven
was the product of neither sheep nor goats. Clay 'stamp-seals',
'lamps' and anthropomorphic and zoomorphic figurines all occur in
the Szakalhát–Lebő assemblages. These objects generally occur more
sporadically further north and are completely absent in settlements
north of the Körös river. The clay anthropomorphic figurines resemble much more closely the small standing figurines of the Vinča–
Tordoš culture with their cylindrical bodies and triangular heads
than those of the Körös culture. Like the Körös houses, the houses
of the Szakalhát–Lebő group were small rectangular one-roomed
structures, 2·5–4m wide, 6–10m long, with a few post-holes round the
edge representing the wooden posts which supported a wattle and
daub wall. The floor of the houses was frequently plastered and was
furnished with a round hearth and/or clay oven. The pottery of the

Szakalhát–Lebő group was similar to the fine mica-tempered black ware of the Vinča-Tordoš culture, but it was decorated by incised lines in curvilinear patterns typical of the Alföld Linear Pottery further north. The surface of the pot was left matt between the incised lines and covered with red paint after firing; outside these bands the surface was burnished as in the Vinča culture. This category of pottery was associated with Vinča–Tordoš pottery incised in the 'winkelband' style and with later incised Alföld Linear Pottery.

LINEAR POTTERY CULTURES NORTH AND EAST OF
THE CARPATHIANS

It would seem from the Carbon 14 evidence from Strzelce (*c.* 4300 B.C.) and the pottery at Zofipole and Bienczyce that, even in the early stages of the evolution of the Linear Pottery culture, agriculturalists from C. Czechoslovakia spread through the passes of the Carpathians to the loess plains of the upper Vistula and Oder rivers in *S. Poland.*[117] The burials at Zofipole and Szczotkowice contain pots whose decoration may be assigned to the initial stages in the development of the 'notenkopf' style. The burial at Szczotkowice[118] also contained a necklace of *Spondylus*, white marble and fired clay beads, showing probably indirect connection with the Mediterranean or Black Sea. The main expansion of agriculturalists to the loess plains north and east of the Carpathians coincided with the middle and later periods in the evolution of the Linear Pottery cultures. The pottery of the settlements in south and central Poland (Fig. 22) is characterised by decoration in the 'notenkopf' and Želiezovce styles.[119] Along the Vistula, sherds decorated in the style of the Bükk variant occur almost always in association with blades of obsidian, and may represent some form of exchange with the settlements in the east Slovak mountains.[120] Thus, although some of the Polish sites may have been territorially closer to Linear Pottery sites with the filled-in band style of decoration of the Elbe–Saale basin, the stimulus for their pottery decoration, and possibly other elements of their material culture, came entirely from central and eastern Czechoslovakia. Apart from pottery, evidence of the Linear Pottery settlements is minimal. The sites are generally located on the upper terraces of rivers or on the loess plain, but there is no evidence of their basic means of subsistence apart from the presence of traces of einkorn and emmer wheat. In the Linear Pottery settlements of central Poland, such as Chełmzia, sporadic 'geometric' microlithic blades occur among the chipped stone artefacts, but whether this indicates contact with or continuation of a local mesolithic hunting and gathering population is impossible to assess without more evidence of the economy and material culture. Microlithic blades are absent from the Linear Pottery assemblages of south Poland, where the chipped and polished stone industry is identical to that of the central European Linear Pottery assemblages. The only traces of habitations recognised so far in the Polish sites are long ovaloid pits, apart from the excavation of long rectangular surface structures at Olszanica.[121]

Settlements of agriculturalists with Linear Pottery assemblages are scattered along the tributaries of the Vistula which rise near the source of the Dniester. Similar settlements occur regularly down the Dniester and its tributaries as far as its confluence with the Reut in the *Ukraine and Moldavian SSRs*.[122] It would seem that the spread of the agriculturalists was via this route, up the Vistula tributaries and down the Dniester. The Linear Pottery settlements were distributed north and west of those of the Bug–Dniester culture (p.101). They are situated in various locations including the middle of the loess plateaus, the upper and lower terraces of rivers and very occasionally on the banks of the rivers themselves. Isolated Linear Pottery sherds occur on a few sites with assemblages of the middle (Samtčin) phase of the Bug–Dniester culture, even as far as Basikov Ostrov on the S. Bug river. The Linear Pottery cultures, however, seem to have had no effect on the subsequent development of the Bug–Dniester culture. In general the two cultures, and presumably the settlements, were isolated from each other with a different material culture and economy. The bone material from the Linear Pottery settlements indicates that domesticated animals were much more important in the economy than in the Bug–Dniester culture, and that fishing was hardly practised at all.[123] Although cattle predominated among the domesticated animals, with pigs in second place, there is evidence on the Linear Pottery settlements of the breeding of ovicaprids, whereas in the Bug-Dniester settlements ovicaprids were always absent. Evidence from Nezviska shows that, as in the central and southeastern European neolithic settlements, both einkorn and emmer wheat was cultivated. At a number of Linear Pottery sites (Floreşti, Nezviska, Novi Ruseşti, and Torskoye), blades of obsidian were discovered. The obsidian must have been obtained from the N. Hungarian–S.E. Slovak mountains (p.128). There is no such evidence of long-range exchange and contacts in the Bug–Dniester assemblages.

The Linear Pottery settlements of the Ukraine and Moldavia, however, show certain differences in their economy from that of their counterparts in central Europe, even though the content and form of their material culture was identical. Hunting activities, particularly of large forest animals such as red-deer, wild pig and aurochs, provided much more food and raw material for the Dniester valley settlements than in central Europe. The relative proportions of the various domesticated species, however, remained the same. The chipped stone artefacts were also very similar to those of the central European Linear Pottery assemblages in spite of the differences in economy. Long wide blades whose distal ends had been carefully shaped by deliberate retouch and which could have been associated with the processing of meat and skins tended to occur more frequently. There is no apparent increase in bone and antler artefacts corresponding with the increase in hunting activities. Apart from a bone spoon from Floreşti, bone implements in the Dniester Linear Pottery settlements were limited to small bone points. Generally the only evidence of habitations in the Linear Pottery settlements of the Ukraine and Moldavia, as in Poland, is in the form of pits. These have been interpreted as the dwellings themselves, since the erosion factor of loess soil has not been recognised. It is very probable, however, that surface houses of central European Linear Pottery type were built by the same methods and with the same dimensions on these sites. At Torskoye and Floreşti, for example, long ovaloid pits have been excavated in rows oriented in the same direction and separated by a distance of *c.* 8 m. Thus, it is possible that traces of long rectangular surface houses originally existed between the pits but have since been completely eroded away. At Nezviska, however, the remains of two surface houses with clay floors have been preserved (p.119). Burials occur, as in central Europe, in the settlement area, accompanied by grave-goods such as a pot and a polished stone artefact.

The spread of agriculturalists with the Linear Pottery culture appears to have been limited to the relatively wet loess basins. No Linear Pottery settlements occur east of the Dniester or in the lower Dniester valley on the drier loess plains, which would have been covered by forest-steppe and steppe grassland. The spread of the Linear Pottery culture, and probably the agricultural population from the Dniester valley, was rather westwards to the Prut and Seret valleys of *E. Rumania* (Moldova and N. Muntenia) and even sporadically back across the Carpathians to C. Rumania (Transilvania).[124] At Perieni in Moldova a culture layer with a characteristic assemblage of the Linear Pottery culture was stratified above a pit containing an assemblage of the Criş culture, from which it was separated by a sterile layer representing a break in occupation.[125] All the Linear Pottery settlements of N.E. Rumania were located on the upper terraces of the river valleys unlike those of the preceding Criş culture. The limited evidence available indicates an identical economy[126] and identical house type to that of the Dniester valley settlements.

The pottery of the Ukrainian, Moldavian and E. Rumanian Linear Pottery settlements comprises the same two categories of ware as in Poland and C. Europe (Fig. 22). The coarse ware was manufactured into globular pots with flaring necks which were decorated by the application of strips of clay. The fine ware was made into three-quarter spherical pots, which were typical of the central European Linear Pottery. Frequently, however, the pots of the regions east of the Carpathians had flat instead of rounded bases and the addition of a cylindrical or flaring neck. The fine ware was decorated by an evolved form of the 'notenkopf' style in which the indentations were much smaller and less regular and were frequently placed carelessly under the incised lines instead of interrupting them. The most popular patterns were the volutes and horizontal lines surrounding not only the rim but also the body of the pot.

It would seem that the groups with the Linear Pottery culture east of the Carpathians remained very isolated from their neighbours and that, in spite of thriving cultures on their eastern and southern borders, they retained their cultural identity. On the other hand, apart from E. Rumania, they had little effect on the cultures surrounding them or on the subsequent evolution of later neolithic cultures in these areas. In E. Rumania, however, it would seem that the Linear Pottery cultures were partly responsible for the formation of the later neolithic cultures. At certain sites a transitional form of pottery has been recognised between the Linear Pottery and that of the later neolithic Boian and Pre-Cucuteni cultures. At Suditi in S.E. Rumania, for example, two pits were excavated in close proximity to each other.[127] The first contained Linear Pottery sherds decorated in the evolved 'notenkopf' style (Fig. 22) typical of E. Rumania. The same pit contained fragments of biconical pots characteristic of the Dudeşti culture (p.108) with a highly burnished surface and decorated by shallow fluting on the upper part of the pot; on the same sherds (Fig. 22) in combination with the fluting were incised lines which were executed in the same patterns as the evolved 'notenkopf' style but without the indentations or with indentations between the lines. It would seem, therefore, that the Dudeşti culture, which predominated in the assemblages of the lower Danube roughly contemporary with the Linear Pottery of E. Rumania, also played an important part in the formation of the later neolithic cultures of E. Rumania. The second pit at Suditi contained pottery in which the amalgamation of Dudeşti and Linear Pottery elements is visible at a slightly later stage; the pottery of this pit has been assigned to the initial stage in the development of the Boian culture. A parallel amalgamation of Linear Pottery and Dudeşti elements is observable further north in Moldova (N.E. Rumania) in the transitional pottery at

Tîrpeşti and the pottery at Traian (Dealul Vieii), both regarded as the initial stages in the development of the Pre-Cucuteni culture.[128] Although Dudeşti elements such as the burnished surface and fluted decoration are not so strong in the more northern settlements, it is interesting to note that the sites are located on the lower terraces of river valleys and that domesticated animals were very important in the economy, as in the Dudeşti settlements.

1. Carbon 14 evidence of the spread of the neolithic and eneolithic cultures into Europe: Ehrich, R. (1965); Clark, J. G. (1965); Gimbutas, M. (1965); Neustupny, E. (1968); id. (1969); Quitta, H. (1967); Renfrew, C. (1970a); id. (1970c); Tringham, R. (1968).

2. After the discovery of preceramic neolithic layers in certain 'tell' settlements in Thessaly, Greece (Milojčić, V., *Die Deutschen Ausgrabungen auf der Argissa-Magula in Thessalien*, I, Bonn, 1962; Theocharis, D., 'Pre-pottery in Thessaly', *Thessalika*, I, Volos, 1958, 70–86), the possibility of contact between the mesolithic and neolithic populations and the idea of a pre-ceramic agricultural population in S.E. Europe was suggested: Berciu, D. (1960a); id. (1967), 30–1; id., 'Neolitic Preceramic în Balcani,' *SCIV*, IX: 1 (1958), 91–100; Brukner, B., 'Die Tardenoisienischen Funde von "Pereš" bei Hajdukovo und aus Bačka Palanka und das Problem der Beziehungen in Donaugebiete', *Arch. Iug.*, VII (1966), 1–12; Grbić, M., 'Starčevo kao najraniji izraz neolitske ekonomike na Balkanu', *Starinar NS*, IX–X (1959), 11–16; Milojčić, V. (1956); id. (1960); Lichardus, J., & Pavuk, J. (1966); Pittioni, R. (1961). These ideas have been refuted by: Nicolaescu-Plopşor, C. S., 'Discuţii pe marginea paleoliticului de sfîrsit şi începuturilor neoliticului nostru', *SCIV*, X: 2 (1959), 221–35; Tringham, R. (1968); Vencl, Sl. (1968).

3. Garašanin, M., 'Ein Beitrag zur Kenntnis der frühneolithischen Verbindungen des Balkans und Vorderasiens', *Arch. Iug.*, IV (1960), 1–3; id., 'Khronologiya i genezis na neolita v centralnata i yugoiztočnata čast na Balkanskiya poluostrov', *Arkheologiya*, VIII: 1, Sofia (1966), 16–30; Mellaart, J. (1965), 115–18; Milojčić, V. (1949b); Nandris, J. (1970); Piggott, S. (1965), 40, 44; Trogmayer, O. (1967); Titov, V. S., *Neolit Grecii*, Moscow (1969), 195–210.

4. Lepenski Vir: Srejović, D. (1966); id. (1969); Nandris, J. (1968). Possibly Padina: Jovanović, B., 'Padina' in Trifunović L., et al., *Anciennes Cultures du Djerdap*, Belgrade (1969), 45–6. Schela Cladovei and Ostrovul Banului: Boroneanţ, V. (in press).

5. Crvena Stijena, S.W. Yugoslavia: Benac, A., & Brodar, M., 'Crvena Stijena— 1956', *Glasnik Z.M. Sar.*, XIII (1958), 26–61. Soroki, Moldavia, SSR: Markyevič, V. I., 'Issledovaniya neolita na Srednem Dnestre', *KSIA*, 105 (1956), 85–90; id., *Neolit Moldavii*, unpublished thesis for Kandidat Istoričeskikh Nauk degree in the Inst. of Archaeology, ANSSSR, Moscow (1968). Cremenea, C. Rumania: Nicolaescu-Plopşor, C. S., & Pop, I., 'Cercetările şi săpăturile paleolitice de la Cremenea şi împrejurimi', *Materiale* VI (1960), 50–6. Dîrţu-Ceahlău, C. Rumania: Vlassa, N., 'In legătură cu neoliticul timpuriu de la Dîrţu-Ceahlău', *Acta Musei Napocensis*, I, Cluj (1964), 463–4; Păunescu, Al., 'Locuirea neolitică de la Dîrţu-Ceahlău', *SCIV*, IX: 2 (1958), 269.

6. Necrasov, O., 'Considerații asupra populațiilor din vîrsta pietrei și de la
   începtul vîrstei metalelor pe teritoriul RPR', *Omagiu lui C. Daicoviciu,*
   Bucharest (1960), 415–26.
7. Renfrew, J. (1969).
8. Ucko, P., & Dimbleby, G., Eds. (1969); Higgs, E., & Jarman, M. (1969).
9. Piggott, S. (1965), 44–5.
10. Childe, V. G. (1929); id. (1957). For general discussion of chronological and
   cultural connections between the two areas: Milojčic, V. (1949a); id. (1952);
   Quitta, H. (1964).
11. Detev, P., 'Opit za različavane na neolitnite bradvi ot dletata, teslite, motikite,
   i polešnisite', *God. Nar. Arkh. Muz.* IV (1960), 61–74; Sonnenfeld,
   J. (1962–3); Semenov, S. A. (1964), 126–34; Vencl, Sl. (1960); id., 'K
   otazce interpretace funkce pravěkych předmětů', *Arch. Rozh.,* XIII: 5
   (1961), 678–93.
12. Tringham, R. (1968).
13. Prehistoric European sickle blades: Behm-Blancke, G. (1962–3); Bibikov,
   S. N., 'Iz istorii kamennikh serpov na yugo-vostok Evropi', *SA,* 3 (1962),
   3–24; Berciu, D. (1967), 40, pl.8 (Valea Răii); Georgiev, G. I., 'Za nyakoi
   orudiya za proizvodstvo ot neolita i eneolita v Bulgarija', *Studia in honorem
   D. Dečev,* Sofia (1958), 369–87; Semenov, S. A. (1964), 115–22; Piggott, S.
   (1965), fig.11.
14. e.g. Gyalaret and Ludvár: unpublished material in Szeged Museum.
15. Georgiev, G. (1961), 57–63.
16. Petkov, N., 'Predistoričeska bojadisana keramika ot Sofiskata Kotlovina',
   God. Plovdiv Nar. Bibl. i Muz. (1928–9), 185–98; id., 'Le décor peint à
   l'epoque du Néolithique dans la region de Sofia', *Arkheologiya,* IV: 3,
   Sofia (1962), 43; Nikolov, B., 'Sites préhistoriques de l'arrondissement de
   Vraca', *Arkheologiya,* IV: 4, Sofia (1962), 65.
17. Garašanin, D. (1954); Makkay, J., & Trogmayer, O. (1966); Jovanović,
   B., 'Keramički tipovi Balkanskog neolita i eneolita', *Starinar,* XIII–XIV
   (1962–5), 14–18.
18. Ucko, P. (1968).
19. Höckmann, O. (1968); Kalicz, N. (1970); Mikov, V., 'Plastic figurines of the
   neolithic in Bulgaria', *IAI,* VIII (1934–5); Renfrew, C. (1969a); Srejović, D.
   (1964–5); id., 'Neolitska plastika Centralnobalkanskog poručja', *Neolit
   Centralnog Balkana,* Belgrade (1968), 177–240; Galović, R. (1966).
20. Nea Nikomedea: Rodden, R. (1966), 11; Ludvár: unpublished in Szeged
   Museum.
21. e.g. Porodin, S. Yugoslavia: Grbić, M. (Ed.), *Porodin,* Bitola (1960), fig. XXIX;
   Karanovo, S. Bulgaria: Georgiev, G. (1961), fig. 3:1.
22. Gorzsa: Gazdapusztai, Gy., 'A Körös kulturá lakótelepe Hodmezövasarhely-
   Gorzsa', *Arch. Ert.,* 84 (1957), 3–12; Bogojevo (Öcsöd): Kutzian, I. (1947),
   fig. XII:10.
23. Selmeczi, L., 'Das Wohnhaus der Körös-Gruppe von Tiszajenő: neuere
   Haustypen des Frühneolithikums', *A Mora F. Muz. Evk.,* 2, Szeged (1969),
   20.
24. e.g. Leţ, C. Rumania: Zaharia, E., 'Considerations sur la civilisation de Criş
   à la lumière des sondages de Leţ', *Dacia NS,* VI (1962), 5–51; Verbiţa,
   S.W. Rumania: Berciu, D. (1961a), 29–32.
25. Early neolithic houses in S.E. Europe: Trogmayer, O. (1966); Stalio, B.,
   'Naselje i stan neolitskog perioda', *Neolit Centralnog Balkana,* Belgrade
   (1968), 83.
26. Selmeczi, L., op. cit. (1969), 20–2.
27. Georgiev, G. (1965).

28. Rapoport, A. (1969).
29. e.g. Ludaš (Budžak), N.E. Yugoslavia: unpublished private communication from Szekeres, L., Subotica Museum; Nosa (Biserna Obala), N.E. Yugoslavia: Garašanin, D., 'Die Siedlung der Starčevokultur in Nosa bei Subotica und das Problem der neolithischen Lehmschermen', *Bericht V Kongress ISPP, Hamburg 1956* (1961), 303–7; Grbić, M., op. cit. (1959).
30. Georgiev, G. (1961), 62.
31. Benac, A. (1961), 31.
32. e.g. Kisajaksor, S.E. Hungary: Trogmayer, O. (1966), 14; Lepenski Vir: Srejović, D. (1966); id. (1969).
33. e.g. Nagyjaksor, S.E. Hungary: Trogmayer, O. (1966), 14.
34. Comşa, E., 'Contribuţie cu privire la riturile funerare din epoca Neolitică de pe teritoriul ţării noastre', *Omagiu lui C. Daicoviciu,* Bucureşti (1960), 84–6; Galović, R., 'Sakhranivanje u Starčevačkoj kulturi', *Starinar,* XVIII (1968), 168–74; Garašanin, M. (1956); Trogmayer, O. (1969).
35. General discussion of the economic basis of neolithic settlements of the Balkans: Glišić, J., 'Ekonomika i sozialno-ekonomski odnosi u neolitu Podunavsko–Pomoravskog baseina', *Neolit Centralog Balkana,* Belgrade (1968), 21–62.
36. e.g. Argissa, Arapi and Otzaki: Boessneck, J., 'Zu den Tierknochen aus neolithischen siedlungen Thessaliens', in Milojčić, V., op. cit. (1962); Nea Nikomedea: Rodden, R. (1965).
37. Hopf, M., in Milojčić, V., op. cit. (1962); Renfrew, J. (1969), 160.
38. Gaul, J. (1948); Georgiev, G. (1961).
39. Krudy, K., 'Settlement types of the Early Neolithic Karanovo–Starčevo–Körös–Criş cultures in S.E. Europe', unpublished thesis for M.A. Hons. degree in the Dept. of Archaeology, Univ. of Edinburgh (1968); Piggot, S. (1965), 41, 44.
40. Azmak: Georgiev, G., 'Glavni rezultati ot razkopkite na Azmaškata selištna mogila 1961', *IAI,* XXVI (1963), 157–76; id. (1965); id. (1969). Kapitan Dimitrievo: Detev, P., 'Selištnata mogila Banjata pri Kapitan Dimitrijevo', *God. Nar. Arkh, Mus. Plovdiv,* II (1950), and 1–25; summarised in Berciu, D., 'Arkheologičeskiye otkritiya v Banjata mogile v svete rumunskikh issledovanii', *Dacia NS,* III (1959), 553–9. Kazanlak: unpublished excavations by Katinčarov, R. (1967–70), Instit. of Archaeology, BAN, Sofia. Karanovo: Mikov, V. (1939); id. (1958); Georgiev, G. (1961). The numbering of the cultural layers by Mikov is rather different from that of Georgiev, whose system is generally now accepted. For a general discussion of the relative chronology of the Bulgarian 'tells' and the neolithic cultures of S.E. Europe: Berciu, D., op. cit. (1959); Garašanin, M. (1961a); id., op. cit. (1966); id., 'Položaj centralnoi Balkana i khronologija neolita jugoistočne Evrope', *Neolit Centralnog Balkana,* Belgrade (1968), 301–38; Georgiev, G. (1961); Piggott, S. (1960).
41. Neustupny, E. (1968); id. (1969); Quitta, H. (1967); Renfrew, C. (1970b).
42. Renfrew, J. (1969), 161.
43. Devetaki cave: Mikov, V., & Džambazov, N., *Devetaškata peštera,* Sofia (1960); Loveč caves: Džambazov, N., 'Loveškite pešteri', *IAI,* XXVI (1963), 195–241.
44. Petkov, N., 'Selištnata Ginova mogila do s. Čelopeč', *God. Nar. Arkh. Muz. Plovdiv,* I (1948), 159–71; id., op. cit. (1928–9); id., op. cit. (1962).
45. e.g. Slatina, W. Bulgaria: Petkov, N., 'Neolitno selište pri selo Slatina', *Arkheologiya,* I, 1–2, Sofia (1959), 100–5: Vršnik, S.W. Yugoslavia: Garašanin, M. & D., 'L'habitat néolithique de Vršnik près de Tarinci', *Zbornik na Štipskog Naroden Muzej,* II, Štip (1960–1), 7–40; Anzabegovo,

140 Hunters, Fishers and Farmers of Eastern Europe

S.E. Yugoslavia: unpublished excavations (1969–70) by Gimbutas, M., for UCLA, Garašanin, M., and Štip Museum. See also: Nandris, S. (1970), 206–7.
46. Hopf, M., in Garašanin, M. & D., op. cit. (1960–1).
47. General discussion of the settlements of the Starčevo culture: Benac, A. (1961); id., 'Neolitski telovi u sjeveroistočnaj Bosni i neki problemi bosanskog neolita', Glasnik, Z.M. Sar., XV–XVI (1961), 39–78; Galović, R. (1964); Garašanin, D. (1954); Garašanin, M. (1958); Grbić, M. (1957); id., 'Nalazišta Starčevačkog i Vinčanskog neolita u Srbiji i Makedoniji', Neolit Centralnog Balkana, Belgrade (1968), 63–76; Jovanović, B., 'Istoriat keramike industrije u neolitu i ranom eneolitu Centralnog Balkana', Neolit Centralnog Balkana, Belgrade (1968), 107–76; Milojčić, V. (1949a); id. (1950).
48. Čović, B., 'Rezultati sondiranja na preistoriskom naselju u Gornjoj Tuzli', Glasnik Z.M. Sar., 16 (1961), 79–139; Garašanin, M. (1958), 8, n. 36.
49. General discussion of the Starčevo culture of N. Yugoslavia and S.W. Rumania and the Körös culture: Brukner, B., 'Einige Fragen über die Verhältnisse der Starčevo und Körös Guppe', Acta Ant. et Arch., X (1966), 7–10; id. (1968); Banner, J. (1942); id. (1961); Gazdapusztai, G. (1962); Kalicz, N., 'Siedlungsgeschichtliche Probleme der Körös- und der Theiss-Kultur', Acta Ant. et Arch., VIII, Szeged (1965), 27–35; id. (1970); Kutzian, I. (1947); id. (1966); Dimitrijević, S., 'Starčevačka Kultura in Slavonsko-Srijemskom', Neolit i Eneolit u Slavonii, Vukovar (1969), 1–96; Milleker, F., 'Vorgeschichte des Banats', Starinar, XIII (1938), 102–66; Makkay, J. (1969); Makkay, J., & Trogmayer, O. (1966); Milojčić, V. (1949a); id. (1950); Garašanin, D. (1954); Trogmayer, O. (1967); id., 'Remarks to the Relative Chronology of Körös group', Arch. Ert., 91 (1964), 67–86; Schmidt, H. (1945).
50. Bökönyi, S., 'Die frühalluviale Wirbeltierfauna Ungarns', Acta Arch. Hung., XI (1959), 39–97; id., 'The vertebrate fauna of the neolithic settlement at Maroslele-Pana', Arch. Ert., 91 (1964), 87–93; id. (1971); id. (forthcoming); id. (1969).
51. Private communication from Bökönyi, S., and Trogmayer, O.
52. The site of Nosa (Biserna Obala), however, had three habitaton levels: Garašanin, D., op. cit. (1961).
53. Bökönyi, S. (1970); Comşa, E., 'Das Banater Neolithikum im Lichte der nemen Forschungen', A Mora F. Muz. Evk., 2 (1969), 29–38; id., 'Materiale de tip Starčevo descoperite la Liubcova', SCIV, XVII: 2 (1966), 355–61; Nandris, J. (1968); Nicolaescu-Plopşor, C. S., et al., 'Cercetările arheologice de la Cazane', SCIV, XVI: 2 (1965), 407–11; Srejović, D. (1966); id. (1969).
54. Single bone fish-hooks also occur at Azmak, S. Bulgaria, and Nea Nikomedea, N. Greece.
55. General discussion of the Criş culture of Rumania: Berciu, D. (1961a); id. (1961b); id. (1967), 39–43; Comşa, E. (1959); Păunescu, Al. (1970), 35–8.
56. Vlassa, N., 'Cultura Criş în Transilvania', Acta Musei Napocensis, III, Cluj (1966), 9–48; Zaharia, E., op. cit. (1962).
57. e.g. Cremenea: Nicolaescu-Plopşor, C. S., & Pop, I., op. cit. (1960); Dîrţu-Ceahlău: Păunescu, Al., op. cit. (1958); Vlassa, N., op. cit. (1964).
58. Berciu, D., 'Săpăturile de la Verbiţa', Materiale, VI (1960), 85–7; Teodorescu, V., 'Cultura Criş în Centrul Munteniei', SCIV, XIV: 2 (1963), 251–74.
59. Petrescu-Dîmboviţa, M. (1959).
60. Danilenko, V. N. (1969); Markěvič, V. I., op. cit. (1965); id., op. cit. (1968); Passek, T. S. (1962); Sulimirski, T. (1970), 64–6; Passek, T. S., & Černyš, E. K., 'Neolit severnovo Pričernomorya', Kamenni Vek na territorii SSSR, Moscow (1970), 122–6.

61. Quitta, H., & Kohl, G., 'Neue Radiocarbondaten zum Neolithikum und zu frühen Bronzezeit Südosteuropas und der Sowjetunion', *Zeitschr. für Arch.* 3, Berlin (1969): *Soroki II,* layer 1—4875±150 B.C. (Bln 586).

62. Childe, V. G., 'The antiquity and functions of antler axes and adzes', *Antiquity,* 16 (1942).

63. e.g. Surskii island and Kamennaya Mogila: Danilenko, V. N. (1969), 9–13, 24–7, 179, figs.1,3; Pidopličko, I. G., *Materiale do Vivčeniya minulikh faun URSR,* Kiev (1956), 54–5, Sulimirski, T. (1970), 80–4; Tringham, R. (1969), 384, 387.

64. Danilenko, V. N. (1969), 30–7; Sulimirski, T. (1970), 113–16; Telegin, D. Ja. (1968).

65. Linear Pottery sherds occur at Basikov ostrov: Passek, T., & Černyš, E. K. (1963), 13; Soroki 5: Markěvič, V. I., op. cit. (1965). Samtčin sherds occur at Novi Rusešti: Markěvič, V. I., 'Mnogosloyinoye poselenie Novi Rusešti I', *KSIA,* 123 (1970), 69–76; private communication from Markěvič, V. I., Kišiněv.

66. Benac, A. (1961).

67. Batović, Š. (1966); Benac, A., & Brodar, M., op. cit (1958); Miroslavljević, V., 'Jamina Sredi', *Arh. Rad. i Raspr.* I (1959), 131–69; id., 'Impresso-cardium keramika na otocima Cresa, Lošina i Krka', *Arh. Rad. i Raspr.,* II (1962), 175–212.

68. Benac, A., 'Zelena Pećina', *Glasnik Z.M. Sar,* XII (1957), 61–92.

69. e.g. Obre I: unpublished; excavated jointly in 1967–8 by Benac, A., Sarajevo, and Gimbutas, M., UCLA, it comprised several habitation levels, the lowest of which (Stratum I) contained a pure Starčevo assemblage, cf. Serbia, and has been dated 4845±150 B.C., Bln 636 (Quitta, H., & Kohl, G., op. cit., 1969, 235). The upper layers have been termed 'Kakanj culture' by Benac (1961), 44, but Gimbutas, M. (private communication) tends to regard the 'Kakanj culture' as the local late variant of the Starčevo culture in Bosnia with Danilo elements in the assemblage. These upper layers of Obre I have been dated 4280±80 B.C., Bln 659 (Quitta, H., & Kohl, G., op. cit., 1969, 236). Also see: Batović, Š. (1966), 111–22.

70. Rodden, R. (1968) Ch. 5; Batović, Š. (1966), 125–42.

71. Benac, A. (1961); Batović, Š. (1966), 157–65; Korošec, J., *Danilo in Danilska Kultura,* Ljubljiana (1964).

72. Cranstone, B., 'Animal Husbandry: The Evidence from Ethnography' in Ucko, P., and Dimbleby, G. (eds.), op. cit. (1969), 247–64.

73. Holmberg, E., 'The Appearance of Neolithic Black Burnished Ware in Mainland Greece', *AJA,* 68 (1964), 343–8.

74. This theory was first put forward by Childe, V. G. (1929), and was supported by: Garašanin, M., op. cit. (1966); id. (1961a); id., op. cit. (1960); id., 'Zur Zeitbestimmung des Beginns der Vinča-Kultur', *Arch. Iug.,* I (1954), 1–6; id. (1961b); id., op. cit. (1968); id. (1958); Grbić, M. (1957), 143–4; Jovanović, B., op. cit. (1962–3); Mellaart, J. (1960); Milojčić, V. (1949a); id. (1949b); id. (1950).

75. Georgiev, G. (1961), 53.

76. Personal communication from Katinčarov, R., Sofia, September 1967.

77. Garašanin, M. (1951); Srejović, D., 'Versuch einer historischen Wertung der Vinča-Gruppe', *Arch. Iug.,* IV (1960), 5–19.

78. e.g. Vršnik: Garašanin, M. & D., op. cit (1960–1); Anzabegovo (see n. 45 above).

79. Vassić, M. (1930–6); Milojčić, V. (1949a); Jovanović, B., 'Stratigrafska podela Vinčanskog nasel', *Starinar,* XI (1960), 9–19.

80. Benac, A. (1961); Garašanin, M. (1951); id. (1958); Grbić, M., op. cit. (1968); Comşa, E., op. cit. (1969).

81. Berciu, D. (1961a); id. (1961b); id. (1967), 46–9; Comşa, E., 'Rezultatele sondajelor de la Dudeşti şi unele probleme ale neoliticului de la sud de Carpaţi', *SCIV*, VII: 1–2 (1956), 41–53; id., 'Săpăturile de la Dudeşti', *Materiale*, V (1959), 96–7; Păunescu, Al. (1970), 40–2.

82. e.g. Turdaş (Tordoš in Hungarian): Roska, M., 'La Stratigraphie du Néolithique en Transilvanie', *Dolgozatek Szeged*, XII (1936), 26–51; Lumea Noua: Berciu, D. & I., 'Săpături şi Cercetări Arheologice în Anii 1944–7', *Apulum*, III, Alba Iulia (1948), 1–18; Tărtăria: Vlassa, N. (1963). For a general description of the neolithic in Transilvania, see also: Schroller, H. (1933).

83. Srejović, D., & Jovanović, B., 'Pregled kamennoj orudja i oružja iz Vinče', *Arch. Vestnik*, 8 (1957), 256–96; id., 'Orudje i oružje od kosti i nakit iz Vinče', *Starinar*, IX–X (1958–9), 181–90.

84. Renfrew, C. (1969a); Srejović, D. (1964–5); id., op. cit (1968); Galović, R. (1966).

85. Detev, P., 'Materiali za praistoriata na Plovdiv', *God. Nar. Arkh. Muz.*, III (1959), 3–80; id., 'Razkopki na selištnata mogila Yasa-tepe v Plovdiv 1959 g.', *God. Nar. Arkh. Muz.*, IV (1960), 5–55; Georgiev, G. (1961), 69–70.

86. Stalio, B., op. cit. (1968), 84–5; Georgiev, G. (1961), 67.

87. Faunal remains from sites in S.E. Rumania (Cernica, Dudeşti, and Draghiceanu) and the Danube gorges (Liubcova) have been analysed.

88. The Tărtăria tablets were used as evidence of the invalidity of Carbon 14 dates. This was a constant theme in Milojčić's studies (e.g. Milojčić, V., 1958–9) and with the evidence from Tărtăria this was stressed afresh by Milojčić and others: Falkenstein, A., 'Zu den Tontafeln aus Tărtăria', *Germania*, 43: 3–4 (1965), 269–73; Hood, S. (1967); Makkay, J., 'Die in Tărtăria gefundenen pictographischen Tafeln und die jüngere Steinzeit Südosteuropas', *A Mora F. Muz. Evk.* (1967), 21–4; Milojčić, V. (1965); Vlassa, N. (1963); id., 'Einige Bemerkungen zu Fragen des Neolithikums in Siebenbürgen', *Štud. Zvesti*, 17 (1969), 513–40. This view of the dating of the Tărtăria tablets has been refuted by: Neustupny, E. (1968b); Dumitrescu, V. (1969), 99–100 & 588 of the same journal. In general they believe that the tablets should be dated not to the Turdaş culture at all, but much later, even to the Baden–Coţofeni culture, c. 2900–2500 B.C. (see Fig. 40). A small clay plaque, inscribed with signs which have been interpreted as primitive writing, has recently been discovered at the late neolithic site of Gradešnitsa, N.W. Bulgaria, synchronous with the Maritsa culture: Nikolov, S., & Georgiev, V., 'Načenky na pismennost prez khalkolitnata epokha v našite zemi', *Arkheologiya*, XII: 3 (1970), 1–9.

89. Piggott, S. (1965), 50–2; Childe, V. G. (1929); id. (1957); Sangmeister, E. (1943–50); Soudsky, B. (1962); id. (1966); Tringham, R. (1968), fig. 7.

90. For a discussion of vegetation on loess deposits see Chapter 1, n. 7.

91. Soudsky, B., has been the main exponent of distinguishing habitation phases in Linear Pottery settlements, mainly on the basis of his excavations at the site of Bylany: Soudsky, B. (1962); id. (1966); id. (1968a); id. (1968b); id. (1969): Soudsky, B., & Pavlů, I. (1971).

92. Müller, H.-H., *Die Haustiere der Mitteldeutschen Bandkeramiker*, Deutschen Akad der Wissenschaft, E. Berlin (1964).

93. Bylany: Soudsky, B. (1966), 63; Soudsky, B., & Pavlů, I. (1971); Clason, A., Biologisch-Archaeologisch Instituut, Groningen, private communication; Györ (Papai Vam), N.W. Hungary: Bökönyi, S. (1959).

94. Tringham, R. (1971b). The author has undertaken the analysis of the chipped

stone industry of Bylany, and these figures are based on the first part of this analysis.

95. General discussion of houses of the Linear Pottery culture: Childe, V. G. (1949); Felgenhauer, F., 'Bandkeramische Grossbauten auf Männsworth bei Wien, *Arch. Aust.*, 27 (1960), 1–10; Waterbolk, H., & Modderman, P. (1958–9); Modderman, P. (1971); Sangmeister, E. (1943–50); Soudsky, B. (1969); Soudsky, B., & Pavlů, I. (1971); Stieren, A. (1943–50); Tringham, R. (1966), Pt. II, ch. 1; Vencl, Sl., 'K otazce interprétace pravěkych staveb', *Arch. Rozh.*, XX: 4 (1968), 490–510.

96. In the reports of early excavations of Linear Pottery settlements (Buttler, W., 'Das bandkeramische Dorf bei Köln-Lindenthal', *Germania*, XV, 1931, 244–52; Buttler, W., & Haberey, W., *Die Bandkeramische Ansiedlung bei Köln-Lindenthal*, Berlin and Leipzig, 1936; Paret, O., 'Vorgeschichtliche Wohngruben?, *Germania*, 26, 1942, 84–103), the pits were interpreted as the dwellings since, with the absence of any culture layer, they contained most of the occupation debris.

97. Černyš, E. K., 'K istorii naseleniya eneolitičeskovo vremeni v srednem Pridnestrovye', *MIA*, 102 (1962), 13, figs.4&8; Passek, T. S., & Černyš, E. K. (1963), 14–16.

98. For a discussion of Early Linear Pottery—Körös culture connections: Kalicz, N., & Makkay, J. (1966); Kalicz, N. (1970); Quitta, H. (1960); id., 'Zur altesten Bandkeramik in Mitteleuropa', *Aus Ur- und Frühgeschichte*, E. Berlin (1962), 87–107; id. (1964); Soudsky, B. (1966), 18–19; id., 'K relativni chronologii volutové keramiky', *Arch. Rozh.*, VIII: 3 (1956), 408–12, 462–3; Tichý, R., 'K nejstarši volutové keramice na Moravě', *Pam. Arch.*, 51 (1960), 415–42; Trogmayer, O., 'Ein Beiträg zur relativen Zeitstellung der älteren Linearkeramik', *Studien zur europäischen Vor- und Frühgeschichte*, Neumünster (1968), 5–9; id., 'Körös-Gruppe—Linearkeramik', *Alba Regia*, Szekesfehervar (in press).

99. Šikulova, V., 'K otazce rybolovu v mladši době kamenne', *Časopis Slezskeho Muzea*, X, Opava (1961), 1–16.

100. Discussion of Linear Pottery burials: Fischer, G., *Die Gräber der Steinzeit im Saalegebiet*, E. Berlin (1956), 24–9; Kahlke, H. (1954); Skutil, J., 'Linearkeramische Gräber in Mähren', *WPZ.*, 28 (1941); Stekla, M., 'Pohřby lidu s volutovou a vypíchanou keramikou', *Arch. Rozh.*, VIII: 5 (1956), 697–723; Pavuk, J. (in press). Discussion of the diffusion of *Spondylus* shells in neolithic C. Europe: Vencl, Sl., 'Spondylové šperky v Podunajském Neolitu', *Arch. Rozh.*, XI: 6 (1959), 699–742; Clark, J. G. D. (1952), 241–3; Shackleton, N., & Renfrew, C., 'Neolithic trade-routes re-aligned by oxygen-isotype analyses', *Nature*, 228: 5270 (1970), 1062–4.

101. e.g. Sondershausen: Kahlke, H. 'Ein Gräberfeld mit Bandkeramik von Sondershausen in Thuringen', *Neue Ausgrabungen in Deutschland*, Berlin (1958), 45–53.

102. Pavuk, J., 'Neolithisches Gräberfeld in Nitra', *Acta VIIe Congrès ISPP*, Prague (1966), 1–11.

103. Chronological classifications of the Linear Pottery culture have generally been based on research in one particular region. W. Czechoslovakia (Bohemia): Neustupny, E., 'K relativni chronologii volutové keramiky', *Arch. Rozh.*, VIII: 3 (1956), 386–407, 461–2; Soudsky, B., 'K methodice třídění volutové keramiky', *Pam. Arch.*, XLV (1954), 75–105; id., op. cit. (1956); id. (1965); Stocky, A., *Pravěk Země Česke*, I, Prague (1926). C. Czechoslovakia (Moravia): Tichy, R. (1961); id., 'Osidleni s volutovou keramikou na Moravě', *Pam. Arch.*, LIII (1962), 245–302. S.W. Slovakia/N.W. Hungary: Pavuk, J., 'Gliederung der Volutenkeramik in der Slowakei', *Štud. Zvesti*,

144   Hunters, Fishers and Farmers of Eastern Europe

9, Nitra (1962), 5–20; id. (1969). S.E. Slovakia/N.E. Hungary: Lichardus, J. (1964); id., 'O periodyzacji i chronologii kultury bukowogorskiej', *Acta Arch. Carp.*, V (1963), 5–25; id. (1969); id. (in press). E. Hungary: Kalicz, N., & Makkay, J. (1966); Kalicz, N. (1970); Korek, J., 'Verbreitung der Linearkeramischen Kultur auf dem Alföld', *A Mora F. Muz. Evk.* (1960), 19–52. S.E. Germany (Saxony/Thuringia): Hoffman, E. *Die Kultur der Bandkeramik in Sachsen*, Berlin (1963); Quitta, H., 'Die Bandkeramische Kultur', *Ausgrabungen und Funde*, III: 4–5 (1958), 173–7; id. (1960). W. Germany/Netherlands: Modderman, P., & Waterbolk, H. (1958–9), 173–83. These various chronological schemes have been summarised in Tringham, R. (1966), Pt. III.

104. Pavuk, J. (1969); Tichy, R., op. cit. (1962); Novotny, B., *Slovensko v Mladšej Době Kamennej*, Bratislava (1958); Draveczky, B., 'Neure Angaben zur Verbreitung der Linearbandkeramik in Ungarn', *Acta Ant. et Arch.*, X (1966), 27–33; Felgenhauer, F., op. cit. (1960); Kutzian, I. (1966a); Dimitrijević, S. (1969).

105. Stekla, M., 'Třiděni vypíchané keramiky', *Arch. Rozh.*, XI: 2 (1959), 207–57.

106. Vencl, Sl., 'Studie o Šareckém typu', *Sbornik N.M. Praha*, XV: 3 (1961), 93–140.

107. Böhm, J., *Domica, jeskyně neolitickeho člověka*, Prague (1933); Lichardus, J., op. cit. (1963); id. (1964); id. (1969); id., *Jaskyňa Domica*, Bratislava (1968); Tompa, F. (1929).

108. General discussion of obsidian as an indicator of trade and exchange: Dixon, J., Cann, J., & Renfrew, C. (1968); Renfrew, C. (1970c). More specifically C. European obsidian: Barta, J., 'Zur Problematik der Höhlensiedlungen in der Slowakischen Karpaten', *Acta Arch. Carp.*, II (1960), 1–39; Gabori, N., 'Quelques problèmes du Commerce de l'obsidienne à l'age préhistorique', *Arch. Ert.*, 77 (1950), 50–3; Kostrzewski, J., 'Obsidian implements in Poland', *Man*, XXX (1939); Kulczycka, A., & Kozlowski, J., 'Pierwsze materialy kultury Bukowogorskiej na Polnoc od Karpat', *Acta Arch. Carp.*, II, 1–2 (1960), 41–54.

109. e.g. Michalovce, S.E. Slovakia: Lichardus, J. (1971); Šiška, S., & Vizdal, J., 'Zachranný výskum na neolitickom sidlisku v Michalovciach', *Arch. Rozh.*, XIII: 6 (1961), 871–4. Ciumeşti (Beria), N.W. Rumania: Comşa, E., 'K voprosu o periodizatsii neolitičeskikh kulturna severo-zapade Rumunskoi Narodnoi Republiki', *Dacia*, VII (1963), 477–83; Păunescu Al., 'Perežitki Tardenuazkoi kulturi v drevnei neolite v Ciumeşti', *Dacia*, VII (1963), 467–75. For N. E. Hungarian sites: Kalicz, N., & Makkay, J. (1966); Kalicz, N. (1970).

110. Lichardus, J. (1964); id. (1971).

111. e.g. Barca III: Hajek, L., 'Nová skupina páskové keramiky na vychodním Slovensku', *Arch. Rozh.*, IX: 1 (1957), 3–6, 33–6.

112. Kalicz, N., & Makkay, J. (1966); Kalicz, N. (1970); Korek, J., op. cit. (1960); Tompa, F. (1929).

113. e.g. Michalovce: Šiška, S., & Vizdal, J., op. cit. (1961); Satoraljaújhely: Tompa, F., op. cit. (1929); Lichardus, J. (1971).

114. Banner, J. (1942); id., 'La troisième période des fouilles au Kökénydomb', *Arch. Ert.*, 78 (1951), 27–36; id. (1960); Banner, J., & Balint, A., 'Die prähistorische Ansiedlung in Szakalhát', *Dolgozatok Szeged*, XI (1935), 76–96; Gazdapusztai, G. (1962); Kalicz, N., & Makkay, J. (1966); Kalicz, N. (1970); Korek, J., op. cit. (1960); Kutzian, I. (1966); Trogmayer, O., 'Ausgrabung auf Tápe-Lebö', *A Mora F. Muz. Evk.*, II (1957), 19–57.

115. e.g. Oszentivan and Csoka: Kutzian, I. (1966).

116. e.g. at Vinča: Garašanin, M., 'Potiska kultura u Banatu', *Starinar*, I (1950), 19–25.
117. Bakker, J., Vogel, J., & Wislanski, T., 'TRB and other C14 dates from Poland', *Helinium*, IX (1969), 210; Wislanski, T., 'Sprawozdanie z prac w Strzelcach, pow. Mogilno', *Spraw. Arch.*, V (1959), 31–40; Kulczycka, A., 'Materialy kultury starszej ceramiki wztęgowej z Zofipola, pow. Proszowice', *Materiale Arch.*, III (1961), 19–29.
118. Krauss, A., 'Grób kultury starszej ceramiki wstęgowej ze Szczotkowice, pow. Kazimierza Wielka', *Stud. i Mat. Neol. Malopolski* (1964), 69–76.
119. Kowalczyk, J. (1969); Jażdżewski, K. (1965), 58–69; Kulczycka, A., 'Ulagi o chronologii kultury starszej ceramiki wstęgowej w Gornym Dorzeczu Wisly', *Stud. i Mat. Neol. Malopolski* (1964), 47–68; Smolczynska, L., 'Kultura ceramiki wstęgowej w Wielkopolśce, *Fontes Praehistorici,* III, Poznan (1952), 1–85.
120. Kulczycka, A., & Kozlowski, J., op. cit. (1960).
121. Excavated 1967–9 by Milisauskas, S., and Machnik, J. See Bakker, J., Vogel, J., and Wislanski, T., op. cit. (1969), 210.
122. Passek, T. S., & Černyš, E. K., (1963); Danilenko, V. N. (1969), 28–30; Gimbutas, M. (1956), 114–15; Passek, T. S. (1962); Sulimirski, T. (1970), 61–3; Svešnikov, I. K., 'Kultura linieno-lentočnoi keramiki na territorii verkhnevo Podnestrovya i Zapadnoi Volyni', *SA*, XX (1954), 100–30. Kričevskii, E. Yu., 'Drevneye naseleniye zapadnoi Ukraini v epokhu neolita i rannei bronzi', *KSIIMK*, 3 (1940), 1–14; Zakharuk, Yu. N., 'O tak nazevayemoi Volynskoi gruppe linieno-lentočnoi keramiki', *SA* (1959), 114–18; Passek, T. S., & Černyš, E. K., op. cit. (1970), 117–22.
123. Analyses have been made of animal bones from Florešti (Passek, T. S., & Černyš, E. K., 1963, 31–2) and Novi Rusešti: David, A. I., & Markěvič, V. I., 'Fauna mlekopitayuščikh poselenia Noviye Rusešti I', *Izvestia Akademii Nauk Mold. SSR*, 4, Kišinev (1967), 3–26.
124. General discussion of Linear Pottery cultures in Rumania: Comşa, E. (1959); id., 'Consideraţii cu privire la cultura cu ceramică liniară de pe teritoriul RPR şi din regiunile vecine', *SCIV*, XI: 2 (1960), 217–42; Nestor, I., 'Probleme noi în legătura cu neoliticul din RPR', *SCIV*, I:2 (1950), 208–19; id., 'Cultura ceramicei liniare în Moldova', *SCIV*, II: 2 (1951), 17–26; Vlassa, N., 'Cultura ceramicei liniare în Transilvania', *SCIV*, X: 2 (1959), 239–45; Paunescu, Al. (1970), 38–40.
125. Petrescu-Dîmboviţa, M., 'Sondajul stratigrafic de la Perieni', *Materiale,* III (1957), 65–82.
126. The animal bones of Traian (Dealul Fîntinilor) have been analysed: Necrasov, O., & Haimovici, S., 'Studiul resturilor de faună descoperite în 1959 la Traian', *Materiale,* VIII (1962), 261–5.
127. Teodorescu, V., 'Date preliminare privind cultura cu ceramica liniară din teritoriul de la sud de Carpaţi al României', *SCIV*, XVII: 2 (1966), 223–34.
128. Discussion of the transition from the Linear Pottery culture to the Pre-Cucuteni culture: Dumitrescu, H., 'Contribuţii la Problema originii culturii Precucuteni', *SCIV*, VIII (1957), 53–73; Dumitrescu, V. (1967a); Marinescu-Bîlcu, S., 'Unele probleme ale neoliticului Moldovenesc în lumina săpăturilor de la Tirpeşti', *SCIV*, XIX: 3 (1968), 395–422; id., 'Quelques aspects du problème de l'apport de la ceramique rubanée à la formation de la civilisation Precucuteni I', *Alba Regia*, Szekesfehervar (in press). Analysis of animal bones from Traian (Dealul Vieii): Necrasov, O., & Haimovici, S., op. cit. (1962).

K

4

ECONOMIC DEVELOPMENT AND

THE EARLIEST USE OF METAL

c. 3800–3000 B.C.

It would seem from the available evidence that, after the initial expansion of the earliest agriculturalists into south-east Europe, there was very little influence on the subsequent evolution of their culture from outside central and south-east Europe. In the previous chapter it has been shown that there is no reason to suspect that the Vinča and Veselinovo and later Linear Pottery cultures were the result of a secondary colonisation from Greece and the Near East. Similarly it seems very likely that the succeeding cultures (referred to generally as the late neolithic and eneolithic cultures) of eastern Europe, including the innovations in their equipment, even the appearance of metallurgy, were the result of internal evolution within eastern Europe, although there is no doubt that there was a certain amount of contact with areas further south. In general, the broad culture areas, which were visible in the earlier neolithic period (described in the preceding chapter), distinguished by similarities in their means of subsistence, settlement and house types and material culture, continued into the later neolithic and eneolithic periods.[1] The regional segmentation in the forms and decoration of pottery and the emergence of local pottery styles which could be seen in the earlier neolithic period became more apparent and crystallised in the later neolithic and eneolithic periods with the result that a large number of small cultures have been distinguished in these periods. These 'cultures' or 'sub-cultures', in fact, frequently reflect only regional variation in the pottery, whereas the rest of the material culture retained its uniformity.

Apart from pottery, cultural changes visible in the material of the

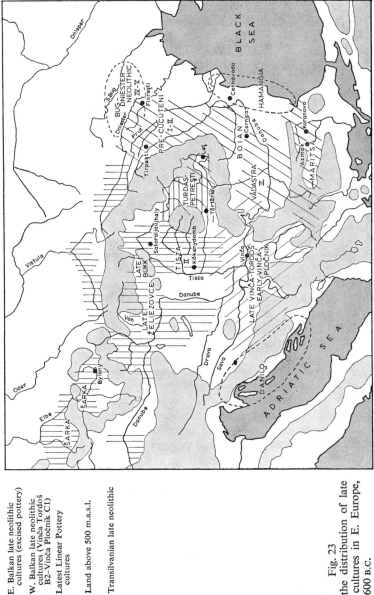

Fig. 23

Map of the distribution of late neolithic cultures in E. Europe, c. 3900–3600 B.C.

E. Balkan late neolithic cultures (excised pottery)

W. Balkan late neolithic cultures (Vinča Tordoš B2–Vinča Pločnik C1)

Latest Linear Pottery cultures

Land above 500 m.a.s.l.

Transilvanian late neolithic

late neolithic and eneolithic cultures of eastern Europe were of
degree rather than kind. In many areas during this period, especially
in south-east Europe, there was an increase in the population (reflected in an increase in the size, number and density of settlements). In
addition, there was an increase in the range of specialised artefacts
which were manufactured in a great variety of materials, including
metal. It is probable that these developments reflect a greater stability and permanence of settlements and the exploitation of a larger
variety of resources for food and raw materials. It is assumed (although there is not very much evidence) that there was an improvement in the techniques associated with the cultivation of grain and
rearing of domesticated animals. There were certainly developments
in the techniques associated with the manufacture of pottery, in particular in its firing. It is possible that this latter process led to the
exploitation of copper resources. Larger and more solid houses were
constructed, and frequently these formed substantial villages with
evidence of deliberate planning and delimitation by various means.
The area included within the sphere of the south-east European
agricultural settlements, or at least within their influence, expanded
in an easterly direction to include the drier loess plains north of the
Black Sea along the Dnieper, southern Bug and lower Dniester
rivers.

Similar developments in the material culture are present, to a
lesser extent, in the later neolithic settlements of central Europe,
especially those within the Carpathian mountain ring, i.e. east
Czechoslovakia and Hungary. It is possible that, by the end of this
period, techniques and equipment associated with agriculture and
stockbreeding had spread beyond the loess sub-soil areas of eastern
Europe to the heavy podsols and podsolised soils of the north
European plain, as seen in the emergence of the Funnel Beaker
cultures (Trichterbecker or TRB cultures).

THE EAST BALKANS

Various 'cultures' have been distinguished among the *late neolithic*
assemblages of the eastern part of south-east Europe.[2] These include
the Maritsa culture in south Bulgaria (as seen in layer V at Karanovo),
the Boian culture in N.E. Bulgaria–S.E. Rumania, the Vădastra
culture in N.W. Bulgaria–S.W. Rumania, and the early Tripolye–
Pre-Cucuteni culture in N.E. Rumania, Moldavia SSR and the
western part of the Ukraine SSR.

The pottery of all these late neolithic cultures consists of three
main categories:

1. Thick, poorly-fired, coarse-tempered ware (Fig. 24) made into globular and biconical flat-bottomed pots, probably used predominantly for storage purposes. The coarse ware was decorated, as in the earlier neolithic cultures, by various forms of rustication, especially

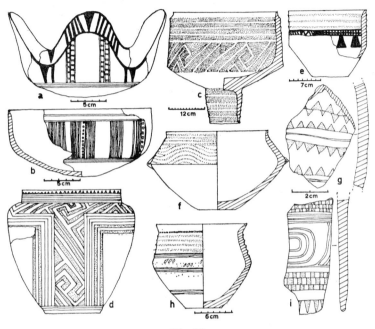

Fig. 24

Pottery of the late neolithic cultures of S.E. Europe.
a Pot with excised and graphite-painted designs. Maritsa culture. Azmak, S. Bulgaria (after Georgiev, 1961).
b Maritsa culture. Azmak, S. Bulgaria (after Georgiev, 1961).
c Pot with negative excised pattern filled with white encrusted paint (dotted area). Kalino, N.E. Bulgaria (after Berciu, 1961).
d Incised and excised (dotted area) decorated pot. Leţ, S.E. Transilvania, C. Rumania (after Zaharia, 1967).
e Pot with channelled and graphite-painted (black area) designs. Late Boian. Tangîru, S.E. Rumania (after Berciu, 1961).
f Fine-channelled ware. Boian culture. Aldeni, S.E. Rumania (Inst. of Arch., Bucharest).
g Sherd with incised and excised (dotted area) decoration. Boian culture. Cernica, S.E. Rumania (after Cantacuzino and Morintz, 1963).
h Fine-channelled, incised and stamped ware. Pre-Cucuteni II culture. Larga Jijia, N.E. Rumania (after Alexandrescu, 1961).
i Sherd with incised and excised (dotted area) decoration. Pre-Cucuteni II culture. Larga Jijia, N.E. Rumania (after Alexandrescu, 1961).

by running the fingers across the surface while it was wet and by finger-impressed strips of applied clay.

2. Less coarse-tempered ware (Fig. 24), but still relatively thick and medium-hard fired to a grey or buff colour with a smoothed or polished surface. This ware was manufactured into straight-sided or globular bowls with a short, wide, cylindrical neck and wide shallow bowls, and was decorated by incised patterns evolved from those of the Vinča and later Linear Pottery cultures. The rectilinear and curvilinear patterns of parallel incised lines were gradually replaced by excised patterns; eventually the whole surface was excised except for a negative pattern formed by the original surface and was filled with white paint applied after firing. This latter method was especially popular in the Maritsa culture, whereas in the Boian culture the patterns consisted more frequently of incised lines bounded on each side by excised triangles, and in the Vădastra culture the patterns were more frequently evolved from the earlier neolithic method of cross-hatched incised squares.

3. Fine-tempered thin pottery (Fig. 24), fired to a grey-black colour, and decorated, as in earlier periods in this region, by narrow shallow channelling or fluting. In the Pre-Cucuteni culture this channelling was combined with incised patterns. In the Maritsa culture this ware was generally decorated by dense parallel incised lines and by excised lines filled with white paint after firing. This category of pottery was most frequently manufactured into wide biconical bowls in which the short upper part was frequently carinated, and the lower part was hemispherical.

Before embarking on a more detailed description of the cultural development and processes in the late neolithic and eneolithic periods in the south-east Balkans, it would be interesting to digress to examine the Hamangia culture. Although this culture did not share the traditions of the south-east European neolithic cultures, it had a profound effect on the development of the subsequent eneolithic Gumelniţa culture.

The Hamangia culture

The majority of 'tell' settlements in the dry region of N.E. Bulgaria and S.E. Rumania (Dobrogea or Dobrudža) date to the eneolithic Gumelniţa culture when this area became densely settled. In the period contemporary with the Boian and Maritsa cultures, however, the Dobrogea was populated by small groups of people living on the low terraces of rivers. The Hamangia culture with which they have been associated has been recognised as far south as Burgas in E. Bulgaria, but the majority of the sites have been excavated in Rumania.[3]

There is evidence of sporadic settlement of the Dobrogea during the mesolithic period in association with the intensive hunting of sheep (p.52). At La Adam, a Hamangia culture layer was stratified above mixed layers containing microlithic blades and pottery decorated by the impressions of *Cardium* shells. Whether the Cardial Impressed Ware represents an intermediate phase of settlement between the aceramic settlement and the pottery-producing Hamangia culture is unclear in view of the confusion in defining the various habitation levels. Apart from this cave, none of the settlements have superimposed occupation layers. The Hamangia settlement sites consist of one thick habitation level. On the basis of a morphological typology of their pottery, however, Berciu has attempted to divide the Hamangia culture into five successive phases, the first of which includes Cardial Impressed Ware. He assumed that this latter group of pottery was contemporary with pottery decorated by a similar method in the early neolithic period of the Aegean and Adriatic coasts (p.102). But there is no stratigraphical evidence to support such a sequence. The upper chronological limit of the culture is fixed by evidence from the stratified site of Hîrşova, where an assemblage of an early phase of the Gumelniţa culture is stratified above a Hamangia culture layer. The general chronological position of the Hamangia culture is indicated by the Carbon 14 date (Fig.40) of *c.* 3930 B.C. from Ceamurlia de Jos, and by the presence in the Hamangia assemblages of sherds of the Boian, Maritsa and Pre-Cucuteni pottery variants of the late neolithic cultures of south-east Europe.

With the general absence of mesolithic sites in the Dobrogea, it is difficult to tell whether there was an analogous situation to that of the Bug–Dniester culture (Chapter 3), in which hunters and gatherers continued to occupy the region, but coming under the strong influence of their pottery-producing agricultural neighbours to the west. It is possible that the Hamangia settlements represent an eastwards expansion of the lower Danube agricultural population. It has even been suggested that the Hamangia culture was formed under the stimulus of 'voyagers' from the eastern Aegean and Anatolia.

The pottery of the Hamangia culture comprises two categories:

1. Thick domestic ware (Fig.25), tempered by organic material and 'grog', and poorly fired to a brick yellow colour. This pottery was made into large storage pots and smaller cylindrical beakers, similar in shape to those of the Veselinovo culture. It was decorated by various methods of roughening the surface, including finger-impressions and the 'wet hand' method.

2. Fine sand-tempered ware (Fig. 25), well fired to a black colour.
The pottery resembles the Boian and Maritsa fine ware, both in the
burnished surface and the forms of some of the pots, in particular
the wide bowls with a carinated upper part and hemispherical lower
part. In addition, however, tall pots were manufactured with a long
flaring upper part and shallow lower part, and these have no analogies in the preceding or contemporary cultures of the Danube basin.
The decoration is the same on both forms of the fine pottery, and

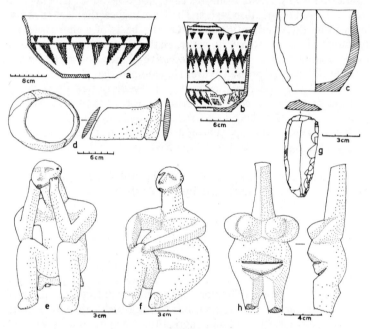

Fig. 25

The Hamangia Culture.
a Fine stamped bowl. Ceamurlia de Jos, S.E. Rumania (after Berciu,
  1966).
b Fine stamped pot. Ceamurlia de Jos, S.E. Rumania (after Berciu,
  1966).
c Coarse-tempered pot. Ceamurlia de Jos, S.E. Rumania (after Berciu,
  1966).
d Bracelet of Spondylus shell. Mangalia, S.E. Rumania (after Berciu,
  1966).
e Clay male figurine—'the Penseur'. Cernavoda, S.E. Rumania (after
  Berciu, 1966).
f Clay female figurine. Cernavoda, S.E. Rumania (after Berciu, 1966).
g Retouched blade of honey-coloured flint. Ceamurlia de Jos, S.E.
  Rumania (after Păunescu, 1970).
h Clay female figurine. Cernavoda, S.E. Rumania (after Berciu, 1966).

consists predominantly of various fine impressions of shells, cords and combs arranged in regular horizontal zones, sometimes in combination with shallow fluting. Most of the impressed patterns such as triangles, chevrons, etc., do not occur in the Danube basin late neolithic pottery. Some, however, especially the close parallel lines forming meanders, are very similar to those of the Maritsa culture and of the pottery of the preceding culture layer (IV) at Karanovo (the Kaloyanovets variant).

There is evidence that both domesticated and wild animals were exploited in the Hamangia settlements. Among the former, as in the contemporary lower Danube settlements, cattle predominated in spite of the dry climate, although sheep and goats were also important. Although domestic animals predominated among the animal remains, hunting forest animals, such as red-deer, and more parkland southern species, such as fallow-deer and wild ass, also provided an important source of food and, presumably, raw materials. In spite of the importance attached to hunting, there are very few artefacts of bone and antler in the Hamangia assemblages. Bone points occur, some of which may have been used for projectile heads, and there are a number of long thin bone points with square cross-sections, which may have been hafted into antler handles, as in the lower Danube settlements. Antler sleeves, and perforated antler 'picks' and 'axes' which form an important part of the equipment in the Boian and Maritsa cultures, occur very infrequently. Polished stone artefacts are also far from common. When they do occur they generally consist of axe-adzes with a quadrangular cross-section, whereas those of the lower Danube late neolithic settlements have an oval or plano-convex cross-section. This however probably reflects a difference in the method of hafting, rather than a wider functional difference. On the basis of the palaeontological evidence, it would seem that sea-fishing and shell-collecting were also important in the subsistence economy. There is no evidence of fishing, however, in the preserved equipment of the Hamangia settlements.

The chipped stone industry of the Hamangia settlements, on the other hand, is much richer that that of the lower Danube late neolithic settlements, in both the quantity and variety of the form and function of the implements. All the blades were manufactured from the local honey-coloured flint which is of very high quality.[4] The area of the Dobrogea, where this variety of flint occurs, is centred round Madara, and it is interesting to note that this district was not settled by people with the Hamangia culture, but by those with the Boian culture. The Hamangia industry comprises predominantly long wide blades which are frequently blunted at their distal and proximal ends (Fig.25), and their surface was retouched by pressure flaking in order to achieve greater thinness. It is possible that this modification of the shape of the blades was the result of cultural preference, but it seems very likely that it was done so that the blades could be used directly by hand, since, on the basis of palaeobotanical evidence, there was a shortage of suitable wood for hafts and handles in the Dobrogea.

The form of burial of the Hamangia culture is quite different from that of the preceding, contemporary and subsequent cultures of the Danube basin and south-east Europe. In these latter, the dead were buried lying on their sides in a contracted position, mostly in rubbish pits among houses.[5] In the Hamangia culture, however, the dead were buried almost exclusively in cemeteries, separate from the settlements, each skeleton lying on its back in a shallow grave pit in an extended position. They were almost always accompanied by a pot of fine black-burnished ware, but of a different shape from those in the settlements (Fig.25), and frequently also by a figurine, as well as beads of copper, stone, shell, etc. The cemeteries were often very large (e.g. at Cernavoda: 300 inhumations). Cemeteries with similarly large numbers of skeletons buried in the same position as those of the Hamangia culture have been excavated in the Dnieper valley.[6] The only grave-goods accompanying these, however, were small beads and pendants. This is very slim evidence on which to base a hypothesis of direct contact between the lower Dnieper sites and the Dobrogea but the possibility cannot be ruled out. It is interesting to note that just west of the Dobrogea, in S.E. Rumania, a similar cemetery was excavated at the site of Cernica.[7] It consisted of 115 inhumations lying on their backs in an extended position in shallow pits and accompanied by polished stone implements of the type found in Boian assemblages, *Spondylus* shells and even two small beads of native copper, as well as coarse Boian pottery, but not a single figurine. A settlement belonging to an early phase in the development of the Boian culture was excavated 100 m away from this cemetery.

The figurines of the Hamangia culture (Fig.25) were excavated exclusively in graves, unlike those of the rest of south-east Europe which come from settlements. Only much later in the east of S.E. Europe, in the late Tripolye culture in the Ukraine and Moldavia, were figurines put into graves. The Hamangia figurines were manufactured from baked clay and marble. Almost all represent humans, and the majority are obviously female in that they have large breasts, and emphasised hips and stomach and a wide incised sexual triangle. Unlike the majority of south-east European neolithic figurines, the arms were carefully portrayed, curving round on to the stomach or under the breasts. The heads were generally portrayed by no more than a prismatic projection. The figurines of the Hamangia culture are superficially of a very uniform shape and either sitting or standing. Two figurines, however, have been made with much more attention to facial and physiological detail.[8] These were found in the same grave at the Cernavoda cemetery. Both are seated; one has been interpreted as a female, for the same reasons as most of the Hamangia figurines. The other has been interpreted as a male, because of the lack of breasts and the narrow straight torso, although there are no positive male sexual features. This figurine has, moreover, been called the 'penseur' because of the thoughtful way in which his elbows rest on his knees and his head on his hands. Two figurines with their arms in a very similar position, and also thought to represent males, have been found north of this area, one in a contemporary and the other in a slightly later settlement.[9] Both the Cernavoda figurines described above have a flat head on which the nose, eyes and mouth were portrayed attached to a long prismatic neck. Prototypes for the Hamangia figurines have been the subject of great speculation; those in the Cyclades and Anatolia have been suggested, as well as the Veselinovo culture of south Bulgaria. The occurrence of perforated *Spondylus* shell beads and bracelets (Fig. 25), as well as marble copies of these and marble figurines, would indicate contact with the east Mediterranean area, since this is the largest source for these commodities. It is not impossible, however, that the marble was obtained from a smaller source in the metamorphosed limestone of the Madara region, the same area from which the yellow flint was obtained. *Spondylus* has yet to be proved to occur outside the Mediterranean Sea.[10]

The various elements which contributed to the formation of the Hamangia culture are still obscure. The Hamangia culture's own contribution to the formation of the subsequent Gumelniţa culture, however, is very clear, for example in the pressure-flaking technique of chipped stone, the exploitation of the yellow Madara flint, certain features of anthropomorphic figurines and the manufacture of these and other objects in marble and alabaster. Apart from these features, the prototypes for the Gumelniţa culture can all be found in the preceding Boian and Maritsa cultures.

Boian–Maritsa–Gumelniţa cultures

In the late neolithic and eneolithic periods, settlements for the first time were located on the banks and lower terraces of the lower Danube and its tributaries, and even on islands in the rivers. The phenomenon of 'tell' formation occurred with increasing frequency and density in south Bulgaria, and spread outside this region during the later Boian and Maritsa and especially Gumelniţa cultures eastwards to the Black Sea coast, and northwards to the lower Danube valley.[11] The 'tell' settlements of south Bulgaria show continuous occupation throughout this period with an increase in the size of the settlements and in the rate of deposition of the occupation debris. The eneolithic layers of the already existing 'tells' and the newly established eneolithic 'tells' are an average of 4–6 m thick and 4–6 m high respectively. They consist of a large number of habitation levels (as many as 21 at Tangîru). At Karanovo, the Maritsa (layer V) and Gumelniţa (layer VI) culture layers consist of a total of 16 habitation levels. It is clear that this must reflect an increase in the length of the duration of the settlements and a greater stability and continuity of their occupation than in the earlier neolithic periods. It is likely that this was made possible by improvement in the techniques of agriculture and rearing domesticated animals, and the exploitation of a large variety of resources for food and raw materials.

At a large number of sites, there is evidence of the cultivation of not only emmer and einkorn wheat, lentils and vicea, but also (for the first time in Europe outside Greece) six-row barley. There is also evidence of the collection of wild plants including nuts and roots. It is possible that the large numbers of perforated antler artefacts with both wide edges and perforated ends, which were found in the late neolithic and eneolithic cultures, were used in the processing of these plants. Almost every house in the settlements contained a saddle quern which, in the Gumelniţa culture, was dug into the floor in a special place next to the oven. In many of the Gumelniţa houses clay box-shaped utensils, 1 m high, 2 m long, 1·5 m wide, and 8 cm thick, were excavated, with the preserved remains of grain still inside them.[12] They may well have been used also to store other vegetable products. Although there is evidence in earlier periods of the use of large pots and pits for storage, it seems possible, from their sharply rectangular shape, that these in the Gumelniţa settlements were derived from wooden prototypes.

The animal-bone material from most of the Bulgarian and south Rumanian late neolithic and eneolithic sites indicates an increasing importance of domesticated animals until, in the Gumelniţa culture, they were overwhelmingly predominant.[13] In all the sites, cattle predominated among the domesticated animals, but on the drier sites of the Dobrogea and north of the Danube delta in south Moldavian SSR, sheep were more important than in the more forested settlements.[14] Wild animals and fishing played a small but important part in the economy, as may be seen from the number of specialised, carefully made implements in durable materials for hunting and fishing. At a few riverside sites wild animals, in particular fish, predominated over domesticated species.[15] The main hunted animals were large forest mammals, in particular red-deer, roe-deer, wild pig and aurochs. For the first time in the history of the early agriculturalists of S.E. Europe, there is definite evidence that the hunting equipment included arrowheads of chipped stone. It is possible that projectiles, including the arrow, were used in earlier neolithic and mesolithic periods, using bone or wooden heads, so that these stone arrowheads need not be associated with the first appearance of the technique and equipment of bows and arrows. The arrowheads of the Gumelniţa culture (Fig. 26) are triangular with straight or concave bases made from flakes of the east Bulgarian honey-coloured flint.[16] They were shaped and thinned by pressure flaking on the surface. This method of constructing arrowheads was completely alien to the south-east European traditions, but it occurs frequently in the steppe and forest-steppe area north of the Black Sea in the Dnieper valley. It is interesting to note that in the late Boian culture, where there was a significant increase in the importance of hunting wild animals, there is no evidence of such arrowheads.

Apart from chipped stone projectile heads, bone and antler points (Fig. 26) occur in the late Maritsa, late Boian and Gumelniţa settlements. These were barbed on one or both sides, with barbs arranged densely or widely spaced depending, presumably, on the nature of the prey on which they were used. Some have swollen perforated bases and could have been used as harpoons. They occur particularly at riverside settlements, although (Chapter 2) this does not preclude their having been used against land mammals as well as fish. Some of the uniserially barbed points were probably used as fish leisters. Very few of the fish-bones from the settlements have been identified. Those that have include large species such as carp and catfish (wels). It is likely also that sturgeon, which formerly abounded in the lower reaches of the Danube, were exploited. A common method of catching this fish was by the use of a hook, but it would also have been possible to pierce its hard skin from above with a strong fish-spear. Unfortunately, sturgeon leave very few identifiable remains on archaeological sites. And in general it is difficult to judge whether the possible use of larger more substantial equipment in fishing was due to the exploitation of a different species of fish, or whether there was a general development of more durable equipment in association with the large-scale exploitation of fish, in particular large meat-producing fish. Fish-hooks (Fig. 26) occur in small numbers on many sites. They are small and barbless, as in earlier neolithic periods, and were made of bone and, from the late Boian and Maritsa cultures onwards, of thin copper strips. It is possible that the long ellipsoid perforated clay objects found on a number of sites were weights for fishing lines, although they could also have been weights for looms.

It would seem, therefore, that in the late neolithic and eneolithic settlements of the lower Danube and Maritsa basins there was not only a continuous improvement of agricultural and animal-rearing techniques, but also that food and raw materials from many sources was assured.

The chipped stone implements of the late neolithic and particularly the eneolithic settlements of the lower Danube and Maritsa valleys were manufactured almost exclusively in the honey-coloured flint of the Madara region of N.E. Bulgaria. The blades are frequently more than 10 cms long and were trimmed or blunted by deliberate retouch (Fig. 26), either to facilitate their use unhafted held in the hand, or to strengthen the hafting of the blades for cutting and scraping. Many of the blades with 'sickle gloss' were much larger than in preceding periods. It is clear that the manufacture of such large blades of standard size and shape was associated with improved techniques in the production of cores and blanks, and with the large-scale exploitation of a high quality source of flint. Polished stone artefacts (Fig. 26), mostly with a lens-shaped cross-profile, occur in large numbers. In the later part of the Boian and Maritsa cultures they were supplemented by polished stone axes (Fig. 26) which were perforated for the attachment of a haft. It is possible that the idea of putting a haft through a perforation in the actual head of the tool was adapted from a similar technique which had been in use on tools with antler heads since the preceding Veselinovo and Vinča-Tordoš cultures. The perforated stone axes were strong enough to have been used in heavy wood-working, including the construction of houses and pos-

---

Fig. 26

Bone, stone and baked-clay artefacts of the eneolithic settlements of the S.E. Balkans.

a Clay lamp with goat's-head terminal. Kapitan Dimitrievo (Banjata), S. Bulgaria. Gumelniţa culture (after Georgiev, 1961).

b–e Barbed spear-heads of antler. *b–d* Bikovo, S. Bulgaria (after Georgiev, 1961). *e* Cascioărele, S.E. Rumania (after Dumitrescu, 1965).

f Knife-blade of flint set in an antler handle. Dennitsa mogila, N.E. Bulgaria (Guide to the National Archaeological Museum, Sofia).

g Polished stone adze set in an antler handle. Zavet, E. Bulgaria (Guide to the National Archaeological Museum, Sofia).

h Perforated polished stone axe. Russe, N.E. Bulgaria (after Georgiev & Angelov, 1948).

i Flaked flint axe-adze. Cascioărele, S.E. Rumania (after Păunescu, 1970).

i Pressure-flaked arrowhead of flint. Vidra, S.E. Rumania (after Păunescu, 1970).

k–l Bone fish-hooks. Russe, N.E. Bulgaria (Russe Museum).

m Polished bone point, possibly a spearhead. Russe, N.E. Bulgaria (Russe Museum).

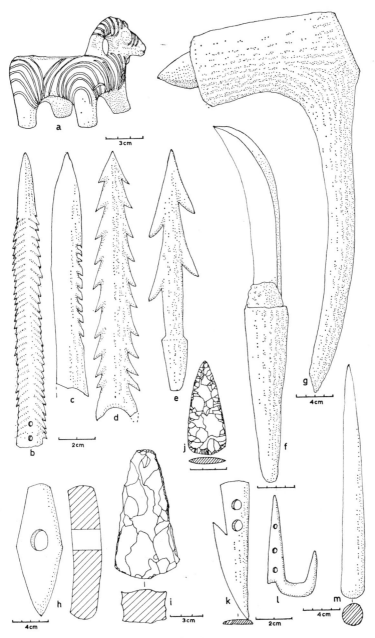

Fig. 26

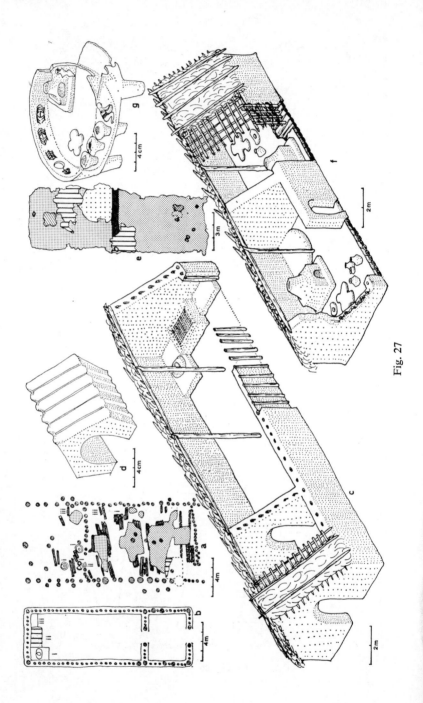

Fig. 27

sibly tree clearance, which expanding crop cultivation would have demanded. In the Gumelniţa culture assemblages, heavy perforated copper axes (Fig. 38) frequently occur, their butt ends blunted and shorter than their cutting ends. It is very likely that they were developed from stone prototypes, but it is uncertain whether they had the same function as these. So far they have not been examined for traces of wear. They were manufactured from pure copper, with no added impurities, such as tin or antimony, to harden them. They would, therefore, have had a limited life if used constantly to chop wood. The copper axes frequently occur in association with unperforated narrow square-sectioned heavy copper tools (Fig. 38) which have a narrow transverse edge at one end, the other end being blunted. These have been interpreted as narrow axes, although they could as easily have been used as chisels for splitting wood, in conjunction with the blunt hammer-end of the perforated copper or stone axes.

The houses of the later neolithic and eneolithic settlements (Fig. 27) were constructed by the same method as those of the earlier settlements of south-east Europe, with the walls built of thick clay on a framework of light wooden posts, and frequently decorated by incised and painted patterns. In the later Boian and Maritsa settlements, and commonly in the Gumelniţa settlements, houses with thick clay floors often covering a layer of horizontal logs have been excavated. The floors had been preserved by burning. The late neolithic houses had the same shape and dimensions as the earlier neolithic houses, comprising small one-roomed structures. Those of the Gumelniţa culture, however, were very commonly built with the addition of a porch area or ante-room at one end (Fig. 27), increasing the length to an average of 12 m, although the width remained a constant 5–6 m. From the large number of small clay house-models

---

Fig. 27
Eneolithic house construction in S.E. Europe.

a Ground-plan of house 2 at Azmak, layer IV, S. Bulgaria. Gumelniţa culture (after Georgiev, 1963).

b Ground-plan of house in layer VI at Karanovo, S. Bulgaria (after Georgiev, 1961). Gumelniţa culture: (i) fixed quernstone, (ii) oven, (iii) ash platform.

c Isometric cutaway reconstruction of house from layer VI at Karanovo.

d Clay house-model. Gumelniţa culture. Kirilometodievo, S. Bulgaria (Guide to Stara Zagora Museum).

e–f House 3 at Vladimirovka, Ukraine SSR. Middle Tripolye culture (after Passek, 1949). *e* Ground-plan of house: vertical lines = oven, light shading = clay floor, dark shading = clay wall, dotted area = clay platform, hatched area = clay 'table', black circle = quernstone.

f Cutaway isometric reconstruction.

g Clay model of interior of a house. Late Tripolye culture. Popudnya, Ukraine SSR (after Passek, 1949).

L

(c. 6×8 cm) which occur in many Gumelniţa assemblages (Fig. 27), it is clear that the houses had gabled roofs of wood daubed with clay or covered in thatch, sometimes with an animal head over the entrance. Some of the models have domed roofs, but these have generally been interpreted as models of ovens. It is not impossible, however, that certain roofs of Gumelniţa houses were of this shape and built on a framework of saplings or other pliable material. None of the house-models shows any division of the interior.

Ovens occur in all the houses of the late neolithic and eneolithic settlements of south-east Europe. Those of the Boian and Maritsa cultures were shaped in plan like a horseshoe, whereas those of the subsequent Gumelniţa culture were square, c. 1 m². They were all built on a solid foundation of stones or slate with thick clay and chaff or clay and reed walls. They were always placed at the back of the houses along with other domestic fixtures such as a fixed quern and clay platform covered in a thick layer of ash. The whole of the back area of the houses was generally littered with sherds of coarse pots. The ovens show signs of having been renewed at frequent intervals. This may have been the result of regular deliberate destruction of the former oven after each pottery-making or even metallurgy session, or it may have been the result of accidental bursting of the ovens. It has even been suggested that the attempts to reach high temperatures in a reducing atmosphere, in order to fuse graphite-painted decoration to pottery or to smelt copper, in ovens which were not strongly enough constructed to withstand the heat, may have been the cause of so many fires in the eneolithic settlements.

Although the late neolithic and eneolithic settlements of the south-east Balkans comprise large villages (up to 50 houses at Karanovo), there is very little evidence of deliberate planning of the houses in rows, circles, or with the same orientation. Evidence of any physical demarcation of the settlement by a bank or a ditch is much less common in the settlements of Bulgaria and S.E. Rumania than in the contemporary settlements of the Cucuteni–Tripolye culture of N.E. Rumania, Moldavia and the Ukraine. The ditches which do occur are c. 2 m deep and 4 m wide, and have been called defensive, but this seems unlikely from their dimensions and the lack of any supplementary strengthening.[17]

The pottery of the Gumelniţa culture is enormously rich in the variety of its forms and decoration. It consists of two main categories:

1. Coarse-tempered gritty and micaceous domestic ware (Fig. 28), fired hard to a buff colour and manufactured into biconical and globular pots. This pottery was decorated by various methods of roughening the surface, as well as incised lines.

2. Fine-tempered ware (Fig. 28), which was manufactured into a large variety of forms (even a 'drinking horn'), the most popular of which was the small biconical bowl with a strongly carinated upper part and hemispherical lower part. The pottery was covered with a self-slip and burnished while it was leather hard. It was then painted with graphite in a variety of rectilinear and curvilinear designs, on the interior as well as the exterior surface. The pottery was then fired in an oxidising atmosphere up to 600°C, and then under very carefully controlled reducing conditions to a temperature of 1050°C.[18] Below this temperature, the graphite would not fuse and fix to the pottery. In this way the pottery was fired to an even dark grey colour, while the graphite paint appears silvery. At Karanovo, as many as 100 pots of the fine pottery were found in one house, and it has been suggested that specialist potters and kilns existed in each settlement. The graphite for the paint was obtained from the metamorphic rocks in the mountains of north and south Bulgaria, often in the same areas which contain copper ore-bearing rocks. Graphite-painted pottery occurred in the later part of the Boian and Maritsa cultures when the patterns were the same as those incised on the majority of pots, but it is essentially a characteristic of the Gumelniţa culture. Outside the area of the Gumelniţa culture it is very rare but occurs in the Salcuţa culture to the west and sporadically as far west as the Morava basin of E. Yugoslavia.

Baked clay spindle-whorls, 'stamp-seals', 'lamps' (Fig. 26) and figurines have been excavated in the later neolithic and eneolithic assemblages. Clay figurines include representations of animals and humans. The anthropomorphic figurines of the Gumelniţa culture may be divided into two main groups:[19]

1. Small, solid figurines (Fig. 28) generally in a standing position which were evolved from those of the earlier neolithic assemblages. Some have rudimentary breasts and an incised sexual triangle, but a large number are entirely devoid of any sexual features. The Boian and Maritsa figurines were frequently decorated all over the body by incised lines like those of the contemporary Pre-Cucuteni culture further north. As in the earlier neolithic figurines, emphasis was laid on the facial features which comprise pinched out noses and incised eyes. For the first time in south-east Europe, excluding Greece, the mouth was represented on figurines of the late Boian, late Maritsa and Gumelniţa cultures, in the form of an incised line frequently with a row of holes underneath. The sides of the face were expanded into 'ears' which were generally perforated from one to six times. The purpose of the perforations may have been to suspend ornaments.

Small copper rings have been excavated still adhering to similar perforations on bone figurines. Or they may have been to suspend the figurine itself. The majority of these figurines have been excavated in a broken state in rubbish pits. A few, however, including seated figurines, which are very rare, were excavated on house floors, and at Vulcaneşti and Kodžadermen they were still seated on small stools. The small clay chairs and tables which frequently occur in the house debris of Gumelniţa settlements may originally have all been associated with such figurines. The evidence indicates that the seated figurines had a different function from the standing figurines with perforated heads and arms. In addition, the seated figurines, along with sporadic seated marble figurines and flat standing marble figurines, would seem to have close connections with those of the immediately preceding Hamangia culture.[20]

2. Large, hollow figurines (Fig. 28) which were made in the same fabric as the fine pottery, but were decorated quite differently. The combination of incised patterns and paint applied, after firing, is much more similar to the decoration of the clay 'lamps'. The heads, when they are incorporated in the hollow body, are similar to those of the solid figurines with expanded perforated 'ears'. On many, however, the head was not attached to the body and if made at all would have been separate (although separate hollow anthropomorphic heads have not been found on any sites). Other hollow figurines had only a very narrow opening at the neck into which, presumably, a solid head of clay or some other material would have been inserted. The large hollow figurines have most frequently been excavated on house floors.

Fig. 28

Pottery and figurines of the Gumelniţa culture.

a Graphite-painted bowl. Kapitan Dimitrievo (Banjata), S. Bulgaria (after Georgiev, 1961).

b Pot with negative excised pattern filled with white encrusted paint (dotted area). Russe, N. Bulgaria (Russe Museum).

c Graphite-painted pot-stand. Azmak, S. Bulgaria (after Georgiev, 1969).

d Bone figurine with copper anklets. Lovetz, S. Bulgaria (after Dimitrov, 1962).

e Small clay anthropomorphic figurine. Russe, N. Bulgaria (Russe Museum).

f Clay hollow male figurine with graphite-painted decoration. Gabarevo, C. Bulgaria (after Gaul, 1948).

g Flat marble anthropomorphic figurine. Sulitsa, S. Bulgaria (after Popov, 1926).

h Large pot with roughened surface. Karanovo, layer VI (after Vajsova, 1969).

i Graphite-painted pot. Karanovo, layer VI, Bulgaria (after Georgiev, 1961).

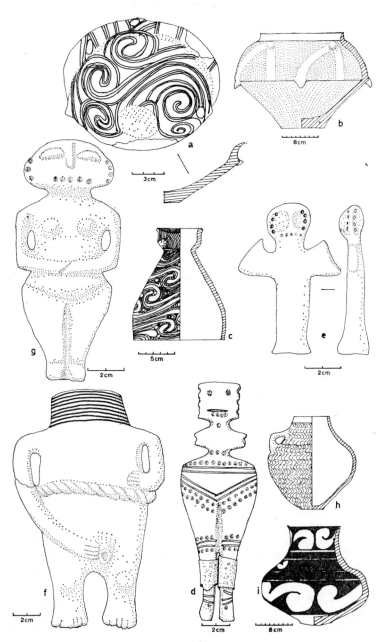

Fig. 28

The zoomorphic figurines may be divided into the same two main groups. The small solid figurines represent especially cattle, the most important domesticated animal. Animal heads also occur as terminals of the clay 'lamps' (Fig. 26), but these generally represent goats or sheep. In addition large hollow zoomorphic figurines were manufactured in the fine-tempered fabric. These were frequently manufactured with a separate hollow head (Pl. 11) which acted as a lid, and represent imaginary animals. It is possible that these provided the prototypes of the 'rhytons' which became typical of the later Gumelniţa and Early Bronze Age cultures of Bulgaria. No zoomorphic figurines of bone or stone have been found.

Small flat anthropomorphic bone figurines are a frequent occurrence in Gumelniţa assemblages.[21] It is questionable whether all those claimed as figurines are in fact human representations. Many, however, have the same perforated heads, arms and hips as the clay figurines. Copper ornaments (Fig. 28) have been found still hanging from the perforations, or attached to the limbs.[22] Generally the only sexual feature represented on these figurines was the incised sexual triangle. Copies of the bone figurines were made in clay and even gold leaf.[23] No copper copies of bone figurines have been found in the area of the Gumelniţa culture.

Cucuteni–Tripolye culture

The Cucutenyi–Tripolye culture which developed in the forest-steppe region north and east of the Gumelniţa culture had many features in common with the lower Danube area including an expansion of the settlement area and an increase in the size and density of the settlements, along with an improvement in agricultural and stockbreeding techniques and an increase in the number and variety of artefacts made in durable materials including stone, bone, antler and copper.[24] None of the Cucuteni–Tripolye settlements, however, formed 'tells' or even shallow stratified mounds of occupation deposits, although many comprise thin stratified habitation levels.

The late neolithic and eneolithic cultural sequence is indicated by a number of stratified sites.[25] At Izvoare, for example, as in the lower Danube basin, there is no visible break in occupation from the late neolithic Pre-Cucuteni culture to the eneolithic Cucuteni culture.

Pre-Cucuteni–early Tripolye culture: At least two and possibly three successive periods (I–III) have veen recognised in the development of the Pre-Cucuteni culture (Fig. 41). Apart from cultural evolution, they reflect the steady eastwards spread of the agriculturalists of S.E. Europe and the diffusion of their techniques and the absorption of the hunting and fishing groups into the cultural traditions of S.E. Europe (Fig. 23).

The Pre-Cucuteni II period, in which the pottery was very similar
to that of the earlier periods of the Boian culture of the lower
Danube (Fig. 24), is found in settlements in S.E. Transilvania west of
the Carpathians, in the Prut and Seret valleys and as far east as the
middle Dniester basin.[26] The settlements in this period were located
especially on the higher terraces of river valleys and on the edges of
plateaus. This location of the settlements, as well as the means of
subsistence, was quite different from that of the settlements of the
contemporary *late Bug–Dniester culture*, which were situated on the
lower terraces and banks of the Dniester and S. Bug rivers, with an
economy based to a very large extent on fishing as well as the exploitation of wild and domesticated animals.

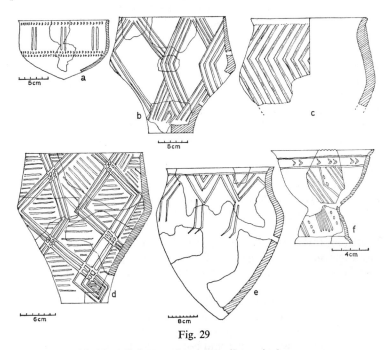

Fig. 29

Pottery of the Bug–Dniester culture. Late (Savran) phase.
a Tsikinovka I, Moldavia SSR (after Markyevič, 1965).
b Savran, S. Bug river, Ukraine SSR (after Danilenko, 1969).
c Černyatka, S. Bug river, Ukraine SSR (after Danilenko, 1969).
d Mikolina Broyanka, S. Bug river, Ukraine SSR (after Danilenko,
    1969).
e Savran, S. Bug river, Ukraine SSR (after Danilenko, 1969).
f Luka Vrublevetskaya, Dniester river, Ukraine SSR. Pedestalled bowl
    of later (Khmelnik) phase, synchronous with Pre-Cucuteni II (after
    Danilenko, 1969).

Assemblages belonging to the late (Savran, Khmelnik, Haivoran) phases of the Bug–Dniester culture are frequently found in habitation layers stratified above those of earlier phases (Chapter 3), and it is presumed that they represent the descendants of these.[27] Unlike the Linear Pottery culture of Moldavia, it would seem that the Pre-Cucuteni culture, even in this early phase of its development, had an influence on the form and decoration of the pottery of the late Bug–Dniester culture. At first the various elements of the Pre-Cucuteni excised patterns were broken up and recombined into quite different patterns, and the flat-based pots were associated with egg-shaped pots (Fig. 29) with stamped decoration. Gradually, however, this latter group of pottery disappeared, and the decoration of the flat-based pottery became much closer to that of the Pre-Cucuteni culture (Fig. 29). By the period of the Pre-Cucuteni III–Tripolye A phase, this process was complete and the pottery of these riverside settlements is indistinguishable from the Pre-Cucuteni III–Tripolye A pottery of the upland settlements from the Seret to the S. Bug rivers.

A similar process of gradual absorption may be seen in other aspects of the material culture in the occurrence on the riverside settlements of clay anthropomorphic figurines, and the complete change in the technology and forms of the chipped stone implements which were also identical to those of the upland Pre-Cucuteni III settlements. However, in the continued location of settlements at these riverside sites, and the continued importance of fishing and shell-collecting in the economy, it is clear that absorption or acculturation was not total. The fishing activities at the Pre-Cucuteni III–Tripolye A riverside settlements, however, were not quite the same as those of the preceding Bug–Dniester culture in that, in addition to roach (which had been the favourite species of the Bug-Dniester fishermen), larger members of the carp family and catfish weighing up to 15 kg were caught. It was possibly in order to catch these large fish that the technique of fishing with a hook and line was favoured. This technique and associated equipment may have been part of the commodities diffused from the lower Danube area at this time. The hooks are barbless and made of copper and bone. There is evidence, too, at the riverside settlements of the domestication of sheep and the cultivation of emmer, both of which had been completely absent from all phases of the Bug–Dniester culture.

The economy of the riverside settlements, however, is very different from that of the upland settlements of the Seret, Prut and the upper Dniester, in which evidence of fishing was almost totally absent.[28] The economy and the location of the upland Pre-Cucuteni and early Tripolye settlements is much more similar to that of the preceding Linear Pottery settlements of Moldavia (Chapter 3). The economy was based on an equal exploitation of wild animals, in particular large forest mammals such as red-deer, and domesticated animals, especially cattle (although sheep and goats and pigs were also present). Many of the Moldavian upland Pre-Cucuteni III sites would seem to have had a continuous occupation from the earlier Pre-Cucuteni phase, but during this period there was an increase in the number and density of settlements on the high terraces and promontories overlooking the Seret, Prut and Dniester rivers. The agriculturalists also spread to the edges of high loess plateaus beyond the Dniester towards the S. Bug as well as south to the lower valley of the Dniester. These settlements, unlike the riverside settlements, which would seem to reflect acculturation of the local population, may represent the spread of an actual population to these steppe and forest-steppe areas.

The pottery associated with the spread of the Pre-Cucuteni III Tripolye A culture was clearly developed from that of the earlier Pre-Cucuteni pottery (Fig. 30). The same three categories of pottery were manufactured (p.149). The main developments were in the form and decoration of the fine polished dark grey ware. In the Pre-Cucuteni III phase this pottery was manufactured into tripartite pots (Fig. 30) each comprising a cylindrical neck decorated by fine fluted horizontal lines, a belly on which deep channelled decoration was arranged around conical lugs in combination with stamped and finely incised lines, and a lower part which was left plain. At almost every site, small bone toothed objects have been found, which may have been used in stamping pottery.

From the earliest phase of the Pre-Cucuteni culture, the assemblages included clay anthropomorphic figurines of a distinctive type (Fig. 30); they were small (rarely more than 10cm long) solid figurines, manufactured almost exclusively in a semi-reclining position, with legs joined together, large buttocks and flat upper part of the body, with short pointed perforated arms, very small breasts and incised sexual triangle. In the earlier Pre-Cucuteni phases, the figurines were generally undecorated, and the heads were much more similar to those of the lower Danube valley in that they had pinched-out noses and incised eyes. The heads of the Pre-Cucuteni III–Tripolye A figurines, however, rarely consist of more than a small conical projection without any facial features. These same figurines were decorated all over apart from their heads with dense patterns of incised lines. Because of their breasts and large buttocks, the majority of the figurines have been claimed as representing females. Very few are obviously male. For example, at Luka Vrublevetskaya, out of a total of more than 300 figurines, only two had male sexual features. The majority of the Pre-Cucuteni figurines were excavated in a broken state in rubbish pits.[29]

As in the lower Danube and Maritsa settlements, an increasing skill in techniques of manufacturing chipped stone implements is observable in the Pre-Cucuteni–early Tripolye settlements.[30] There was clearly a large-scale exploitation of the local grey Dniester and Prut flint from which long regular polyhedral cores were manufactured. This enabled the striking of large numbers of wide blades of standard size and shape. These were shaped at their distal ends by deliberate retouch (Fig.30), and many were then used as cutting

Fig. 30

The Pre-Cucuteni–Cucuteni–Tripolye culture.

a Fine-tempered pot. Early Tripolye culture. Luka Vrublevetskaya, Dniester river, Ukraine SSR (after Bibikov, 1953).

b Incised pedestalled bowl. Early Tripolye culture. Solončene I, Dniester river, Ukraine SSR (after Passek, 1961).

c Chipped flint blade used as an end-scraper. Early Tripolye culture. Luka Vrublevetskaya, Ukraine SSR (after Bibikov, 1963).

d Chipped flint blade used as a sickle-blade. Dotted area denotes 'sickle-gloss'. Early Tripolye culture. Luka Vrublevetskaya (after Bibikov, 1963).

e Reconstruction of the method of hafting the early Tripolye sickle-blades (after Semeonov, 1964).

f Clay anthropomorphic figurine with incised decoration. Early Tripolye culture. Bernovo-Luka, Dniester river, Ukraine SSR (after Passek, 1961).

g Bowl painted in white and black. Dotted area denotes the red unpainted surface. Ariusd-Cucuteni A. Ariusd, C. Rumania (Sfînte Georghe Museum).

h Pot painted with white (black lines) patterns on dark-red surface. Proto-Cucuteni style. Stoicani, E. Rumania (after Dumitrescu, 1953).

i Pot decorated by incised designs. Middle Tripolye B1 culture. Nezviska, Dniester river, Ukraine SSR (after Černyš, 1962).

j Pot-stand decorated by white and black paint. Dotted areas denote brick-red unpainted surface; dotted lines denote red paint. Middle Tripolye B1–Cucuteni A culture. Cucuteni-Cetatuia, N.E. Rumania (after Petrescu-Dîmbovița, 1966).

k Pot painted with black designs on a buff ground. Middle Tripolye B2 culture. Nezviska, Dniester river, Ukraine SSR (after Černyš, 1962).

l Flint arrowhead. Cucuteni A culture. Hăbășești, E. Rumania (after Păunescu, 1970).

m Pot painted in black on buff ground. Middle Tripolye culture B2. Vladimirovka, S. Bug river, Ukraine SSR (after Passek, 1949).

n Incised pot. Middle Tripolye B2 culture. Kolomiiščina II, Dnieper river, Ukraine SSR (after Passek, 1949).

o Shell-tempered pot, decorated with comb-impressions. Middle Tripolye B2 culture. Nezviska, Dniester river, Ukraine SSR (after Černyš, 1962).

p Clay anthropomorphic figurine. Middle Tripolye B2 culture. Polivanov Yar, Dniester river, Ukraine SSR (after Passek, 1961).

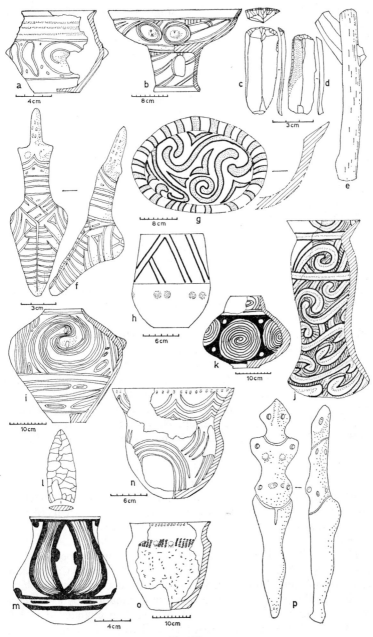

Fig. 30

implements to harvest grain, either singly as reaping knives or compositely as sickles.

It is interesting to note that even in the Pre-Cucuteni II phase
probably direct contact with the lower Danube is indicated by the
presence of beaten copper square-sectioned awls and, in the Pre-
Cucuteni III–Tripolye A phase, contact with the same area is indicated by beaten copper square-sectioned awls (Fig. 38) and fish-hooks
(p. 197)[31] and sporadic triangular pressure-flaked arrowheads manufactured in the yellow flint of the lower Danube.

In a few of the Pre-Cucuteni III assemblages, especially from settlements in S. Moldavia,[32] there occur sherds of fine pottery covered in
a dark red burnished slip, painted before firing (Fig. 30) with white
patterns comprising fine parallel lines. This type of painted pottery
also occurs in assemblages of the latest Boian–earliest Gumelniţa
culture in the lower Danube basin. For this reason, assemblages
which contain this type of painted pottery have been referred to as
Proto-Gulmeniţa (Figs. 31, 41) or *Proto-Cucuteni*.[33] The white-painted
patterns are very similar to those incised on Maritsa and Boian
pottery, and later painted in graphite on the late Boian and early
Gumelniţa pots. The forms of the pots on which they occur, however, are much more similar to the fine-tempered Hamangia culture
pots. It is interesting to note, in this respect, that at the site of
Hîrşova, in S.E. Rumania, the Hamangia culture layer was overlain
by just such a Proto-Gumelniţa assemblage.[34] In the Proto-Cucuteni
assemblages of Moldavia the red-slipped ware painted with white
lines is associated with pottery identical in form and decoration to the
Pre-Cucuteni III fine-tempered pottery described above, but with the
addition of the application of white paint before firing to emphasise
the channelling, and a dark red slip. The occurrence of white-painted
pottery in Moldavia would seem to have been associated with the
northwards diffusion of other elements from the lower Danube, for
example triangular pressure-flaked arrowheads and sickle blades
manufactured in the honey-coloured flint of the Dobrogea and large
hollow anthropomorphic figurines, as well as artefacts made of
copper. As noted above, however, these objects occur in Pre-
Cucuteni–Tripolye A settlements where there was no painted
pottery.[35]

Cucuteni A–Middle Tripolye culture: On the western edge of the
Pre-Cucuteni culture area on the western side of the Carpathians
(S.E. Transilvania) in stratified sites the Pre-Cucuteni II assemblages
were overlain, generally after a break in occupation, by layers containing pottery which was incised, excised and channelled in late
Pre-Cucuteni style, in many cases covered with a dark red slip and
painted in white. The white painted patterns comprising thin parallel

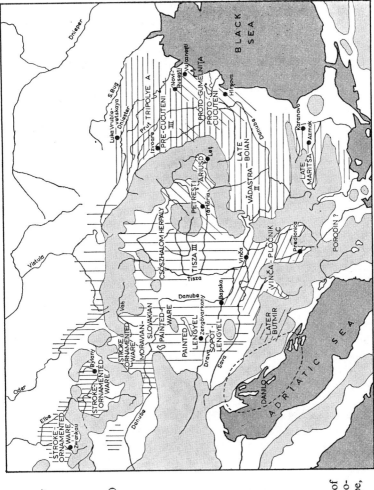

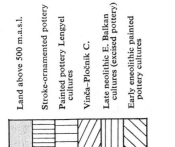

Land above 500 m.a.s.l.

Stroke-ornamented pottery

Painted pottery Lengyel
cultures

Vinča–Pločnik C.

Late neolithic E. Balkan
cultures (excised pottery)

Early eneolithic painted
pottery cultures

Fig. 31
Map of the distribution of
transitional late neolithic-eneo-
lithic cultures in E. Europe,
c. 3700–3600 B.C.

lines was entirely absent. In addition there was a thick fine-tempered ware, fired at a low temperature to a light orange colour; white and black rectilinear and curvilinear patterns were painted on its un-slipped surface. This trichrome painted pottery, which is known in Transilvania as the *Ariuşd* or Erösd style (Fig.30), became wide-spread in the western part of the Cucuteni–Tripolye culture area, from Transilvania to the S. Bug river, and became one of the charac-teristic features of the middle phase of the culture (Cucuteni A–Tripolye B1). In Moldavia, it occurs in assemblages stratified im-mediately above those with Proto-Cucuteni painted ware, which sur-vived but quickly lost popularity and disappeared in the face of the new trichrome style. It is difficult to prove trichrome pottery occurred in Transilvania earlier than in Moldavia, but it is certainly impossible to find prototypes for the forms and decoration of this pottery in Moldavia. In Transilvania, on the other hand, the development of painted pottery of this type may be followed through from the late neolithic Turdaş–Petreşti culture (p.188).[36] In central Transilvania the main development of the Turdaş–Petreşti painted ware was into the bichrome painted pottery of the Petreşti culture, although in the upper layers of certain stratified Turdaş–Petreşti sites of Central Transil-vania and in open sites there is evidence of the early development of trichrome painted ware. The forms of the Ariuşd and the Moldavian Cucuteni A painted pottery included especially wide deep bowls on hollow pedestals, which was a form also popular in the Petreşti and Turdaş–Petreşti cultures of central Transilvania.

As in the preceding Pre-Cucuteni III period, the majority of settle-ments in the western part of the Cucuteni–Tripolye culture area as far as the S. Bug river were located on high terraces and promontor-ies overlooking rivers (Fig. 32). It has frequently been suggested that these types of location were chosen for their defensive value. This hypothesis gained favour especially because in a large number of settlements the neck of the promontories on which the settlements were located were cut by a shallow ditch 11–13 m deep and 3–5 m wide.[37] At Tîrpeşti, an earlier Pre-Cucuteni III settlement on the same site had a shallower ditch which was deepened in the later occupa-tion. There is no evidence, however, to indicate that these ditches were to protect the settlements from human intruders. It is possible that they served some purpose beyond that of demarcating the terri-tory of the settlement, for example to control the wanderings of animals, either those inside or those outside the settlement.

It is possible that such locations were chosen, as in the preceding Linear Pottery and Pre-Cucuteni settlements of Moldavia, to facili-tate exploitation of the drier areas for pasture and agricultural land. As in the preceding settlements there was an equal exploitation of

7. Clay anthropomorphic figurine. Szegvár-Tűzköves, E.C. Hungary. Tisza culture. 25·6 cm high. (Szentes Museum)

8. Clay anthropomorphic figurine. Divostin, E. Yugoslavia. Vinča-Pločnik culture. About 25 cm high.

9. Burned clay floor of a house showing traces of internal divisions and hearths. Divostin, E. Yugoslavia. Vinča-Pločnik culture, c. 3200 B.C. About 12 m long. (Reproduced by courtesy of A. McPherron, from *Expedition*, 1970)

wild animals, especially red-deer, and domesticated animals, especially cattle.[38] Hunting was carried out in many cases by the bow and arrow utilising the triangular pressure-flaked arrowheads manufactured in imported honey-coloured Dobrogea flint and local grey flint. There were also many small bone points which may also have been used in hunting.

There is very little evidence in the upland Cucuteni A–Tripolye B settlements of the exploitation of river resources, although at this time in the lower Danube Gumelniţa culture a marked increase in fishing activities is observable both in the bone material and equipment (p.157). It is, therefore, very interesting to note that the majority of those settlements in Moldavia which show direct connection with the lower Danube area by the presence of white-painted Proto-

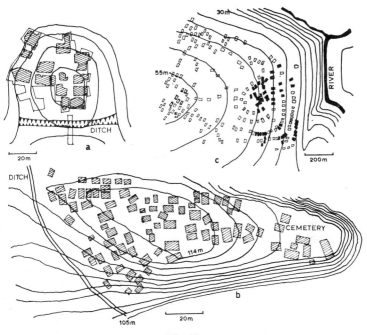

Fig. 32

Eneolithic settlements of S.E. Europe.
a Radovanu, S.E. Rumania. Gumelniţa culture (after Comşa, 1969): hatched blocks = excavated houses.
b Truşeşti, N.E. Rumania. Cucuteni A culture (after Florescu, 1969): hatched blocks = houses.
c Vladimirovka, S. Bug river, Ukraine SSR. Middle Tripolye B2 culture (after Passek, 1949): solid blocks = excavated houses, white blocks = surveyed houses.

Cucuteni–Proto-Gumelniţa pottery, copper objects, etc. are located on the banks and lower terraces of rivers. In their bone material they show evidence of the exploitation of a large variety of fish and forest mammals, and in their equipment have produced evidence of fishing in the presence of copper and bone fish-hooks and (at Frumuşica) a biserially barbed antler harpoon.[39]

From grain impressions and carbonised grain, it is clear that both wheat and barley and possibly millet (at least in the later phases) were cultivated in the Cucuteni A–Tripolye B settlements, as in the lower Danube eneolithic settlements. Flint blades with sickle gloss, similar to those of the preceding Pre-Cucuteni–early Tripolye culture, and querns occur in large numbers in all the settlements, as well as per-forated antler implements with pointed ends and with transverse edges and polished stone trapezoid axe-adzes. In addition, there were perforated axes of polished stone, as in the lower Danube late neo-lithic and eneolithic settlements, and sporadic copper 'hammer-axes' and quadrangular-sectioned narrow copper 'chisels' (p. 202).

Throughout the development of the Cucuteni and Tripolye cul-tures, there were three main categories of pottery whose relative proportions changed during the evolution of the cultures:

1. Thick ware with a smooth surface (Fig. 30) decorated by broad incised lines which formed the bulk of the pottery of the earlier part of the middle period of the Cucuteni A–Tripolye B1 as in the early period. In the Cucuteni AB–Tripolye B2 phase it lost popularity.

2. In this western area from Transilvania to the S. Bug, the chan-nelled and stamped fine-tempered pottery was superseded by the fine-tempered thick ware which was decorated by trichrome painted patterns before firing (Fig. 30). At first (Cucuteni A–Tripolye B1) the painted patterns were the same as those of the Transilvanian Ariuşd style; slightly later, however, a style in which the white paint was applied as a slip in negative patterns with black lines bordering bands of unslipped orange surface became more popular. There was a continuous evolution of the painted pottery into the Cucuteni AB–Tripolye B2 period in which white painting dropped out of use, and large areas were painted in black on the unslipped orange surface (Fig. 30) with thin black or red stripes in between.

3. The third category of pottery occurred at first sporadically in the western area of the Cucuteni–Tripolye culture, but increased in fre-quency and quantity in the later phases of the culture. It comprised a thick soft ware (Fig. 30), tempered predominantly with shells, which was fired to a light buff colour with a pockmarked surface. The forms were predominantly globular pots with short cylindrical collars which were decorated by shallow vertical fluting by stroking

the wet surface with a comb or by comb-impressions. This category of pottery had no prototypes in the neolithic cultures of south-east Europe, but it was common in settlements on the steppes of the lower Dnieper valley and beyond. It has been suggested that it represents the first indication of elements from this area coming into contact with the agricultural settlements of south-east European tradition.[40]

The anthropomorphic clay figurines associated with the earlier trichrome painted pottery are identical to those of the preceding Pre-Cucuteni–early Tripolye culture, but occur in rather fewer numbers. With the disappearance of incised ware, however, in the Cucuteni AB–Tripolye B2 phase, the manufacture of figurines with incised decoration also tended to cease. They were replaced by a rather different set of figurines (Fig. 30), undecorated in a standing position with pointed joined legs, large stomachs and buttocks and very small breasts, perforated arms and hips, and flat-faced heads with pinched-out noses and perforated eyes.[41] These figurines first occur in settlements in association with Proto-Gumelniţa–Proto-Cucuteni painted pottery. It seems likely that the original source of stimulus for these figurines was the lower Danube basin. At Kostiši, a figurine of Cucuteni AB/B–Tripolye B2 type was found still standing in a small clay perforated stand. No bone or stone figurines have been found in Cucuteni–Tripolye culture assemblages, although some of the copper pendants have been claimed as copies of bone figurines.[42] Small clay zoomorphic figurines, generally not very carefully made and representing predominantly cattle, were found on a large number of sites.[43]

From the S. Bug river eastwards, the time-lag in the diffusion of the Tripolye culture is emphasised by the fact that the incised ware of the S. Bug and the S. Bug–Dnieper interfluve, referred to as Tripolye A, was probably contemporary with the early trichrome pottery west of the S. Bug, and trichrome pottery itself was never diffused east of the S. Bug river. The earliest painted pottery associated with the Tripolye settlements east of the S. Bug is also called Tripolye B2, but is quite different from the Tripolye B2 painted pottery west of the S. Bug (Fig. 30). The painted patterns of what may be termed the 'eastern' Tripolye B2 pottery were evolved directly from the incised patterns of the S. Bug Tripolye A and were painted in black on the orange surface of the pots. Unlike the western Tripolye B2 culture the manufacture of incised ware did not cease during this period, but continued to be an important category of pottery, alongside the coarse shell-tempered ware. The development of the bichrome painted pottery east of the S. Bug coincided with the

M

eastwards diffusion of the Tripolye culture as far as the Dnieper and the absorption of the predominantly hunting and fishing groups of these valleys. The majority of Tripolye settlements east of the S. Bug river, however, were located on high ground, especially on the edges of wide loess plateaus overlooking rivers. The settlements were generally larger than those in the west (up to 150 houses at Vladimirovka) and did not comprise superimposed habitation levels. They seem to have been one-period settlements. None of the settlements was surrounded by ditches, but several had their 30 or more houses arranged in concentric circles (Fig. 32) around a large open space in which there was only one or two large houses.[44] This settlement plan, in fact, may have served the same purpose as the ditches in the more western sites, that is to demarcate the territory of the settlement and to protect the domestic animals, rather than as defence against human agency. The economy of the Tripolye settlements from the S. Bug eastwards was similar to that of the western Tripolye sites in that there was an equal exploitation of wild and domesticated animals, but there was an increase both in hunting horses and other parkland and steppe animals and also in keeping domesticated sheep, which thrive in the drier parkland conditions that would seem to have prevailed in the more eastern sites.[45]

The houses of the Tripolye culture were of homogeneous form and construction from Transilvania to the Dnieper, but they tended to be longer in the later phases and further east. They were constructed with walls of wattle daubed with a thick layer of clay on a framework of relatively large wooden posts. The houses (Fig. 27) were rectangular with an average length of 10–12 m (8 m in Transilvania and up to 22 m on the Dnieper), with a constant width of 5–8 m as in the Linear Pottery houses of central Europe (Chapter 3). This constant width was presumably very much controlled by factors such as the average length of available trees for the cross-beams, rather than any survival of cultural tradition from the Linear Pottery culture. Unlike the Linear Pottery houses, there was only one central interior row of posts to support the long gabled roof, most of the support undoubtedly coming from the substantial wattle and daub transverse walls which divided the interior of the house into two to four rooms. Evidence of the elaborate moulding of daub on the gabled end of houses comes from Transilvania (Ariuşd) and from a house-model from Kolomiiščina II. On this latter, the incised decoration may possibly represent some form of thatching. The interior and exterior walls of a house model from Vladimirovka were painted and may indicate that the walls of actual houses were similarly decorated.

The floors of many of the houses, which consisted of a thick clay layer covering a base of horizontal logs, had been preserved by fire.

This characteristic feature of Cucuteni and Tripolye sites, as well as those of the Gumelniţa, Petreşti and Vinča–Pločnik cultures, is referred to as 'ploščadki' or low platform (Pl. 9).[46] It has frequently been suggested in the literature that the floors must have been deliberately set alight before the main construction of the houses in order to protect them from damp and erosion. It is possible, however, that with the increasing number of ovens in which higher temperatures were reached, and the increasing density of the houses themselves, there was a greater risk of the houses accidentally catching fire. Most of the clay house-models of the Cucuteni–Tripolye culture stand on short legs, but there is no evidence as yet that the Tripolye houses themselves were constructed on low stilts. It is more likely that the short legs were a part of the function of the house-models.

Several of the house-models of the Cucuteni–Tripolye culture consist of a view into one room of the house with the interior arrangement of its furniture, rather than a view of the exterior of the house.[47] The interior arrangement (Fig. 27) corresponds exactly to that excavated in the houses themselves. Unlike the houses of the Gumelniţa and Vinča–Pločnik cultures, the Cucuteni-Tripolye houses did not consist of one main room and an ante-chamber or porch. The houses were divided into two to four rooms of equal size, each with an oven and domestic working area, as was speculated for the Linear Pottery culture. Whether this interior arrangement of the house should also be interpreted in terms of an extended family-based social system is open to question. As in the Gumelniţa culture, the ovens were built up against a wall on a large square base of stone slabs covered in clay; the dome was built up of wattle and reeds daubed with clay and, by analogy with the house models, was provided with a narrow chimney in the centre. As in the Gumelniţa houses, there was a platform covered in ash next to the oven. The house model from Popudnya shows a figurine of schematised type with pinched-out nose and perforated eyes sitting next to the oven. Another figurine of more realistic form was kneeling in another corner of the room grinding with a quern. Generally only one saddle quern was found in each room. Unlike those of the Gumelniţa culture, this was moveable. The function of the clay platform with four lobes usually located in the centre of each room is uncertain. There is no positive evidence to support the suggestion that it was a 'sacrificial table', although it may have acted as a table for some purpose. All round the sides of each room were large pots, presumably used for storing various commodities.

THE WEST BALKANS

Many features of the late neolithic and eneolithic settlements of the western part of the Balkan peninsula—the development of food-producing techniques, enrichment in the variety and forms of artefacts made in more durable materials including copper, the enlargement of houses and settlements—echo those already described in the east Balkans. There were at least two important differences, however, from the situation in the south-east Balkans. First, there was no westwards expansion of the 'tell' type of settlement corresponding to its expansion from the Maritsa to the lower Danube basin. The late neolithic and eneolithic settlements were frequently stratified above earlier neolithic settlements, but only with considerable breaks in occupation and horizontal displacement of the occupation area. This must reflect a lack of long occupation on one site and possibly a lower level of production from domesticated animal and cultivated plant sources, or a lesser exploitation of a variety of wild and domesticated resources. Secondly, there was a marked absence of the method of decorating pottery by the application of paint before firing.

The *Salcuţa* culture of N.W. Bulgaria and S.W. Rumania, derived from the late neolithic Vădastra culture, is to a certain extent transitional between the east and west Balkans in that a few settlements formed 'tells' and a small percentage of the pottery on almost every site is graphite-painted.[48]

Vinča–Pločnik culture

West of the area of the Salcuţa culture, in the valley of the Morava and the Danube above the gorges, many of the settlements of the Vinča-Tordoš culture were overlain by thick habitation layers of the late neolithic and eneolithic *Vinča–Pločnik* culture, and many other settlements were founded at the time of the Vinča–Pločnik culture on the same locations, that is the lower terraces of rivers. On the basis of pottery typology and stratigraphy, the culture has been divided into two phases, Vinča–Pločnik C, roughly contemporary with the Boian and Maritsa cultures (Fig. 23), and Vinča–Pločnik D, roughly contemporary with the Gumelniţa culture (Fig. 33).[49] There is evidence of a significant increase in hunting activities in the late neolithic and eneolithic settlements of the west Balkans from the animal bone remains, in which red-deer, wild pig and aurochs formed a high proportion, and hunting equipment made in durable materials such as antler and bone points (Fig. 34), and including biserially and uniserially barbed bone antler harpoons (Fig. 34) as in the Gumelniţa culture. In addition there were bone fish-hooks (Fig. 34), some of

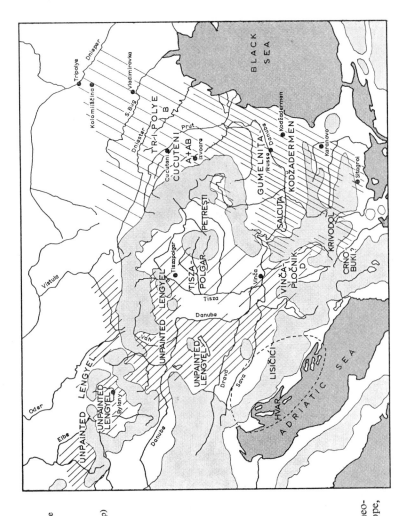

Fig. 33
Map of the distribution of eneolithic cultures in E. Europe,
c. 3600–3200 B.C.

Graphite-painted ware
cultures

Cucuteni–Tripolye culture
(middle phase)

W. Balkan eneolithic
cultures

W. Balkan eneolithic
cultures (Lengyel group)

them barbed, which would indicate either an increase in fishing activities or a change of fishing methods similar to that of the Gulmeniţa culture.[50] Domesticated animals, however, still predominated, and cattle continued to be the most important domesticated species as in the preceding Vinča–Tordoš culture, although sheep, goats and pigs were also kept.

No analysis of cultivated grain samples from any Vinča-Pločnik sites has yet been made. From the fact, however, that barley as well as wheat was cultivated in the late neolithic settlements to the west (Butmir culture) and east of the Vinča–Pločnik culture, we may assume that both these species were cultivated in the late neolithic and eneolithic settlements of the Vardar–Morava basin.

Perforated antler artefacts (Fig. 34), some with pointed ends, others with wide cutting edges, have been found on all the Vinča–Pločnik settlements from its earliest phases of development, along with polished stone flat trapezoid axes or adzes and perforated 'hammer-axes'. In the later phase of the culture, these were supplemented at one or two sites by perforated copper 'hammer-axes' and narrow quadrangular-sectioned copper 'chisels'.

The houses of the Vinča–Pločnik culture were built, as in the south-east Balkans, of thick clay and chaff walls on a framework of small upright wooden posts with a central row of heavy posts in the interior of the house to support the gabled roof.[51] The houses were of rectangular shape (Fig. 34), c. 15 m long and 6–8 m wide. As in the Gumelniţa culture, the later Vinča–Pločnik houses consisted of a main room with an ante-chamber. Very interesting evidence for the

---

Fig. 34

The Vinča–Pločnik culture.

a Ground-plan of a house at Banjica, layer III, E. Yugoslavia (after Todorović and Cermanović, 1961): hatched = post-holes, dotted = surviving wall-plaster, shaded = surviving burnt clay floor, dotted 'horseshoe' = hearth.

b Fafos, E. Yugoslavia (after Jovanović, 1968).

c Petrovaradin, N.E. Yugoslavia (after Brukner, 1968).

d Clay anthropomorphic figurine. Decorated by burnishing and covering with red encrusted paint (dotted area). Vinča, N.E. Yugoslavia (after Vassić, 1932–4).

e 'Cat-face' lid. Vinča, N.E. Yugoslavia (after Vassic, 1932–4).

f Antler perforated axe. Banjica, N.E. Yugoslavia (after Todorović and Cermanović, 1961).

g Antler harpoon. Žarkovo, E. Yugoslavia (after Garašanin, M. & D., 1952–3).

h Bone fish-hook. Vinča, N.E. Yugoslavia (after Srejović & Jovanović, 1958–9).

i Bone double fish-hook. Vinča, N.E. Yugoslavia (after Srejović & Jovanović, 1958–9).

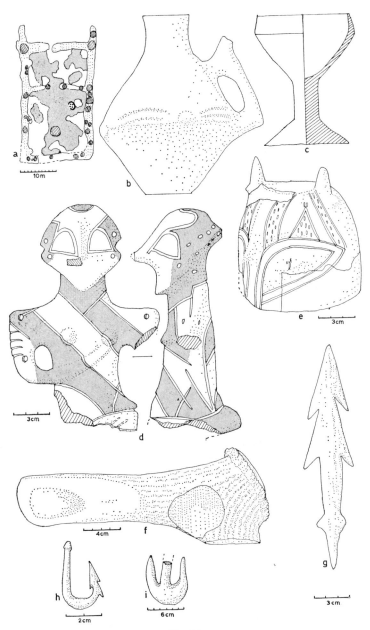

Fig. 34

external decoration of houses was excavated at the site of Kormadin near the Danube, where two massive heads of clay which had been burnt accidentally were found among the house debris. It was suggested that they were originally 'totem heads' which were fixed to the gable ends of the house.[52] It would seem that the heads were representations of cattle, the most important domesticated animal. At the back of the heads instead of horns were large holes, possibly for attaching real horns. A large fragment of wall-plaster from the same site indicates that the walls of the houses were incised and coloured as in other eneolithic settlements of south-east Europe. Many of the houses had thick clay floors built on a layer of horizontal logs and preserved by burning. Each house contained an oven, but this was placed in the centre of the floor rather than against one wall. It is possible that the ovens were not fired to very high temperatures and therefore did not need the extra support or shelter of a house wall. Or, their different position from the east Balkan ovens may be due to factors such as the social organisation in the interior of the house. The Vinča–Pločnik ovens were built up into a dome shaped from a stone or clay base of horseshoe or circular shape, unlike the very solid square-based ovens of the eneolithic settlements of the east Balkans.

The pottery of the Vinča–Pločnik culture was evolved from that of the preceding Vinča–Tordoš culture. The coarse-tempered ware (Fig. 34) was decorated by roughening the surface or by incised 'winkelband' patterns and was manufactured into globular biconical pots of various sizes. The fine-tempered black burnished ware continued to be made into biconical bowls, in particular on tall solid flaring pedestals (Fig. 34), which were decorated on their upper parts by deep rilling or fluting, although in the later periods of the Vinča–Pločnik culture decoration tended to disappear, apart from the sporadic use of pattern-burnishing. The decoration of Vinča–Pločnik clay figurines and 'lamps' in the form of stripes of red paint, applied after firing on to the matt surface, alternating with stripes of the black burnished surface separated by incised lines which were filled with white paint, never occurred on the pottery of the Vinča–Pločnik culture. It is interesting to note, however, that it was characteristic of the pottery of the Szakalhát–Lebö group of the Linear Pottery (Chapter 3) and the Late Tisza and Early Lengyel pottery, both of which were contemporary with the early part of the Vinča–Pločnik culture.

The clay anthropomorphic figurines (Fig. 34) of the Vinča–Pločnik culture were predominantly small, solid, seated or standing figurines.[53] All had small bodies in proportion to the head. Great detail and care was given to the portrayal of the face, which comprised a well-formed elongated nose and large bulging eyes, but no mouth. The face was polygonal with a sharp perforated projection at the back of the head which has prompted the suggestion that these represent masked figures. The arms were also perforated, even those of the seated and kneeling figurines. Many also have garments and ornaments including arm-rings, belts and pendants incised on them. As with pottery, decoration of the figurines tended to disappear in the later part of the Vinča–Pločnik culture. The majority of the figurines had standardised schematised facial and body features. A few, however, had more personalised facial features. Most of the figurines were no higher than 16 cm but several sites near the Morava–Vardar watershed area have produced large figurines (up to 30 cm high) carefully manufactured and decorated (Pl. 8). Two heads, 18 cm high, must have come from figurines of an original height of *c*. 50 cm. Semi-human figurines were a feature of Vinča–Pločnik assemblages, for example anthropomorphic heads attached to four legs. Zoomorphic figurines, as in other late neolithic and eneolithic settlements of S.E. Europe, comprise small solid figurines, mostly cattle, as well as zoomorphic terminals of clay 'lamps'.

West of the Drina river, the Vinča-Pločnik culture was bordered by the *Butmir* culture which evolved from the preceding Danilo culture (Chapter 3) with strong influence from the area of the Vinča culture.[54] The fine pottery of the Butmir culture, however, was decorated by incised patterns developed from those of the Danilo culture, in combination with the application of red and white paint after firing. Further west, on the Adriatic coast, the *Hvar* culture, which was also evolved from the preceding Danilo culture, shows no Vinča influence.[55]

On the southern periphery of the Vinča–Pločnik culture, the late neolithic and eneolithic settlements of the Vardar basin in *Macedonia*, as far as it is possible to tell from the small amount of research carried out there, were connected culturally much more to the eneolithic settlements further south in Greek Macedonia and Thessaly than to the Vinča-Pločnik culture of the Morava basin. The sites comprise thick stratified habitation deposits, none of which formed 'tells'. The coarse ware was occasionally decorated by incised 'winkelband' patterns, as in the Vinča-Plocnik culture, but the fine ware was painted after firing without incised patterns. Two main periods in the development of this painted pottery have been recognised in Macedonia, but their chronological position in relation to the cultures of Serbia and Greece is still very uncertain. The first was characterised by white on red painted patterns, as at Porodin, and the second was characterised by white or black on red painted patterns, as at Crnobuki.[56]

Tisza culture

Immediately north of the area (Fig. 23) of the Vinča-Pločnik culture, two distinct cultures evolved from the Linear Pottery variants of the Great Hungarian plain (Alföld).[57] One of these was centred on the Tisza valley, in which, as in preceding periods, the settlements were located on alluvial mounds rising above the flood plain. As in a number of other late Linear Pottery variants (e.g. Želiezovce and Bükk), the pottery of this region was characterised by an increase in the number and density of the incised lines which decorated the whole of its surface in complicated meander and other rectilinear patterns. The incised lines formed a base for the application of red, yellow and white paint after firing (Tisza II) (Fig. 35). Gradually, contemporary with Vinča–Pločnik C, decoration by incised lines decreased and disappeared (Tisza III), and finally, contemporary with a similar phenomenon in the Vinča–Pločnik D phase, all decoration on pottery disappeared. As in the preceding Linear Pottery variants of this region, many features link the culture with the contemporary cultures further south in the Danube–Morava area—for example, the presence of large 'monumental' and large hollow figurines (Pl. 7) or of anthropomorphic pots, such as the two from Kökénydomb which were lying together by the hearth of a house.[58] The houses were small and rectangular one-roomed structures as in the preceding period in this region. Near the house at Szegvár–Tűzköves a large clay zoomorphic head was discovered which, like those found at Kormadin (p.184), may originally have been attached to the gable end of the house above the entrance.[59]

In addition, the manufacture of hunting and fishing equipment in durable materials, for example bone and antler points and biserially barbed harpoons, increased in the Tisza valley settlements, as in other late neolithic settlements of S.E. Europe. This was associated, on the basis of the evidence of the animal bone material, with a significant increase in the exploitation of wild animals, including wild pig and cattle and red-deer, and large fish such as catfish and carp.[60] Among the domesticated animals, only pig and cattle were domesticated in this period. Sheep and goats were almost absent from the bone material of Lebő, although on this site and many others the manufacture of clay objects interpreted as spindle whorls and loom weights continued. It was either an accident of sampling that the bones of sheep and goats were absent, or the 'spindle-whorls' were used in spinning some other material (possibly nettles?), or the objects themselves have been misinterpreted.

In the late neolithic settlements in the middle of the Great Hungarian plain, there is also evidence of a significant increase in hunting activities, not from the presence of hunting equipment in durable materials, but in the animal bone material of which over three-quarters are from wild animals, almost all from wild cattle, in particular old or mature male animals. The domesticated animals also comprised predominantly cattle. It has been suggested by Bökönyi that the wild animals were killed not so much for food, but either so that the young animals could be captured alive and domesticated, or as a means of controlling the breeding rate and quality of a semi-wild herd to which a human group had attached itself.[61] In either case,

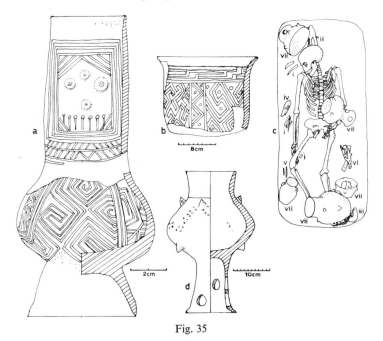

Fig. 35

Late neolithic and eneolithic cultures of the east Hungarian plain.
a Anthropomorphic pot. Szegvar-Tűzköves, E.C. Hungary. Tisza culture (after Kalicz, 1970).
b Incised pot. Aszod-Papai földek, E.C. Hungary. Tisza culture (after Kalicz, 1969).
c Burial 67 of a 60-year-old man. Tiszapolgar-Basatanya, E. Hungary. Tiszapolgar culture (after Kutzian, 1963): (i) flint blades, (ii) wild-boar mandible, (iii) skeleton of a dog, (iv) perforated axe of antler, (v) polished bone awl, (vi) bones of cattle, deer, and pig, probably fallen out of pot, (vii) pedestalled bowls, pots and cup.
d Pedestalled bowl from grave 67 at Tiszapolgar-Basatanya, E. Hungary. Tiszapolgar culture (after Kutzian, 1963).

this would indicate local domestication of cattle on a scale unprece-
dented in the prehistory of temperate Europe. The pottery of the late
neolithic settlements of the Great Hungarian plain falls into two
groups. In both groups the forms are identical, including especially
wide bowls on tall hollow pedestals. In the more western or Csöz-
halom group, the pottery was painted in red and white after firing
(Fig.35) in patterns much more reminiscent of the contemporary
Lengyel culture to the west. In the more eastern or Herpaly group,
the light orange surface was either unslipped or covered by a self or
white slip and painted before firing in thin dark brown parallel lines
(Fig.35). There is no doubt that this group had close connections
with west and central Transilvania to the east, but its chronological
relationship with the late neolithic and eneolithic cultures of this
region is not clear.

Transilvania

Many of the late neolithic and eneolithic settlements of *W. and C.
Transilvania* comprised thick habitation deposits stratified above
earlier neolithic Turdaş culture settlements (Chapter 3). There is no
evidence, as yet, of the economic basis which could support such a
relatively continuous occupation of the same site. Any such stratified
deposits were a very rare occurrence in the late neolithic and eneolithic sites of the east Hungarian plain. The late neolithic *Turdaş–
Petreşti* culture was evolved to a large extent from the Turdaş culture,
but its fine pottery was decorated by the application of paint before
firing, for which it is difficult to find prototypes in the preceding
cultures of Transilvania. The pots were covered in a white or less
frequently a bright red or orange slip, and painted in red, black or
dark brown designs. It was claimed that the painted designs could
be the result of a reflowering of the painted Criş pottery or an evolution of the practice in the Turdaş culture of applying a coloured slip
to the pottery. Much more likely, however, is the possibility that the
Turdaş-Petreşti painted ware was evolved partially, if not wholly,
from the painted pottery of the late Linear Pottery Esztar and
Szamos groups of the Great Hungarian plain (Chapter 3).[62]

The succeeding *Petreşti* culture was characterised by thin fine-
tempered ware fired at high temperatures to a light orange colour;
the surface was covered with a self-slip and painted in dark brown,
parallel, thin and thick lines before firing. The patterns would seem
to have been evolved from those of the Turdaş–Petreşti culture. It is
not impossible, however, that there was further influence from the
Great Hungarian plain, from the culture which succeeded the Esztar
and Szamos groups, that is the Herpaly group, or even that the
Petreşti culture had some effect on the development of the distinctive

thin hard-fired fabric and patterns of the Herpaly pottery. These questions can only be resolved, however, by clarification of the relative chronological positions of these cultures.

In the northern part of the Great Hungarian plain, and the north Hungarian limestone mountains, the later phases of the Bükk culture are, like the Tisza culture, characterised by increased density of incised lines forming a base for the application of red, white and yellow paint after firing; subsequently the area covered by incised decoration gradually decreased and finally decoration disappeared altogether.[63]

Tiszapolgar

Out of these various late neolithic groups in the east Hungarian plain there emerged, contemporary with the Vinča–Pločnik D culture, the *Tiszapolgar* culture (Fig. 33), characterised by a uniform pottery style over the whole plain and Tisza valley. The culture is also frequently referred to as the *Early Copper Age* because of the occurrence of copper perforated 'hammer-axes', 'chisels' and square-sectioned awls (Fig. 38) in its assemblages. The pottery is distinguished by a complete lack of decoration (Fig. 35), apart from the application of small warts and lugs. The fabric was fine-tempered but thick and fired to a light grey colour. The forms were evolved from those of the late neolithic pottery of the Great Hungarian plain and the Tisza valley, and comprise deep biconical pots and wide bowls on tall flaring, hollow, perforated pedestals.

Most of the settlements of the Tiszapolgar culture are small and consist of a single habitation level.[64] At Crnokalačka Bara, however, the Tiszapolgar culture layer comprised five superimposed habitation levels. The animal bone material from the settlements shows a sharp decrease of wild animals from the late neolithic settlements, and an overwhelming majority of domesticated animals, especially cattle, although sheep, goats and pigs were also present. It is possible that this reflects a further stage in the process of local domestication of cattle. The economy, however, is quite different from that of the Vinča–Pločnik culture, and there are many other features of the Tiszapolgar culture which distinguish it from the other eneolithic cultures of south-east Europe. Not only was there a lack of thick habitation levels, but the settlements and the houses were much smaller. For example, at Tibava, the rectangular houses were 11 m long, but only 4·5 m wide. In addition to the obvious differences in pottery, there was a complete absence of anthropomorphic figurines although sporadic zoomorphic clay figurines and zoomorphic pots occur.

One of the most significant features of this culture is the presence of separate burial places from the settlements, quite different from the S.E. European eneolithic practice of burying the dead among the rubbish pits and houses of the settlements. Some of the Tiszapolgar cemeteries (e.g. Tibava) are associated with a nearby settlement. The largest cemetery was that of Tiszapolgar–Basatanya in N.E. Hungary in which 156 people had been buried, each in their own shallow grave pit, on their sides in a contracted position. Each burial contained a pot, and frequently also a long flint blade, perforated stone axe or copper perforated 'hammer-axe', beads, gold pendants, etc.

On the basis of stratified habitation layers at Szekely,[65] it would seem that the Tiszapolgar culture of the east Hungarian plain developed, with very little outside influence, into the *Bodrogkeresztur* culture or *Middle Copper Age* at the same time as the middle period of the Cucuteni–Tripolye culture was developing into the later period (Tripolye B2/C1).[66] Graves of the Bodrogkeresztur culture occur in the same burial sites as in the Tiszapolgar culture. The Bodrogkeresztur inhumations were buried in the same position as those of the Tiszapolgar culture and were accompanied by undecorated globular pots on a low pedestal and with a long cylindrical neck provided with two ribbon lugs at the rim. Some of the graves also contained, besides blades and axes of stone, distinctive copper perforated 'axe-adzes' (Fig.38) and, rather less frequently, copper 'chisels' and square-sectioned awls.

The pottery from the Bodrogkeresztur settlements, unlike that from the graves, was decorated by characteristic 'stab-and-drag' (*Furchenstich*) designs in chequerboard and hatched patterns and filled with white encrusted paint. The economy was based on the exploitation of domesticated cattle, as in the preceding period, but it is interesting to note in the Bodrogkeresztur culture the importance of sheep and goats in the economy increased at the expense of domesticated pig.[67] This has been interpreted as indicating the first elements of the westwards diffusion of the Yamno (Pit-Grave) culture from the south Russian steppes to reach east Hungary. At a time contemporary with the Tiszapolgar culture such elements (it is argued) had already reached the Cucuteni–Tripolye settlements of Moldavia (p.177). The increase in sheep-breeding could, however, be a reflection of the transition to light forested or grassland conditions on the Great Hungarian plain resulting from the transition from the Atlantic to the sub-Boreal vegetational period which has been dated by Carbon 14 to about this time (Chapter 1). The occurrence of a copper 'axe-adze' in a grave at Decea Mureşului in Transilvania in which the burial was covered with red ochre has been attributed to stimulus from the same area where the practice of covering burials with ochre was very common.[68] It will be remembered, however, that ochre was already known in burials in S.E. Europe from the early neolithic period (p. 88).

Lengyel culture

On the Pannonian plain, west of the Danube, a similar evolution of pottery decoration to that east of the Tisza took place in the late neolithic and eneolithic settlements (Figs. 23, 33). The various pottery groups of this region have been grouped together under the name *Lengyel* culture.[69] In general, in the whole of this region there was an evolution from the use of incised patterns in combination with red, yellow and white paint after firing (Fig. 22) (e.g. Želiezovce group) to decoration without incised lines with red, white and yellow paint applied after firing (Moravian–Slovakian Painted Ware) (Fig. 36), then by white paint only, and finally to the disappearance of decoration (Fig. 36), contemporary with a similar disappearance of decoration on pottery in the Tiszapolgar culture (Late Lengyel culture). It was suggested that the earliest development of the Lengyel culture took place in the south, in N.W. Yugoslavia in the Bapsko–Lengyel (also called Sopot-Lengyel) culture, and thence diffused northwards.[70] It would seem, however, that the Sopot–Lengyel group was a local hybrid of Vinča, late Linear Pottery and Butmir elements, and had little effect on the subsequent development of the late neolithic and eneolithic pottery of the more northern part of the Pannonian plain.

Certain features connect the settlements of the Slovak–Moravian Painted Ware group with those of the Tisza valley (Tisza II–III) and with the late neolithic cultures of south-east Europe, including the forms of the pots, the presence of elaborate spindle-whorls, clay house-models (Fig. 36) and clay anthropomorphic and zoomorphic figurines (Fig. 36). The anthropomorphic figurines occur in much larger numbers (over 100 at Střelice) and with much greater frequency than in the Tisza valley.[71] They are unlike any of the preceding or contemporary figurines of south-east Europe in that the arms are frequently long and bent forward and up in a supplicating position. Portrayals of human figures with their arms bent upwards, however, have been found applied in relief to coarse pottery of early neolithic settlements in C. and S.E. Europe.[72] They are generally an average height of 15cm, in a standing position, with legs and feet large in proportion to the rest of the body. The small head perched on a long neck rarely had any facial features portrayed on it. So far no satisfactory explanation has been found for the sudden appearance and popularity of clay figurines in an area in which, during the earlier neolithic Linear Pottery culture, they had been significantly absent. If they were not locally evolved or adapted from figurines manu-

factured in a perishable material, it is likely that their appearance is
the result of diffusion possibly from south-east Europe. Apart from
clay house-models, the one commodity which would show contact
with this area is the occurrence of copper 'hammer-axes' in central
Europe, but these only occur in the Late Lengyel culture, by which
time the figurines were generally not manufactured on the Pannonian

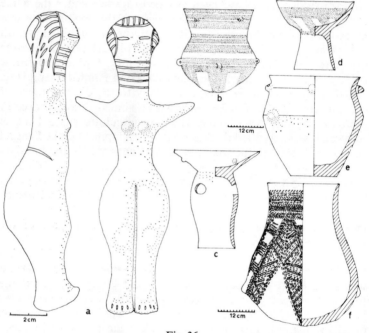

Fig. 36

Late neolithic and eneolithic cultures of the Pannonian and Bohemian
plains.

a Clay anthropomorphic figurine. Střelice, S.C. Czechoslovakia. Early
   Lengyel culture (Moravian-Slovakian Painted Ware) (after Skutil,
   1940).
b Pot decorated by red and yellow encrusted paint (dotted area). Svodin,
   S.C. Czechoslovakia. Early Lengyel culture (after Točik, 1969).
c Pedestalled bowl. Undecorated. Brodzany, S.C. Czechoslovakia. Late
   Lengyel (after Točik, 1969).
d Pedestalled bowl decorated by white-painted encrusted patterns
   (dotted area). Svodin, S.C. Czechoslovakia. Middle Lengyel culture
   (after Točik, 1969).
e Undecorated pot. Bylany, W. Czechoslovakia. Late Lengyel culture
   (after Soudsky, 1966).
f Decorated pot. Buštěhrad, W. Czechoslovakia. Stroke-ornamented
   Ware (after Neustupny, 1961).

10. Clay tablets with engraved designs interpreted as 'writing': *above,* clay tablet from Tărtăria, C. Rumania (see p. 114), 6·1 cm diameter (reproduced by courtesy of N. Vlassa from *Dacia VII,* 1963); *right,* clay tablet from Gradešnitsa, N.W. Bulgaria, late neolithic, 12·5 cm long. (Reproduced by courtesy of B. Nikolov from *Arkheologiya XII,* 1970)

11. Hollow clay zoomorphic figurine with detachable head. Golyam Izvor, N.E. Bulgaria. Gumelniţa culture. About 12 cm high. (Razgrad Museum)

12. Late neolithic house in which the clay tablet (Pl. 10 *right*) was found. Gradešnitsa, N.W. Bulgaria. (Reproduced by courtesy of B. Nikolov, from *Arkheologiya* XII, 1970)

plain. Another possible source of diffusion of the figurines was from the area of the Cucuteni–Tripolye culture. Pottery painted in red, yellow and white in a very similar style to that of the Moravian–Slovakian Painted Ware occurs on settlements north of the Carpathians in S.E. Poland and as far as the upper Dniester valley, bordering on the area of the Cucuteni–Tripolye culture.[73] No figurines, however, have been found in these Lengyel culture settlements north of the Carpathians.

Further west (Fig. 23), in N. Moravia, the Bohemian plain, and the Saale–Elbe basin of S.E. Germany, and S.W. Germany (Bavaria), the pottery of the later Linear Pottery cultures was not characterised by incised decoration combined with the application of paint after firing. In these areas, the late 'notenkopf' and filled-in band designs evolved into the *Stroke-ornamented Ware* (Stichbandkeramik) (Fig. 36). Stroke-ornamented Ware also occurred north of the Carpathians in S. Poland, but generally west of sites with the Moravian–Slovakian Painted Ware. On some sites in Moravia sherds of both of these late neolithic cultures occurred in the same assemblage. There was a general absence of clay figurines and artefacts made of copper in the settlements of the Stroke-ornamented Ware culture. As in the preceding Linear Pottery culture, however, burials containing ornaments made of the Mediterranean *Spondylus* shells would indicate a certain amount of contact with S.E. Europe, probably indirect and possibly for this specific commodity.[74] At the same time as the Tiszapolgar and Late Lengyel cultures were emerging, there was a similar disappearance of decoration on pottery in the Bohemian and Saale–Elbe basins. This pottery has been called Late Lengyel also in Bohemia, but it is still not clear whether, in fact, it was the result of diffusion from the Late Lengyel culture of Moravia, or whether it was a parallel process of the gradual disappearance of pottery decoration.

The settlements of the Stroke-ornamented Ware and Lengyel cultures were located in the same areas, and frequently on the same sites as those of the preceding Linear Pottery Culture. It seems likely that they represent the continuation of the same population. The houses were constructed by the same method as the Linear Pottery houses, with three interior rows of posts to support the roof.[75] In the later periods it was very common for the posts to be dug deep into the ground and the wall embedded in a deep trench. There was a tendency for the houses to become narrower at one end so that they became trapezoidal in plan. The average length of the houses remained 20–30 m throughout this period. In the later periods, in association with undecorated pottery, the houses were frequently built with an ante-chamber separated by a thick wattle and daub

N

wall as in the contemporary Gumelniţa and Vinča–Pločnik culture. At Postoloprty, a house with such an ante-chamber also had four domed ovens down the length of the interior. Thus, unlike the Gumelniţa houses, it is possible that the Postoloprty house was divided into four smaller rooms, even though it had a solid wall separating off the ante-chamber. Similar trapezoidal houses have been excavated in S. Poland in settlements dating to a very late phase of the Lengyel culture, called *Jordanowa*, contemporary with the Bodrogkeresztur culture of E. Hungary and S.E. Czechoslovakia, and the Funnel-Beaker culture (TRB) of the N.W. European plain.[76]

Evidence of territorial demarcation of the settlements occurs in particular in settlements dating to the earlier period of the Lengyel culture, contemporary with similar phenomena in the area of the Cucuteni–Tripolye culture of Moldavia. There is evidence that the settlements were surrounded by wattle fences and shallow cause-wayed ditches.[77] These features have been generally interpreted as defensive fortifications, but they may only have been to protect the domesticated stock from wild animals. The animal bone material indicates that domesticated animals were a very important element of the economy and that, among these, cattle predominated, as in the earlier Linear Pottery culture. However, since the whole settlement was surrounded and the ditches were sometimes laboriously dug into the bedrock, it would seem that there was less frequent move-ment of the settlement and pasturing area than was speculated for the Linear Pottery culture, and that the movements and breeding of the domesticated animals were more carefully controlled, possibly in association with their exploitation for other purposes besides a ready supply of meat.

The use of copper in the Lengyel culture of the Pannonian plain and S. Poland was limited to sporadic copper beads and ornaments until the Late Lengyel culture when copper 'hammer-axes' of the same type as those of the Tiszapolgar culture, and less frequently 'chisels' and square-sectioned awls, appear. In the latest phase, con-temporary with the Bodrogkeresztur culture, large cemeteries in S. Poland have produced many copper objects, in particular ornaments such as spiral armlets, spiral terminals, copper beads, beaten copper 'plaques', copper 'axe-adzes' and quadrangular chisels.[78] These were associated in the graves with beads of perforated animal teeth, amber from the Baltic coast and stone and bone arm-rings decorated by excised patterns. It is clear, therefore, that there was some form of exchange of commodities between the Late Lengyel–Bodrogkeresztur settlements of central Europe and settlements on the Baltic coast, either with hunting-gathering settlements which still existed in the east Baltic (Narva culture) where there was extensive exploitation of local amber, or with hunting and fishing settlements and early agricultural settlements of the west Baltic coast. It is interesting to note that similar copper objects to those found in the Jordanowa group cemeteries have been found in settlements of the early Funnel-Beaker culture (TRB) of the W. Baltic coast in association with the earliest occurrence of a food-producing economy in this region.[79]

COPPER METALLURGY

Native copper and copper ore-bearing rocks have a limited distribution in eastern Europe. They occur, for example, in the eastern Carpathians in Transilvania, in the Danube gorges area, the Balkan mountains of Bulgaria, the Slovak Ore mountains, the Hungarian Matra mountains, the N. Austrian Alps, and very rich deposits in the Harz and Bohemian Ore mountains. From the present state of analysis of trace elements in the metal objects, it is possible to tell that the copper artefacts of the late neolithic and eneolithic cultures of S.E. and C. Europe were made of copper from Carpathian–Balkan sources, but it is not yet possible to identify the particular source among these.[80] It has been suggested that the distribution (Fig. 37) of the artefacts themselves indicates to a certain extent the source of the raw material, but it is just possible that the ores were collected in one area and processed and used in an entirely different area.[81] It is also possible that the ores were not collected by the population living closest to them. In the early stages of the exploitation of ores and native metal, however, it seems unlikely that very distant sources were used. If we assume this is the case, the complete absence of artefacts of copper and the raw material itself in the late neolithic and eneolithic settlements of W. Czechoslovakia, S. Germany and N. Austria would indicate that the rich copper deposits of the Harz and Bohemian Ore mountains, along with those of the northern Alps, were not exploited. The reason why these sources were not used and why there is no evidence of the early development of metal-working in these areas is due to a number of factors, including the relative inaccessibility of the ores in these mountains and a lack of the development of high-temperature pottery-firing techniques. It is also possible that for some reason the metallurgical innovations were rejected, even if the sources or techniques themselves were known, in favour of a continuing manufacture of heavy implements exclusively in stone and bone.

The earliest copper artefacts in eastern Europe are small beads of native copper which occur in the early Boian culture graves at Cernica, *c.* 3900 B.C. Slightly later, square-sectioned copper 'awls'

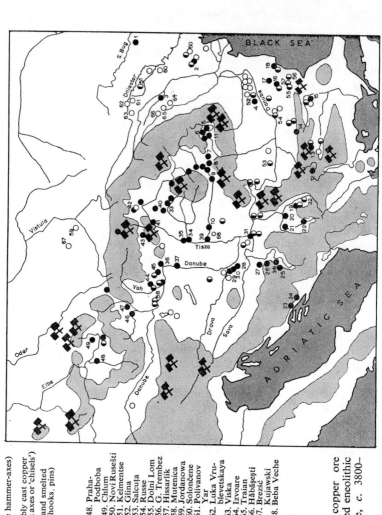

Legend (upper left):

- ● Cast copper objects (shaft-hole hammer-axes)
- ◑ Artefacts of smelted and possibly cast copper (heavy pendants and solid flat axes or 'chisels')
- ○ Hammered artefacts of native and smelted copper ('plaques', awls, fish-hooks, pins)
- ✠ Copper ores

1. Berezov-skaya Gez
2. Karbuna
3. Cucuteni
4. Vidra
5. Reci
6. Teleac
7. Seica Mica
8. Şura Mica
9. Turdaş
10. Lippa
11. Teiu
12. Slivenitsa
13. Gabarevo
14. Trnovo
15. Karanovo
16. Kodžader-men
17. Studenets
18. ? Sava
19. Pločnik
20. Kruševac
21. Stolac
22. Gruvevtsi
23. Split
24. Gorica
25. Travnik
26. Vrbac
27. Laktaši
28. Dereza
29. Vukovar
30. Cerovac
31. Velika
32. Drenoveč
33. Apatkeresz-tur
34. Alsoilosva
35. Apagy
36. Balassa Gyarmat
37. Tápioszecsö
38. Oraşje
39. Csoka
40. Toti
41. Tiszapolgar
42. Tibava
43. Szendre
44. Nitra
45. Trgina
46. Zdonin
47. Rošice
48. Praha-Podboba
49. Chlum
50. Novi Ruseŝti
51. Kelmentse
52. Glina
53. Salcuta
54. Russe
55. Dolni Lom
56. G. Trembez
57. Hissarlik
58. Mutenica
59. Jordanowa
60. Solončene
61. Polivanov Yar
62. Luka Vru-blevetskaya
63. Viska
64. Izvoare
65. Traian
66. Hăbăşeşti
67. Brezść
68. Beba Veche

Fig. 37

Map of the distribution of copper ore resources and cast and hammered eneolithic copper artefacts in E. Europe, c. 3800–3200 B.C.

(Fig. 38) occur with increasing frequency in settlements of the Boian, Maritsa, Pre-Cucuteni II/III–Tripolye A, and Vinča–Pločnik C cultures (c. 3800–3700 B.C.) (Figs. 23, 31), as well as in the late neolithic settlements of the Tisza valley. These were most likely cold-hammered or annealed from native copper. A copper fish-hook (Fig. 38) from this period from Solončene (Tripolye A) was analysed and found to have been heated to 300°C and subsequently hammered and bent into shape.[82] This treatment was basically the same technique already used in the manufacture of stone, bone and antler artefacts in that the composition of the metal was not changed by any special techniques. From the evidence of the Solončene fish-hook, it is clear that the manufacturers not only recognised that copper could be softened, thinned, expanded and shaped by hammering, but also that too much hammering would make the metal brittle and that in order to regain its malleable property it was necessary to heat the metal slightly. No very complex firing techniques were needed, since the metal could be heated up to the necessary temperatures in an open hearth. The exploitation of native copper resources could have taken place in many areas provided that the raw material was available and that there was a need for small copper artefacts such as awls, beads and fish-hooks. Bone prototypes for the awls, possibly used in leatherwork or basketry, occur in all areas where those of copper have been found. In Bulgaria bone awls in antler handles (Fig. 38) were discovered, which were identical in shape and size to the copper awls. These latter were also frequently found with their antler handles still attached (Fig. 38). The advantage of copper fish-hooks over those of bone was that it was easier to achieve the curved shape. It would seem, however, that there was a great problem in manufacturing hooks of sufficient strength which would not bend back under strain, and particularly in finding a suitable method for attaching the metal hooks to a line. Generally at the attachment end the metal strip was coiled several times to form a loop, but on most examples this end has been broken off. The range of objects which could be made of native copper was also severely limited by the small size of the nuggets.

The exploitation of copper ores by the development of techniques of smelting to reduce the metal from the ores did not necessarily follow as a result of the exploitation of native metals. There is very little visual connection between the ore-bearing minerals and the native metal nuggets. The reduction of copper from the ore will take place if it is heated under controlled conditions to 800°C.[83] With certain impurities present this process will take place at a slightly lower temperature. Without a controlled draught, either by the use of bellows or a specially constructed kiln, it is difficult to reach 800°C.

Judging by the temperatures at which the pottery was fired, these conditions could be met in a much more restricted area of eastern Europe at the time when the first smelted copper objects appeared in prehistoric assemblages. This included the areas of the Gumelniţa, Salcuţa, Vinča–Pločnik, Cucuteni–Tripolye, Tiszapolgar and possibly Lengyel cultures (Fig. 33). The potters of all these cultures were potentially able to smelt copper ores.

The process of the discovery of the metal content of ore-bearing rocks may have happened in many ways, probably in several places within this area. It is possible, for example, that ore-bearing rocks were used as the base of pottery ovens, or that ore-bearing rocks were brought back as potential stone artefacts and put in the pottery ovens so that they would break up into manageable pieces. In its reduced state at 800°C, the metal does not liquefy, but forms a soft fused malleable mass. In this state it is possible to hammer and anneal the metal in the same way as native copper.

The earliest evidence in eastern Europe of smelted copper artefacts, hammered into shape, occurs in the late Boian, the Proto-Cucuteni

---

Fig. 38

Early copper metallurgy in E. Europe.

a Copper hammer-axe. Slivnitsa, W. Bulgaria. Gumelniţa culture (after Popov, 1921).

b Copper flat axe or 'chisel'. Russe, N. Bulgaria. Gumelniţa culture (Russe Museum).

c Copper axe-adze. Late Salcuţa–Bodrogkeresztur culture. Timişoara, S.W. Rumania (Timişoara Museum).

d Copper square-sectioned awl. Yasa Tepe, S. Bulgaria. Gumelniţa culture (Plovdiv Museum).

e Square-sectioned awl in a bone handle. Azmak, S. Bulgaria. Gumelniţa culture (Stara Zagora Museum).

f Polished bone awl in an antler handle. Kazanlak, C. Bulgaria. Gumelniţa culture (Kazanlak Museum).

g Small thick pot, probably a crucible. Azmak, S. Bulgaria. Gumelniţa culture (Stara Zagora Museum).

h Copper fish-hook. Solončene, Dniester river, Ukraine SSR. Early Tripolye culture (after Passek, 1961).

i Copper fish-hook. Azmak, Bulgaria. Gumelniţa culture (Stara Zagora Museum).

j Ingot of smelted copper. Polivanov Yar, Dniester river, Ukraine SSR. Middle Tripolye B1 culture (after Rendina, 1961).

k Perforated clay object called a 'phallus', but possibly the tuyère of bellows. Khotnica, C. Bulgaria. Gumelniţa culture (after Angelov, 1958).

l–u The Karbuna hoard, Moldavia SSR (after Sergeyev, 1962–3, and Klein, 1968). *l* The large incised pot with small one acting as a lid which contained the hoard. *m* perforated copper hammer-axe. *n* copper flat axe or chisel. *o–r* heavy copper plaques. *s* copper bracelet. *t* greenstone perforated axe. *u* marble perforated axe. All objects in the hoard are drawn to the same scale.

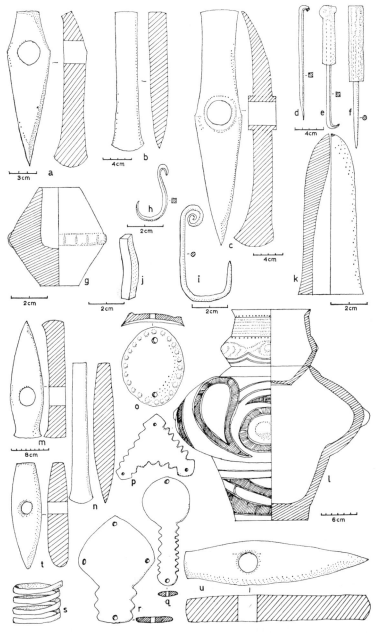

Fig. 38

and the end of the Tripolye A cultures (Fig. 31).[84] It is interesting to note this early occurrence of copper objects of smelted metal in the area of the Cucuteni–Tripolye culture since this culture area is distinguished by a lack of available ore-bearing rocks (Fig. 37) apart from the ores in the mountains of S.E. Transilvania on the western edge. There is no evidence to indicate whether or not the resources of Transilvania were exploited in this period, but it is interesting to note that in the late neolithic and eneolithic period, S.E. Transilvania was connected culturally very closely to the Cucuteni–Tripolye culture of Moldavia, and did not follow the general cultural development of the rest of Transilvania. It is possible that this connection was stimulated by the exploitation of the S.E. Transilvanian copper ores. In this light, it is very interesting to note the presence of ingots (Fig. 38) of smelted copper in the settlement of Polivanov Yar (Tripolye B1).[85] The copper has been identified as from a Carpathian–Balkan source, and would seem to have been brought to the Dniester valley in ingot form, already smelted. Copper objects very rarely occur in the eneolithic settlements of the Ukraine east of the Dniester, and never east of the S. Bug river.

By a simple technology of hammering and annealing the smelted copper, and cold-welding the ingots together, it would have been possible to produce many of the artefacts which occur in late neolithic and eneolithic settlements of eastern Europe including quadrangular-sectioned 'chisels', square-sectioned 'awls', fish-hooks and some of the 'plaques'. In the case of the smelted copper artefacts the size of the artefacts is not limited so much as their shape and complexity.

The area in which the melting and casting properties of copper ores and native metal could have been discovered is very restricted in eastern Europe. Copper will not liquefy until it is heated to a temperature of 1050°C. According to analyses of pottery from eastern Europe, these temperatures were reached during the firing of pottery in only one region of eastern Europe at this time—the south-east Balkan Gumelniţa culture. It was originally suggested by Childe, and more recently by Piggott, that the impetus to develop 'this novel technology (exploitation of metals, in particular casting molten copper) must have come from outside, and in the contemporary circumstances a broadly Anatolian or Aegean origin is almost inevitable and has archaeological support'.[86] Furthermore, they saw the impetus as the result of the activities of prospectors and metalsmiths from the Aegean area and Anatolia in search of raw materials in the Carpathians. This idea is dependent on the assumption that the native population of S.E. Europe was 'conservative' in comparison to the 'innovating' societies of the Near East, but there is, in fact, no evidence to support this concept. The picture becomes much clearer if, as with the introduction of a food-producing economy, S.E. Europe is regarded as part of the Near Eastern cultural area.

All the archaeological evidence points to S.E. Europe and not the Aegean as the area where large-scale melting and casting of copper objects was earliest developed.[87] It would seem that the early development and experimentation in the melting and casting of copper ores and native metal was closely associated with the development of the techniques of the application of metallic paint, in particular graphite, to pottery. As was described earlier (p. 163), this method of decorating fine pottery was characteristic of the Gumelniţa culture, and would seem to have been evolved in the lower Maritsa and Danube basin during the late phases of the Boian and Maritsa cultures. As with the melting and casting of copper, the application and fixing of graphite-paint requires very exacting skills and firing conditions to reach the required temperature of 1100°C. From the occurrence of graphite-painted ware in the late neolithic cultures of the south-east Balkans, it is clear that these firing techniques were developed for the manufacture of pottery before they were ever applied to metallurgy. Apart from the development of the required firing conditions, there were other factors which could have encouraged the local evolution of copper metallurgy in the area of the Gumelniţa culture. These included the presence of abundant supplies of local ores (and possibly native copper) in the nearby Balkan mountains (e.g. at Burgas and Pazardžik) in just those regions where the graphite could have been obtained (Fig. 37); a long tradition of hammering and annealing copper artefacts and the reduction of metal from the ores in the area; an available supply of suitable fuel in the surrounding forests and a developed food-producing economy which was able to support permanent settlements of 'tell' type (the only occurrence in Europe at this time of settlements of this type). Although one or more of these factors may have been present in other eneolithic cultures of eastern Europe, it was only in the area of the Gumelniţa culture where they could *all* interact.

The process of the discovery of the melting properties of copper is, of course, impossible to reconstruct. It may have been the result of trying to 'anneal' native copper or smelted copper in the high-temperature pottery kilns; it may have been the result of using ore-bearing rocks in the construction of these kilns. Or it may have been the result of deliberate experimentation or curiosity to see what happened if the annealing process was taken one step further. There may even have been attempts to decorate pottery by the application of powdered copper ores as with graphite. No direct evidence of metallurgy in the form of metal slag, or fragments in ovens, or smelted ingots of copper has yet been found at any Gumelniţa settlement. At a number of Gumelniţa settlements, however, small (c. 6 cm high), very thick-walled pots (Fig. 38) have been excavated in the house debris; it has been suggested that these were used as crucibles in the melting and casting process.[88] On the basis of the present evidence of the ovens in Gumelniţa houses, it is difficult to see how such high temperatures were achieved without the aid of an artificial draught. There is no evidence of the use of bellows in the form of holes in the surviving structure of the oven. On many settlements, however, there are long cylindrial clay objects (Fig. 38) perforated longitudinally, which have been interpreted as 'phalluses' and 'net- or loom-weights', but which may have acted as the *tuyères* of bellows. As yet there is no evidence to show whether the roofs of the kilns were pro-vided with a funnel to produce the necessary draught, as in the Cucuteni–Tripolye culture. If this had been the case, there would have been no need of bellows.

The most conclusive evidence of the development of melting and casting techniques in copper metallurgy is the analyses of the metal objects themselves. These analyses show that the molten metal was poured into a rough open mould (none of which have ever been found in the settlements). Perforations in the implements were pro-duced by means of charcoal cores.[89] After cooling, the more detailed shape of the implement was obtained by hammering and annealing, as with uncast smelted and native copper artefacts. Large objects, such as the earlier eneolithic perforated 'hammer-axes' (Fig. 38) and 'chisels' (Fig. 38) and later eneolithic perforated 'axe-adzes' (Fig. 38) of south-east and central Europe were made in this way. Proto-types of at least the perforated copper axes occurred in earlier and contemporary assemblages of S.E. Europe in the perforated antler 'picks' and 'axes' and perforated polished stone hammer-axes. Although, even after cold hammering, the copper axes are unlikely to have been as durable as their stone equivalents, they would un-doubtedly have been superior to these in sharpness and suitability for such purposes as delicate wood-working. Thus there is the para-doxical situation of the widespread distribution of cast copper objects and their prototypes in the Gumelniţa, Vinča–Pločnik, Salcuţa, Cucuteni A–Tripolye B1, Tiszapolger, and Lengyel assemblages (Fig. 37), and yet the evidence of the required techniques of firing comes only from the Gumelniţa culture.[90] The only explanation of the paradox is that the cast copper objects were highly exchangeable commodities and that they were diffused to the other eneolithic cultures of central and south-east Europe by some means of ex-change, without a general diffusion of the techniques and equipment associated with melting and casting of copper. Further examination of the distribution of the cast copper objects would seem to support this hypothesis.

The cast copper objects of the Gumelniţa, Salcuţa, Vinča–Pločnik and Cucuteni–Tripolye cultures (Fig. 33) were found almost exclusively in the occupation debris of settlements. Their frequency and quantity was greatest in the settlements of the Gumelniţa culture. In the Vinča–Pločnik and Salcuţa cultures, cast copper objects were rare except for the collection from Pločnik itself. They were also rare in the Cucuteni–Tripolye culture where they were frequently associated with other intrusive features such as pressure-flaked chipped stone arrowheads made of the honey-coloured flint from the Dobrogea, large hollow figurines and *Spondylus* shells.[91]

An exceptional find was made at Karbuna (Moldavia SSR) not far from the Gumelniţa settlement of Vulcaneşti.[92] There a large pot decorated in late Tripolye A–early Tripolye B1 incised style was excavated with a smaller pot resting on top of it as a lid (Fig. 38). The large pot contained 443 objects manufactured in copper and a large number of objects made in other materials. The collection included one perforated cast copper 'hammer-axe' of the type found in the Gumelniţa culture, one cast copper narrow 'chisel', two heavy metal plaques (similar to one from the Tripolye B1 level at Novi Ruseşti not far away) which were probably cast, and a large number of hammered and annealed copper objects, such as bossed copper discs (similar to one from the late Cucuteni A settlement of Hăbăşeşti), spiral armbands, and a large number of copper heads. These hammered copper objects were similar to those found in graves of the Tiszapolgar and Bodrogkeresztur (Jordanowa group) graves but were very rarely found further south. In addition, there were two polished stone perforated hammer-axes, one of which was made of white marble, and beads of animal teeth, bone and *Spondylus* shells. Apart from the axes and chisel which may be regarded as valuable or 'novelties' because of the rarity of their raw material, the objects in this collection are all what is termed 'non-productive'. Various theories have been put forward to explain the presence of this extraordinary and unique collection. It cannot be simply a 'founder's hoard' because it contained other materials. It has been suggested that it was the collection of an itinerant trader since many of the objects could have originated in the lower Danube and have been on their way to more northern sites, but there is no evidence in the eneolithic settlements of eastern Europe to indicate that objects were distributed and diffused in such a way through the medium of any long-distance trader. It is much more likely that diffusion of this type was through a series of short-distance indirect exchanges.[93] There is a possible explanation that the collection was the equipment of a shaman-like personage, comprising a large number of objects which could have been applied to or suspended from a textile garment, as on modern Siberian shamans' costumes.

In temperate central Europe, in particular in the Tiszapolgar culture (Fig. 33), cast copper objects occur almost exclusively in graves. For example, almost every grave at Tibava contained either a perforated cast copper or polished stone hammer-axe; whereas in south-east Europe no copper objects larger than beads occur in any graves on eneolithic sites. It would seem, therefore, that in central Europe copper objects had a rather different significance and function from those of S.E. Europe. There is no evidence of the diffusion of any other commodity from the lower Danube area to temperate central Europe, apart from *Spondylus* shells (which also occur exclusively in graves). There is no evidence of local working of copper in central Europe although it has been claimed that the copper oxide ores of the Slovak Ore mountains were being exploited at this time.

In the subsequent Bodrogkeresztur culture there is evidence of the local working of smelted ingots, although the presence of ingots in E. Hungary does not necessarily indicate the local reduction of metal from ores.[94] In addition in the Late Lengyel culture (Balaton group) of west Hungary, clay crucibles have been found. The characteristic copper axe-adzes, which were made by the same techniques as the earlier hammer-axes, occur especially in the area of the Bodrogkeresztur culture, but by no means exclusively in this region. They occur sporadically in the area of the Cucuteni AB–Tripolye B2 culture, the Salcuţa culture, and in Yugoslavia, even on the Adriatic coast. They were very rare, however, in settlements of the later Gumelniţa culture. It seems possible therefore that in this period there was local casting of copper in the eastern part of temperate central Europe, and the cast objects may possibly have included the perforated axe-adzes.

Compared with artefacts made of other materials, those made of copper, whether of native metal or ores, whether beaten or cast, are very small in number and are unlikely to have made any significant difference in the economy of the late neolithic and eneolithic cultures of eastern Europe. It is possible that they made more of a social impact. Metallurgical activities, including casting, were presumably carried out on a small scale and it is unlikely that there were any specialists engaged full-time as metal-smiths on the settlements. If there were any specialist skilled craftsmen at all, they would probably have combined the roles of potter and metal-smelter and/or caster.[95] There is in fact no evidence in eastern Europe at this time, in the form of a concentration of kilns or pots, to indicate that any settlement employed a specialist potter. Possible exceptions to this include a house at Karanovo in which 100 pots, were excavated and the house at Kolomiiščina in which three ovens were found in one room (p.163). In general, in the Gumelniţa houses, all the ovens were equally large and solid. Presumably at this early stage in the development of skilled potting and metallurgy, there was no special house or social status for the smith or potter, and the metal objects were produced only on demand. The ore could have been supplied by the customer, the village or the smith himself.

The end of the Copper Age

It is not expected that the year 3000 B.C. will be taken seriously as an actual year in which all the settlements and cultural phenomena discussed in this chapter suddenly ceased and disappeared. But it is interesting to note that throughout Europe, especially eastern and central, in the first half of the third millenium B.C. (according to radiocarbon dates) profound environmental and cultural changes took place.

In northern Europe, the cultural changes reflected in the development of the Funnel–Beaker cultures and the diffusion of agricultural techniques and a food-producing economy are associated with environmental changes reflected in the transition from Vegetation Zone VII (VIIa—Atlantic) to Zone VIII (VIIb—Sub-Boreal), in which there was a decrease in certain arboreal species, such as elm, and an increase in certain plants, especially grasses, which favour a drier environment. It is still under discussion whether these vegetational changes were the result of climatic changes, or whether they represent the adjustment of the vegetation to changes in other parts of the eco-system, possibly the activities of Man. Whatever the cause, however, the vegetational changes would seriously have affected the available floral and faunal resources for raw materials and food supply of the prehistoric communities.

Further south and east, with the lack of pollen analyses, it is difficult to distinguish corresponding vegetational changes to those in northern Europe. There is evidence, however, on the east Hungarian plain, of an increase in steppe grassland and open parkland conditions.[96] In addition, a very important change is observable in the means of subsistence of the settlements of this period (Baden, Ezero, Cernavoda and late Tripolye cultures) in the increasing exploitation of domesticated sheep and the first evidence of the exploitation of the domesticated horse in this area.[97] This was associated with the earliest occurrence in Europe of wheels and evidence of wheeled vehicles (it should be remembered, however, that these were not necessarily drawn by horses), a phenomenon which must have revolutionised the transport of humans, animals and goods over land.[98] It has been suggested that the preference for the exploitation of these animals and the diffusion of the techniques and equipment of wheeled transport was the result of strong influences, if not invasion, from the steppes of the east Ukraine. It has been successfully shown by Piggott that the technology of wheeled vehicles was diffused from the Caucasus via the east Ukraine steppes, but it is difficult to prove any associated change of population. It is possible that the greater exploitation of sheep and horses was a cultural response of the local population to environmental changes of increasing grassland. It is equally possible that the economy based on the exploitation of these animals was diffused from the east Ukraine steppes, but without any 'invasion theory' being necessary.

The changes which took place in the agricultural settlements of central and south-east Europe in this period were not only economic. Changes in the settlement pattern also occurred, as is reflected in the abandonment of many of the eneolithic 'tells' of the lower Danube and Maritsa basins, although not, it is true, at Dipsisca and Karanovo, for example, where houses were constructed of the same materials and by the same method as before, if anything of increased size and solidity. There was, too, a general disappearance of clay artefacts which had long been manufactured in the agricultural settlements of south-east Europe—'stamp-seals', anthropomorphic and zoomorphic figurines, 'altars', etc.—as well as objects whose manufacture required firing at high temperatures—graphite painted pottery and artefacts of cast and smelted copper.

The fabric, forms and decoration of the pottery of the S.E. and C. European cultures of the Late Copper Age–Early Bronze Age also reflect a complete change. Painted pottery generally disappeared, and plain grey ware predominated. Earlier in this chapter (p. 176) we saw how pottery identical to that of the E. Ukraine steppes occurred with increasing frequency in the Tripolye culture. In the late Tripolye culture, this type of pottery became one of the characteristic features of the assemblage, but again this need not be associated with any invasion or intrusion of a 'steppe' population. It is interesting to note that in the late Tripolye settlements alone in S.E. Europe, the technique of painting pottery before firing survived alongside the coarse shell-tempered ware. In addition, in the late Tripolye culture alone in this period, the techniques of smelting and casting copper were preserved. The copper used, however, and the forms into which it was manufactured, were not of Carpathian origin, but came predominantly from the Caucasus.[99] Figurines also continued to be manufactured in the late Tripolye culture, long after they had disappeared in the rest of S.E. Europe.

What caused the change of settlement pattern and pottery types, the disappearance both of features long associated with the agricultural settlements of S.E. Europe and of the techniques of metallurgy and high-temperature firing of pottery, is still very obscure and would demand another book.

1. For a general discussion of the cultural development and chronological evidence in S.E. and C. Europe in this period see Ch. 3, n. 1; also see: Berciu, D. (1961a); id. (1961b); id. (1961c); id. (1967); Childe, V. G. (1929); id. (1956); Georgiev, G. (1961); id. (1969); Garašanin, M., 'Khronologiya i genezis na neolita v centralnata i yugoistočnata čast na Balkanskiya poluostrov', *Arkheologiya,* VIII: 1, Sofia (1966), 16–30; Milojčić, V. (1949a); Piggott, S. (1960); Vajsova, H. (1969).
2. Maritsa culture: Georgiev, G. (1961), 71–86; id. (1969); Vajsova, H. (1969). Boian culture: Berciu, D. (1961a), 363; id. (1961c), 112–14; Comşa, E. (1957). Vădastra culture: Berciu, D. (1961a), 155; id. (1961c), 109–12; Mateescu, C., 'Fouilles archéologique de la Vădastra', *Materiale,* V (1959), 189–201. Pre-Cucuteni I–II culture: Alexandrescu, A., 'O vtoroi faze dokukutenskoi kulturi', *Dacia,* V (1961), 21–37; Dumitrescu, H., 'Contribuţii la problema originii culturii Precucuteni', *SCIV,* VIII (1957), 53–73; Dumitrescu, V. (1967a); Marinescu-Bîlcu, S., 'Unele probleme ale neoliticului Moldovenesc în lumina săpăturilor de la Tîrpeşti, *SCIV,* XIX: 3 (1968), 395–422; id., 'Quelques aspects du problème de l'apport de la céramique rubanée à la formation de la civilisation Precucuteni I', *Alba Regia,* Szekesfehervar (in press); Passek, T. S. (1961b); Zaharia, E., 'Angaben über die Boian-Giuleşti Kultur; die Siedlung von Leţ', *Dacia,* XI (1967), 5–38; Comşa, E., 'Cultura Boian în Transilvania', *SCIV,* XVI: 4 (1965), 629–45.
3. Discussion of the Hamangia culture: Berciu, D. (1961a); id. (1967), 55–5; id. (1966); id., 'La civilisation neolithique "Hamangia" en Bulgarie', *Arkheologiya,* V: 1, Sofia (1963), 5–7.
4. Comşa, E., 'Über die Verbreitung und Herkunft einiger von den jungstein-zeitliche Menschen auf dem Gebiete Rumäniens vewendeten Werkstoffe', *A Mora F. Muz. Evk.,* Szeged (1967), 26–8; Păunescu, Al. (1970), 47–8.
5. For a discussion of the method of burial in the late neolithic and eneolithic cultures of the Danube Basin and S. E. Europe: Comşa, E., 'Contribuţie cu privire la riturile funerare din epoca Neolitică de pe Teritoriul ţării noastre', *Omagiu lui C. Daicoviciu,* Bucharest (1960), 87–99; Dumitrescu, H., 'Découvertes concernant un rite funéraire magique dans l'aire de la civilisation de la céramique peinte du type Cucuteni–Tripolye', *Dacia, NS,* I (1957), 97–116; Movša, T. G., 'K voprosu o Tripolskikh pogrebeniyakh s obryadom prutopoloženiya', *MIA YuZSSSR & RNR,* Kišinev (1960), 59–76.
6. e.g. at Vilnyi, Nikolski and Mariupol, belonging to the Dnieper–Donetz culture: Sulimirski, T. (1970), 113–16; Telegin, D. Ja. (1968), 175–90; id. (1969); Gimbutas, M. (1956), 46–51.
7. Cantacuzino, G., & Morintz, S., 'Die jungsteinzeitliche Funde in Cernica'. *Dacia,* VII (1963), 27–89.
8. Berciu, D. (1960); id. (1961a), 507; id. (1967), pls. 4–5.
9. The first, from Tîrpeşti, in N.E. Rumania, dates to the contemporary Pre-Cucuteni III culture: Marinescu-Bîlcu, S., 'Reflets des raports entre les civilisation de Hamangia et de Precucuteni dans la plastique precucutenienne de Tîrpeşti', *Dacia,* VIII (1964), 307–12). The second is from Vulcaneşti in S.W. USSR and is dated slightly later, to an early phase of the Gumelniţa

208 Hunters, Fishers and Farmers of Eastern Europe

culture (Passek, T. S., & Gerasimov, M. M., 'Novaya statuetka iz Vulcaneşti', *KSIA*, 111, 1967, 38–42); fragments of a similar figurine were also possibly found in the Proto-Cucuteni layer at Novi Ruseşti, north of Vulcaneşti (Markyevič, V. I., 'Mnogosloyinoye poselenite Noviye Ruseşti I', *KSIA*, 123 1970, fig. 15:3). For a general discussion of 'penseur' figurines see: Marinescu-Bîlcu, S., 'Die Bedeutung einiger Gesten und Haltungen in der jungstein-zeitlichen Skulptur der ausskarpatischen Gebiete Rumäniens', *Dacia*, XI (1967), 47–58.

10. A possible workshop of articles of *Spondylus* shell was found at the site of Hîrşova, nr. Constanţa: Galbenu, D., 'Neolitičeskaya masterskaya dlya obrabotki ukrašenii v Hîrşove', *Dacia*, VII (1963), 501–9. For a discussion of Aegean versus Black Sea sources of *Spondylus* see: Shackleton, N., & Renfrew C., 'Neolithic trade-routes re-aligned by oxygen-isotope analyses', *Nature*, 228; 5270 (1970), 1062–4.

11. General discussion of the Gumelniţa culture: Berciu, D. (1961a), 363; id. (1961c), 115–19; id., 'Arkheologičeskiye otkritiya v Banjata mogile v svete Rumunskikh issledovanii', *Dacia*, III (1959), 553–9; Dumitrescu, V. (1966); Gaul., J. (1948); Georgiev, G. (1961), 73–86; id. (1969); Vajsova, H. (1969); Passek, T. S., & Černyš, E. K., 'Otkritiye kulturi Gumelnitsi na territorii SSSR', *KSIA*, 100 (1965), 6–18.

12. e.g. Bikovo, S. Bulgaria: Detev, P., 'Selištnata mogila pri s. Bikovo', *Godištnik na Muzeite v Plovdivski okrug*, I, Plovdiv (1954), 151–94; Banjata, S. Bulgaria: Detev, P., 'Selištnata mogila Banjata pri Kapitan Dimitrievo', *God. Nar. Arkh. Muz.*, II, Plovdiv (1950), 1–25.

13. Analyses of animal bone material have been carried out at Tangîru, Gumelniţa, Bikovo and Ezero: Necrasov, O., & Haimovici, S., 'Etude de la faune de la station néolithique de Tangîru', *Dacia*, III (1959), 111; id., 'Studiul restorilor de faună neolitică descoperite în staţiunea Gumelniţa', *SCIV*, XVII: 1 (1966), 101–8; Georgiev, G., & Merpert, N. Ja., 'Raskopki mnogosloyinovo poseleniya u sela Ezero', *IAI*, XXVIII (1965), 129–59.

14. e.g. Vulcaneşti and Bolgrad: Tsalkin, V. I., 'Fauna iz raskopok poselenii kulturi Gumelnitsi v SSSR', *KSIA*, 111 (1967), 43–9; Tringham, R. (1969), 388.

15. e.g. Cascioărele, on an island in the Danube: Dumitrescu, V. (1965); Russe, on the south bank of the Danube: Georgiev, G., & Angelov, N., 'Razkopki na selištnata mogila do Russe prez 1948–9 god', *IAI*, XVIII (1952), 119–94; id., 'Razkopki na selištnata mogila do Russe prez 1950–3 god', *IAI*, XXI, (1957), 112–21.

16. General discussion of the chipped stone implements of the Gumelniţa culture, including arrowheads: Comşa, E., op. cit. (1967); Georgiev, G., 'Za nyakoi orudiya za proizvodstvo ot neolita i eneolita v Bulgaria', *Studia in Honorem D. Dečev*, Sofia (1958), 369–87; Păunescu, Al. (1970), 49–52.

17. e.g. Spanţov, Vidra and Radovanu, S.E. Rumania: Comşa, E., 'Quelques données nouvelles sur la phase de transition de la civilisation de Boian à celle de Gumelniţa', *Štud. Zvesti*, 17 (1969), 75–6, fig.1; Florescu, A., 'Befestigungsanlagen der Spätneolithischen in Donau-Karpatenraum', *Štud. Zvesti*, 17 (1969), 121–3; Morintz, S., 'Tipuri de aşezării şi sisteme de forti-ficaţie şi de împrejumire în cultura Gumelniţa', *SCIV*, XIII: 2 (1962), 273–84; id., 'Oaşezare Boian fortificaţii', *SCIV*, XIV: 2 (1963), 275. Evidence of a possible surrounding wooden fence has been found at Azmak, S. Bulgaria (Georgiev, G., 1969) and Russe, N. Bulgaria (Georgiev, G., & Angelov, B., op. cit. (1957), 15–16.

18. Frierman, J., 'The Balkan graphite ware' in Renfrew, C. (1970a), 42–3.

19. Discussion of the anthropomorphic clay figurines of the Gumelniţa and

Boian cultures: Dumitrescu, V. (1932–3); id. (1964a); Höckmann, O. (1968); Jovanović, B. (1964); Mikov, V., 'Plastičnite figuri na neolita v Bulgaria', *IAI*, VIII (1934–5); Neustupny, J., 'Studie o eneoliticke plastice', *Sbornik NM*, X: 1–2, Prague (1956); Popov, R., 'Idoli i životinski figuri na predistoričeskata mogila pri Kodža–Dermen', *IAD*, II, Sofia (1911), 70–80; Rosetti, D., 'Steinkupferzeitliche Plastik aus einen Wohnhügel bei Bukarest', *IPEK*, XII (1938), 29–50.

20. e.g. from Azmak and Hissarlik, S. Bulgaria: Georgiev, G. (1965).

21. Angelov, N., 'Atelier d'idoles plates en os dans le tell près du village Khotnica', *Arkheologiya*, III: 2, Sofia (1961); Petkov, N., 'Klasifikacija na plastike kostni idoli v Balkano-dunavskata oblast', *God. Nar. Arkh. Mus.*, II, Plovdiv (1950); Dumitrescu, V., 'La plastique anthropomorphe en os du sud-est de l'Europe pendant la periode eneolithique', *Revue Internationale des Etudes Balcaniques*, III (1937–8), 374–5.

22. e.g. Azmak, Karanovo and Hissarlik.

23. There is a clay copy from Blagoyevo. Copies in gold leaf occur at Kašla depe, Pazardžik, Khaskovo and possibly Khotnica. For a discussion of the occurrence of pendants of gold leaf and the use of gold in the eneolithic settlements of central and south-east Europe see: Angelov, N., 'Zlatnoto sukrovište ot Khotnica', *Arkheologiya*, I: 1–2, Sofia (1959), 38–46; Dumitrescu, H., 'Connections between the Cucuteni–Tripolye cultural complex and the neighbouring eneolithic cultures in the light of the utilisation of golden pendants', *Dacia*, V (1961), 69–95; Gazdapusztai, Gy., 'The copper age golden treasure at Hencida', *A Deri Muzeum Evkönye*, Debrecen (1968), 33–52; Kutzian, I. B. (1963), 483–4; Patay, P., 'Kupferzeitliche Goldfunde', *Arch. Ert.* 85 (1958), 37–45.

24. For a discussion of the synchronisation of the Cucuteni–Tripolye culture with the Gumelnița culture see: Berciu, D. (1961a); id. (1961c); Dumitrescu, V. (1964b); id. (1969); Nestor, I., 'Zur periodisierung der späteren Zeitstufen des Neolithikums in der Rumänischen Volksrepublik', *Dacia*, IV (1960), 53–68; Roman, P., 'Ceramica precucuteniană din aria culturilor Boian-Gumelnița și semnificata ei', *SCIV*, XIV: 1 (1963), 33–50.

25. For general discussion of the late neolithic and eneolithic cultural sequence in N.E. Rumania, Moldavia SSR and Ukraine SSR see: Dumitrescu, V. (1959); Gimbutas, M. (1956), 99–110; id. (1965), 462–3; Briussov, A. (1957), 266–86; Passek, T. S., 'La Ceramique Tripolienne', *Izvestia Gosudarstvenni Akademii Materialnoi Kultury*, 122, Leningrad (1935); id. (1949); id. (1961a); id. (1961b); id. (1962); Sulimirski, T. (1970), 66–74, 108–9 Stratified sites include: S.E. Transilvania (C. Rumania)—Leț (Zaharia., E., op. cit. 1967; Nestor, I., 'Raport asupra sondajelor de la Leț–Varhegy', *Materiale*, III, 1957); Prut valley (N.E. Rumania)—Izvoare (Vulpe, R. 1957), Cucuteni (Petrescu–Dîmbovița, M., 1966; Schmidt, H., 1932), Tîrpești (Marinescu–Bîlcu, S., 'Sondajul de la Tîrpești', *Materiale*, VIII, 1962, 235), Traian (Dealul Fîntînilor) (Dumitrescu, V., 'Traian', *Dacia OS*, IX–X, 1941–4); Dniester valley (Moldavia SSR)—Polivanov–Yar (Passek, T. S., 1961a, 105–39); Nezviska (Černyš, E. K., 'K istorii naseleniya eneoličeskovo vremeni v srednem Pridnestrovye', *MIA*, 102, 1962, 5–85); Novi Rusești (Markyevič, V. I., op. cit., 1970).

26. See n. 2 above for Pre-Cucuteni I–II culture. For Dniester valley sites, e.g. Florești, see: Passek, T. S. (1961a), 192–203; id. 'Noviye otkritiya na territorii SSSR i voprosi pozdneneoličeskikh kultur Dunaisko–Dnestrovskovo meždurečya', *SA*, 1 (1958), 28–46.

27. Danilenko, V. N. (1969), 121–47; Markyevič, V. I., 'Issledovaniya neolita na Srednem Dnestre', *KSIA*, 105 (1965), 85–90; id., *Neolit Moldavii*, unpublished

O

210 Hunters, Fishers and Farmers of Eastern Europe

thesis for the degree of Kandidat Istoričeskikh Nauk in the Inst. of Archaeology, ANSSSR, in Moscow (1968); Passek, T. S. (1962); Sulimirski, T. (1970), 66. The Savran phase of the Bug–Dniester culture has been dated by Carbon 14 from a sample from the site of Soroki (Trifautski les 5), 4545 ± 100 B.C., Bln 589: Quitta, H., & Kohl, G., 'Neue Radiocarbondaten zum Neolithikum und zur frühen Bronzezeit Südost-europas und der Sowjetunion', Zeitschr. für Arch., 3, Berlin (1969), 250.

28. Analyses of animal bone material from lowland sites (Bernova Luka, Solončene and Sabatinovka II) and upland sites (Luka Vrublevetskaya, and Lenkovtse): Bibikov, S. N. (1953), 170–92; Bibikova, V. I., 'Iz istorii golocenovoi fauni pozvonočnikh v Vostočnoi Evrope', Prirodnaya Obstanovka i Fauna Prošlovo, I, Kiev (1963), 122; Černyš, E. K., Rannotripilske poselennya Lenkivtse na serednomu Dnistri, Kiev (1959); Passek, T. S. (1961a), 31–100; Tringham, R. (1969), 388.

29. Bibikov, S. N. (1953), 204–75.

30. Bibikov, S. N. (1953), 78–91; Černyš, E. K., 'Tripolskiye masterskiye po obrabotke kremnya', KSIA, 111 (1967), 60–6; Păunescu, Al. (1970), 53–5; Semeonov, S. A. (1964).

31. Copper artefacts in Pre-Cucuteni II sites occur e.g. at Izvoare and Floreşti. Copper awls and fish-hooks occur in early Tripolye sites, e.g. at Bernovo Luka and Solončene: Rendina, N. V., 'K voprosu o tekhnike obrabotki Tripolskovo metalla', MIA, 84 (1961), 204–9.

32. e.g. Frumuşica, E. Rumania: Mataşa, C., Frumuşica, Bucharest (1941); Stoicani, E. Rumania: Dumitrescu, V., 'Cetăţuia dela Stoicani', Materiale, I (1953), 13–15; Novi Ruseşti, S. Moldavia SSR: Markyevič, V. I., op. cit. (1970), fig.13:10,16; Izvoare, Layer II: 1a, E. Rumania: Vulpe, R. (1957).

33. For a discussion of the Proto-Cucuteni–Proto-Gumelniţa assemblages and the problem of the transition from late neolithic to eneolithic in the lower Danube see: Comşa, E., 'K voprosu o perekhodnoi faze ot kulturi Boian k kulture Gumelniţa', Dacia, V (1961), 39–68; id., 'Unele probleme ale aspectului cultural Aldeni II', SCIV, XIV: 1 (1963), 7–32; id. (1969).

34. Galbenu, D., 'Aşezarea neolitica de la Hîrşova', SCIV, XIII: 2 (1962), 285–306.

35. e.g. Luka Vrublevetskaya, Bernovo Luka and Solončene. At Novi Ruseşti, however, painted pottery, copper artefacts and a large hollow clay figurine were associated: Markyevič, V. I., op. cit. (1970), figs.12–14.

36. The problem of the origin of Ariuşd painted ware and painted pottery in Transilvania has been discussed in: Dumitrescu, H., 'Cîteva probleme legate de cultura Petreşti', SCIV, XVII: 3 (1966), 433–4; Dumitrescu, V. (1958a); Berciu, D. (1967), 64; Laszlo, F., 'Les types de vases peints d'Ariuşd', Dacia OS, I (1924), 1–27; Passek, T. S. (1949), 42–3; Paul, I., 'Der Forschungsstand über die Petreşti Kultur', Štud. Zvesti, 17 (1969), 325–44; Roska, M., 'La Stratigraphie du Néolithique en Transilvanie', Dolg. Szeged, XII (1936), 26–51; Vlassa, N. (1963); id., 'Einige Bemerkungen zu Fragen des Neolithikums in Siebenburgen', Štud. Zvesti, 17 (1969), 513–40; Schroller, H. (1933); Tringham, R. (1966), Pt. IV: 1.

37. e.g. Ariuşd, Tîrpeşti, Truşeşti, Hăbăşeşti, and Polivanov-Yar. For a discussion of 'defence' barriers see: Dumitrescu, V. (1967b), 43–5; Florescu, A., 'Sistemul de Fortificare al Aşezărilor Cucuteniene din Moldova', Arch. Mold., IV (1966), 23–37; id., op. cit. (1969), 112–21; Passek, T. S. (1961), 133; Tringham, R. (1971).

38. Animal bone analyses from Traian (Dealul Fîntînilor), Novi Ruseşti, Sabatinovka I and Polivanov Yar: Necrasov, O., & Haimovici, S., 'Studiul resturilor de Fauna descoperite în 1959 la Traian', Materiale, VIII (1962), 261–5; Bibikova, V. I., op. cit (1963), 122; Passek, T. S. (1961a), 98–9, 138–9;

David, A. I., & Markyevič, V. I., 'Fauna mlekopitayuščikh poseleniya Noviye Rusešti I,' *Izvestia Akademia Nauk Mold. SSR.*, IV, Kišinev (1967), 3–26; Pidopličko, I. G., *Materiale do Vivčeniya minulikh faun URSR*, Kiev (1956), 77–8; Tringham, R. (1969), 388.

39. e.g. Frumuşica: Mataşa, C., op. cit. (1941); Cucuteni (Băiceni): Petrescu-Dîmboviţa, M. (1966); Novi Rusešti: Markyevič, V. I., op. cit. (1970) and David, A. I., & Markyevič, V. I., op. cit. (1967).

40. Movša, T. G., 'O svyazakh plemen Tripolskoi kulturi so stepimi plemennami Mednovo Veka', *SA*, 2 (1961), 186–99; Gimbutas, M. (1965), 470; Sulimirski, T. (1970), 108.

41. Makarenko, N., 'Sculpture de la civilisation Trypilienne en Ukraine', *IPEK* (1927), 119–29; Movša, T. G., 'Ob antropomorfnoi plastike Tripolskoi kulturi', *SA*, 2 (1969), 15–34.

42. e.g. from Hăbăşeşti: Dumitrescu, V. (1967b), fig. 51, and Karbuna: Klein, L. S., 'O date Karbunskovo klada', *Problemi Arkheologii*, I, Leningrad (1968), 5–74.

43. Popova, T. A., 'Zoomorfnaya plastika Tripolskovo poseleniya Polivanov Yar', *KSIA*, 123 (1970), 8–14.

44. e.g. Vladimirovka, Kolomiiščina and Taburišče: Passek, T. S. (1949), 54–108; Gimbutas, M. (1956), 102–3; Tringham, R. (1971).

45. Analyses of animal bone material from Vladimirovka, Kolomiiščina II and Khalepye: Bibikova, V., op. cit. (1963); Passek, T. S. (1961a), 98–9; Pidopličko, I. G., op. cit. (1956); Tringham, R. (1969); Bibikov, S. N., 'Khozaistvenno-ekonomičeskii kompleks razvitovo Tripolya', *SA*, 1 (1965), 48–62.

46. For a discussion of Tripolye houses with special reference to 'ploščadki' floors, see: Kričevskii, E. Ju., 'Tripolskiye ploščadki', *SA*, VI (1940), 20–45; Passek, T. S. (1949), 58–66; Paul, I., 'In legătura cu problem locuinţilor de suprăfaţa cu platforma din aşezările culturilor Petreşti si Cucuteni-Tripolye', *SCIV*, XVIII (1967), 3–24.

47. e.g. Vladimirovka and Popudnya: Passek, T. S. (1949), figs. 50:4, 54, 69.

48. For a more detailed description of the Salcuţa culture see: Berciu, D. (1961a), 155; id. (1961b); id. (1967), 58–60; Păunescu, Al. (1970), 52–3.

49. For a discussion of the relative chronology and cultural sequence of the Vinča–Pločnik culture see: Garašanin, M. (1951); id., 'Zur Zeitbestimmung des Beginns der Vinča–Kultur', *Arch. Iug.*, I (1954), 1–6; id., op. cit. (1966); id., 'Položaj centralnoi Balkana u khronologija jugoistočne Evrope', *Neolit Centralnog Balkana*, Belgrade (1968), 301–38; id. (1958); Jovanović, B., 'Stratigrafska podela Vinčanskog nasel', *Starinar*, 11 (1960), 9–19; id., 'Keramički tipovi Balkanskog neolita i eneolita', *Starinar*, 13–14 (1962–3), 14–18; id., 'Istoriat keramike industrije u neolitu i ranom eneolitu Centralnog Balkana', *Neolit Centralnog Balkana*, Belgrade (1968), 107–76; Grbić, M., 'Nalazišta Starčevačkog i Vinčanskog neolita u Srbiji i Makedoniji', *Neolit Centralnog Balkana*, Belgrade (1968), 63–76; Renfrew, C. (1969); Srejović, D., 'Versuch einer historischen Wertung der Vinča–Gruppe', *Arch. Iug.*, IV (1960), 5–19.

50. Glišić, J., 'Ekonomika i socialno-ekonomski odnosi u neolitu Podunavsko-pomoravskog basena', *Neolit Centralnog Balkana*, Belgrade (1968), 21–62; Srejović, D., & Jovanović, B., 'Pregled kamennoj orudja i oružje iz Vinče', *Arh. Vestnik*, 8 (1957), 256–96; id., 'Orudje i oružje od kosti i nakit iz Vinče', *Starinar*, 9–10 (1958–9), 181–90.

51. Stalio, B., 'Naselje i stan neolitskog perioda', *Neolit Centralnog Balkana*, Belgrade (1968), 77–88; Todorović, J., & Cermanović, A., *Banjica*, Belgrade (1961).

52. The material from Kormadin is unpublished in Zemun Museum. Similar

zoomorphic heads occur on the gable ends of house-models from earlier (Röszke–Körös culture) and contemporary (Cascioărele–Gumelniţa culture) settlements.

53. Galović, R. (1966); id. *Predionica*: *neolitsko naselje kod Priština*, Priština (1959); Höckmann, O. (1968); Jovanović, B. (1964); Letica, Z. (1964); Renfrew, C. (1969); Srejović, D., 'Neolitska plastika Centralnobalkanskog poručja', *Neolit Centralnog Balkana*, Belgrade (1968), 177–240; id. (1964–5).

54. For a more detailed description of the Butmir culture see: Benac, A., *Prehistorijsko naselje Nebo-Bila i Problem Butmirske Kulture*, Ljubljiana (1952); id., 'Grenzonne der Vinča-Kultur in Ostbosnien', *Arch. Iug.*, III (1959), 5–10; id., 'Die Entwicklungsphasen der Butmir–Kultur', *Štud. Zvesti*, 17 (1969), 19–30; id. (1961). A recent series of Radiocarbon dates from Obre give a range of *c*. 4200–3700 B.C. for early and middle phases of the Butmir culture: Quitta, H., & Kohl, G., op. cit. (1969), 236.

55. Benac, A. (1961); Novak, G., *Prethistorijski Hvar*, Zagreb (1955).

56. Garašanin, M. (1958); Grbić, M. (Ed.). *Porodin—kasno neolitsko naselje na tumbi kod Bitolja*, Bitolj (1960).

57. For a general discussion of the late neolithic and eneolithic cultures of the Great Hungarian plain see: Kalicz, N. (1970), 38–64; Kutzian, I. B. (1961); id. (1963); id. (1966a), 265–9; id. (1971); Kutzian, I. B., &. Banner, J. (1961); Milleker, F., 'Vorgeschichte des Banats', Pt. 5, *Starinar*, 14 (1939), 129–40; Milojčic, V. (1949a); Trogmayer, O., 'Beiträge zur Chronologie des Neolithikums auf dem Mitteltheissgebiet', *Štud. Zvesti*, 17 (1969), 467–80.

58. e.g. figurine from Szegvár–Tűzköves: Csalog, J., 'Die anthropomorphen Gefässe und Idolplastiken von Szegvár–Tűzköves', *Acta Arch. Hung.*, XI (1959), 7–38; id., 'Sur quelques problèmes de la plastique d'idoles', *Arch. Ert.*, 87 (1960), 188–94. For a discussion of the anthropomorphic pots from Kökénydomb see: Banner, J., 'Anthropomorphe Gefässe der Theisskultur von der Siedlung Kökénydomb bei Hódemzővásárhely', *Germania*, 37 (1959), 14–37; Kalicz, N. (1970), 40–1.

59. Unpublished in Szentes Museum. See also: Banner, J., 'La troisième période des fouilles au Kökénydomb', *Arch. Ert.*, 78 (1951), 27–36; Csalog, J., 'Das Wohnhaus "E" von Szegvár–Tűzköves und seine Funde', *Acta Arch. Hung.*, IX (1958), 95.

60. On the basis of the analysis of animal bones from Lebö: Bökönyi, S., 'Die Frühalluviale Wirtbeltierfauna Ungarns', *Acta Arch. Hung.*, XI (1959); id. (1971); id. (forthcoming).

61. Analysis of bone material from Berettyószentmárton and Herpály: Bökönyi, S. (1969), 223–4.

62. For a discussion of the origins of painted pottery in Transilvania, see n. 36 above. For evidence of connections between the east Hungarian plain and west Transilvania see: Vlassa, N., 'O contribuţie la problema legăturilor culturii Tisa cu alte culturi neolitice din Transilvania', *SCIV*, XII: 1 (1961), 17–23.

63. Lichardus, J., 'O periodizacji i chronologii kultury Bukowogorskiej', *Acta Arch. Carp.*, V (1963), 5–25; id., 'Beitrag zur chronologischen Stellung der rot und gelb inkrustierten Bükker keramik', *Štud. Zvesti*, 17 (1969), 219–32; Tompa, F. (1929).

64. e.g. Tibava: Šiska, S., 'Tiszapolgarska Kultura na Slovensku', *Slov. Arch.*, XVI: 1 (1968), 61–176); and Bodzaspart: Kutzian, I. B. (1971).

65. Kalicz, N., 'Copper Age stratigraphy in the outskirts of the village of Szekely', *Arch. Ert.*, 85 (1958), 3–5. The Copper Age sequence of east Hungary has also been based on the 'horizontal stratigraphy' of graves in cemeteries such as Tiszapolgár–Basatanya: Kutzian, I. B. (1963). The dangers of using such

a method of defining cultural sequence has been pointed out in: Ucko, P. (1969), 276–7.

66. For a more detailed description of the Bodrogkeresztur culture see n. 57 above and: Kutzian, I. B., 'Probleme der mittleren Kupferzeit im Karpatenbecken', *Štud. Zvesti*, 17 (1969), 31–60; Patay, P., 'Ornamente der Keramik der Ungarländischen kupferzeitlicher Bodrogkereszturer Kultur', *Swiatowit*, XXIII (1960), 363–87; Vlassa, N., 'Contribuţii la cunoaşterea culturii Bodrogkeresztur în Transilvania', *SCIV*, XV: 3 (1964), 351–67.
67. On the basis of analysis of the animal bone material from Tarnabod: Bökönyi, S. (forthcoming).
68. Zirra, V., 'Kultura pogrebenii s okhroi v Zakarpatskikh oblastyakh RNR', *MIA YuZ SSSR & RNR* (1960), 97–125 (see p. 97).
69. For a general discussion of the late neolithic and eneolithic settlements of the Pannonian plain and the development of the Lengyel culture see: Kalicz, N. (1969); id. (1970), 50–2; Kutzian, I. B. (1961); id. (1963); id. (1966a); id. (1966b); Ohrenberger, A., 'Die Lengyel-Kultur in Burgenland', *Štud. Zvesti*, 17 (1969), 301–14; Pavuk, J., 'Anteil des Želiezovce-Typus an der Genesis der Lengyel-Kultur', *Štud. Zvesti*, 17 (1969), 345–60; Palliardi, J., 'Die relative Chronologie der jüngeren Steinzeit in Mähren', *WPZ* (1914), 256–77; Točik, A., 'Erforschungsstand der Lengyel-Kultur in der Slowakei', *Štud. Zvesti*, 17 (1969), 437–54; Vildomec, F., 'O Moravske neoliticke keramice malovane', *Obzor Prehistoricky*, VIII, Praha (1929), 1–40; Tichý, R. (1961); Neustupny, E. & J. (1961), 53–8; Točik, A., and Lichardus, J., 'Staršia faza Slovensko-Moravskej Malovanej Keramiky na juhozapadnom Slovensku', *Pam. Arch.*, LVII (1966), 1–90.
70. For the problem of the relationship of the Lengyel and Vinča cultures and the possible genesis of the Lengyel culture in N.W. Yugoslavia see: Brukner, B., 'Zur Frage der territorialen Beziehungen der Vinča- und Lengyel-Grupper', *Štud. Zvesti*, 17 (1969), 61–72; Dimitrijević, S., *Sopotsko–Lendjelska Kultura*, Zagreb (1968); Dombai, J. (1960); Korošec, J., 'Lengyelska kulturna skupina v Bosni, Sremi i Slavoniji', *Arch. Věstnik*, VIII (1957), 179; Srejović, D., 'Danilo-Butmir-Lengyel', *Starinar*, XVIII (1968), 1–10; id., 'Die genetischen und chronologischen Beziehungen der Vinča- und der Lengyel-Gruppe', *Štud. Zvesti*, 17 (1969), 383–92.
71. Kalicz, N., 'Über die Probleme der Beziehungen der Theiss- und der Lengyel-Kultur', *Acta Arch. Hung.*, XXII (1970), 13–23; Palliardi, J., op. cit. (1914); Skutil, J. (1940); Vildomec, F., op. cit. (1929).
72. Antoniewicz, W., 'Le motif d'orant dans l'art neolithique', *Arch. Polski.*, XI (1969), 199–219; Niţu, A., 'Reprezentari umare pe ceramica Criş şi Liniara din Moldova', *SCIV*, XIX: 3 (1968), 387–93; Kutzian, I. B. (1947), 1.
73. The upper Dniester sites, e.g. Zimne, are unpublished in Lvov Museum. For Lengyel painted ware in S. Poland, e.g. Sandomierz, see: Kamienska, J., 'Frühe Entwicklungsphase der Lengyel-Kultur in Kleinpolen', *Štud. Zvesti*, 17 (1969), 207–18; Kozlowski, J., 'Proba klasyfikacji materialow zaliczanych do kultury Lengyelskiej i Nadcisanskiej w Polsce poludniowej', *Arch. Polski*, XI: 1 (1966), 7–27; Gimbutas, M. (1956), 116.
74. For a more detailed description of the Stroke-ornamented Ware culture see: Stekla, M., 'Třideni vypíchané keramiky', *Arch. Rozh.*, XI: 2, (1959) 207–57; id., 'Pohřby lidu s volutovou a vypíchanou keramikou', *Arch. Rozh.*, VIII: 5 (1956), 710–16 (graves); id. (Zapotocka, née Stekla, M.,) 'Die Stichbandkeramik zur Zeit des späten Lengyelhorizontes', *Štud. Zvesti*, 17 (1969), 541–74. Stroke-ornamented Ware in Poland, e.g. Zlota: Gimbutas, M. (1956), 116.
75. Soudsky, B. (1969), 64–93; id., 'Trapezförmige und absidale Bauten des

Spätlengyeler Horizontes der Stichbandkeramik', *Štud. Zvesti,* 17 (1969), 375–82.

76. For a more detailed description and discussion of the Jordanowa variant and its relationship with the early Funnel-Beaker culture of the N.W. European plain see: Bakker, J., Vogel, J., & Wislanski, T., 'TRB and other C14 dates from Poland', *Helinium,* IX (1969), 3–37, 209–38; Driehaus, J., & Behrens, H. (1961), 257–62; Kowalczyk, J. (1961); Gabalowna, L., *Ze studiow nad grupa Brzesko–Kujawska kultury Lendželskiej,* Lodz (1966); Gimbutas, M. (1956), 118–22; Neustupny, E., & J. (1961), 59–67; Novotny, B., 'Jordanovska skupina a jihovychodni vlivy v českem neolitu', *Obzor Prehistoricky,* XIV: 1, Prague (1950), 163–260; Neustupny, E., 'Der Übergang vom Neolithikum zum Äneolithikum und der Ausklang der Lengyel Kultur', *Štud. Zvesti,* 17 (1969), 271–92.

77. e.g. Bylany (fence): Soudsky, B. (1966), 70; Hluboke Mašůvky (ditch): Neustupny, E., & J. (1961), 54–5; Křepice (ditch): Tichý, R., 'Village fortifié néolithique à Křepice, près de Znojmo', *Investigations Archeologiques en Tschechoslovaquie,* Praha (1966); Tringham R. (1971).

78. See n. 76 above and Kostrzewski, J., 'Copper implements and ornaments found in Poland and East Germany', *Man,* XXIV (1924), 83–7.

79. Narva culture and exploitation of E. Baltic amber: Gurina, N. N., 'Drevnyaya istoriya severo-zapada Evropeiskoi časti SSSR', *MIA,* 87 (1961); Loze, I., 'Novi centr obrabotki yantarya epokhi neolita v vostočnoi pribaltike', *SA,* 3 (1969), 124–34. For the occurrence of copper in early TRB settlements see: Gimbutas, M. (1956), 118, 120.

80. For a discussion of the identification of copper sources and its validity see: Driehaus, J. (1955); Černikh, E. N., 'Istoriya drevneišei metallurgii Vostočnoi Evropi', *MIA,* 132 (1966); id., 'O drevneišeikh očagakh metalloobrabotki yugo-zapada SSSR', *KSIA,* 123 (1970), 23–41; Junghans, S., Sangmeister, E., & Schroder, M., 'Metallanalysen kupferzeitlicher Bodenfunde aus Europa', *Studien zu den Anfängen der Metallurgie,* I, Berlin (1960); Novotna, M., 'Medené nástroje a problem najstaršej ťažby medi na Slovensku', *Slov. Arch.,* III (1955), 70–98; Patay, P., Zimmer, K., Szabo, Z., & Sinay, G., 'Spektographische und metallographische Untersuchung kupfer- und frühbronzezeitlicher Funde', *Acta Arch. Hung.,* XV (1963), 37–64; Pittioni, R., 'Zweck und Ziel spektralanalytischer Untersuchungen für die Vorgeschichte des Kupferbergwesens', *Arch. Aust.,* XXVI (1959), 67–95; Rosenfeld, A. (1965), 133–8; Waterbolk, H., & Butler, J. (1965).

81. Rowlands, M. (1970).

82. Rendina, N. V., op. cit. (1961), 204.

83. Hodges, H., *Artifacts,* London (1964), 66–7; Rosenfeld, A. (1965), 147–51.

84. Černikh, E. N., op. cit. (1970); Rendina, N. V., op. cit. (1971), 206.

85. Rendina, N. V., op. cit. (1961), 206; id., 'Mednyi import epokhi razvitovo Tripolya' *KSIA,* 123 (1970), 15–22; Černikh, E. N., op. cit. (1970); Nestor, I., 'Sur les debuts de la métallurgie du cuivre et du bronze en Roumanie', *X-ème Congrès des Sciences Historiques à Rome,* Bucharest (1955).

86. Childe, V. G. (1956); Piggott, S. (1965), 73.

87. Renfrew, C. (1969b).

88. e.g. at Yasa Tepe, Azmak, Karanovo, Kazanlak and Russe: Detev, P., 'Razkopki na selištnata mogila Yasa Tepe v Plovdiv', *God. Nar. Arkh. Muz.,* IV (1960), 5–55; Georgiev, G., & Angelov, N., op. cit. (1952); Georgiev, G., 'Glavni rezultati ot razkopkite na Azmaškata selištna mogila', *IAI,* XXVI (1963), 157–76; id., op. cit. (1958).

89. Charles, J., 'Metallurgical examination of south-east European copper axes' in Renfrew, C. (1970a), 40–2.

90. For a discussion of the distribution of copper artefacts in the late neolithic and eneolithic settlements of central and south-east Europe see: Driehaus, J. (1955); Kutzian, I. B. (1963); id. (1971); Nestor, I., op. cit. (1955); Roska, M., 'Uber die Herkunft der kupfernen Hacken, Axthacken, Hammeräxte und Pickelhacken von ungarischen Typus', *Közlemenyek*, II, Cluj/Kolozsvar (1942), 15–77; Schubert, F. (1965).
91. Rendina, N. V., op. cit. (1970).
92. Klein, L. S., op. cit. (1968); Sulimirski, T. (1970), 71–2; Černikh, E. N., op. cit. (1970), 25; Sergeyev, G. P., 'Rannetripolskii klad u s. Karbuna', *SA*, 1 (1962–3), 135–51.
93. Rowlands, M. (1970).
94. Ingots from Tiszapolgár–Basatanya: Kutzian, I. B. (1963), 500. See also: Patay, P., 'Prispevky k spracuvarim kovov v dobĕ medenej na Slovensku', *Slov. Arch.*, VI (1958), 301–13; Novotna, M., op. cit. (1955); Roska, M., op. cit. (1942).
95. Rowlands, M. (1970).
96. Vadasz, E., 'Zur prähistorischen Siedlungs- und Klimageschichte des Bezirka von Kalocsa', *A Mora F. Muz. Evk.*, 2 (1969), 90.
97. Bökönyi, S. (1969), 227; id. (in press).
98. Piggott, S. (1965), 92–6; id., 'The Earliest Wheeled Vehicles and the Caucasian evidence', *PPS*, XXXIV (1968), 266–318.
99. Černikh, E. N., op. cit. (1966); id., op. cit. (1970).

CONCLUSION

The evidence available to an ethnographer is complete, for it can give information about the sum total of the activities of a human social group, whereas that available to a prehistorian reflects only a very small part of these activities. But the advantage which the prehistorian has over an ethnographer is that his evidence covers a much broader time-scale, involving in some cases many thousands of years. Thus, this prehistoric evidence can indicate, over a much longer period of time than is ever available to ethnographers, the gradual processes of technological, economic and even social change as a result of the diffusion, rejection, acceptance and adoption of innovations. It is unfortunate that at present the methods used by prehistorians are subtle enough to distinguish only the end rather than the beginning of these processes.

The evidence of some of these processes has been set out in this book by showing the diffusion of certain techniques and equipment over an area of c. 1,400,000 km² during a period of 3,000 years, their acceptance in certain places and periods and their rejection in others. Thus, it is possible to see that in the period c. 5500–4000 B.C. (Carbon 14 years) the techniques of agriculture and stockbreeding and a food-production economy were diffused from the Near East throughout the Danube Basin probably as a result of the expansion of an actual population. From there, the spread of these agricultural techniques, along with those of pottery manufacture, was furthered by the indigenous hunters and gatherers of, for example, Moldavia, the Adriatic and Black Sea coasts and the N. European plain, who partially accepted the new techniques and partially absorbed the culture of the expanding agricultural population. In the period *c.* 4000–3000 B.C. (Carbon 14 years), the techniques and equipment associated with firing pottery at high temperatures and with copper metallurgy were diffused, though over a much smaller area than agriculture and not associated with any population movements.

The acceptance or rejection of these and other techniques was dependent on various factors: firstly, the availability of a suitable environment (in the case of agriculture) or necessary raw materials (in the case of metallurgy), which would make the large-scale adoption of the new technique feasible; secondly, the necessary level of technological skill and economy to be able to exploit the new technique and recognise its potential; thirdly, a need for the new technique, means of subsistence or piece of equipment. Even with these qualifications, however, an innovation will not necessarily be adopted if it is culturally or socially acceptable. Conversely, even though the environment, level of technological skill or economy should logically prevent the acceptance of a particular innovation, a society may still choose, illogically, to adopt it.

The preceding chapters have shown that both the diffusion of agricultural techniques and the tradition of manufacturing painted pottery and clay objects, with which early agriculture was associated in south-east Europe, were absent in the material culture of the early agriculturalists of temperate central Europe. It is possible that suitable clay and firing techniques for the manufacture of painted pottery were not available or were forgotten in the northwards spread of the early agricultural population. Figurines, however, could have been made with the available clay and techniques; the fact that they are absent is very likely the result of cultural rejection, the cause of which is very difficult to reconstruct. In Moldavia, it is clear that the hunters and fishermen of the Dniester river valley (Bug–Dniester culture) were in contact with an early agricultural population (Criş culture) of south-east European tradition, from whom they accepted the innovation of pottery manufacture in certain forms. On the basis of environmental, economic and technological factors, it would have been possible for them to accept in full the economic innovations of their neighbours in the Prut river valley, but they chose to adopt only some of the agricultural innovations and to retain most of their own hunting and fishing activities. Conversely, as the intrusive agricultural population spread northwards from south-east Europe to temperate central Europe, and the environment became cooler and more humid, it would have been economically more logical to depend more on the products of cattle-keeping rather than sheep-keeping; but the settlements of the Körös culture, to whom the techniques of cattle-keeping were available, chose to retain their basically sheep-keeping activities, even though these must have dislocated their economy.

In the later period (c. 4000–3000 B.C.) a similar pattern of logical and illogical choice is evident in the diffusion of the techniques of metallurgy and pottery fired at high temperatures. For example, it is logical that there should have been no large-scale metallurgical activities in the area of the Cucuteni–Tripolye culture in which there was almost no necessary raw material. On the other hand, in areas where the raw material, in this case copper ore, was available, for example the Austrian Alps, there were almost no early metallurgical activities, even though, on the basis of the eneolithic pottery (Lengyel) of E. Austria and W. Hungary, it would have been possible with the available techniques to smelt copper. It is possible either that the rich copper sources were unknown, or that the need for copper objects was not sufficient to stimulate their manufacture. It is unlikely, however, that the rich copper resources of the Bohemian Ore and Harz mountains could have been exploited with the available level of technological skill at this time, even if their presence had been known and even if there had been a need for metal objects. It is interesting to note, too, that in the more western areas—Hungary and E. Yugoslavia—to which cast copper objects were diffused (always assuming that metallurgical techniques were not locally evolved) there was no corresponding diffusion of the techniques of firing pottery at very high temperatures or of painting pottery before firing. Whether this may be interpreted as the result of lack of available raw material or fuel, or of cultural independence in retaining their undecorated pottery on the part of the Tiszapolgar and late Vinča–Pločnik cultures, or a complex preservation of the secrets of the technique on the part of the Gumelnţia culture, is still very much open to question.

The region discussed in this book may be broadly divided into two culture areas: south-east Europe and temperate central Europe. South-east Europe in many respects forms the northern edge of the Near Eastern culture area, for features characteristic of contemporary cultures in Greece and Anatolia were retained here. It may however be referred to as a culture area in its own right; its cultures do not blindly mimic those in the north and south but have clearly gone through a gradual process of cultural evolution to adopt or reject a long series of innovations. Between south-east Europe and temperate central Europe was a 'buffer' culture area comprising the East Hungarian plain and to a certain extent the more easterly regions of the Pannonian plain. Between south-east Europe and the steppes of shuth Russia was another 'buffer zone' which at the beginning of the period under discussion was located in Moldavia (Bug–Dniester culture), but by 3500 B.C. had gradually shifted towards the Dnieper river. During the whole period 5500–3000 B.C. these culture areas retained roughly the same boundaries.

Apart from the more dramatic diffusion of techniques and equipment from one area to another, mentioned above, the cultures within these areas evolved continuously by gradual or sudden processes of trial and error, by internal rather than external innovation, by the applications of certain techniques to different functions, by the manufacture of objects in different raw materials, by the gradual morphological change in the preferred shape of an object such as pottery and houses. Although some of these internal processes have been described in this book, it should be stressed that prehistoric evidence can never show more than the tip of the iceberg, and that the unobtainable knowledge of the processes of social change which accompanied those of technological and economic change and the reasons for the choice to adopt or reject new ideas and objects could alter our whole idea of prehistoric societies.

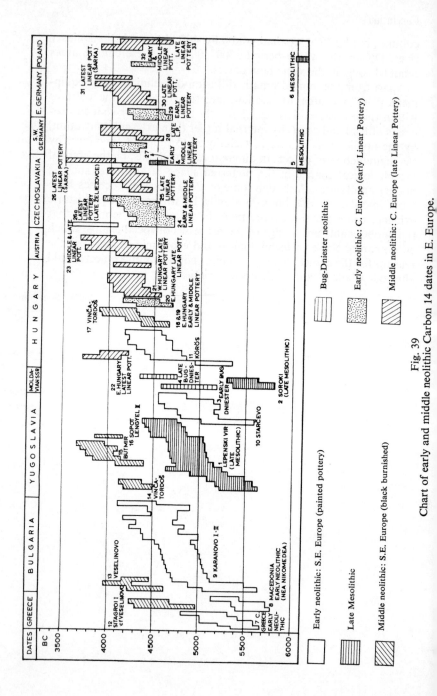

Fig. 39

Chart of early and middle neolithic Carbon 14 dates in E. Europe.

GENERAL BIBLIOGRAPHY

BANNER, J. (1942), *Das Tisza-Maros-Körös Gebiet*, Budapest.
——(1960), 'The Neolithic settlement on the Kremenyak Hill at Csoka', *Acta Arch. Hung.*, XII, 1–57.
——(1961),' Einige Probleme der ungarischen Neolithforschung', *Le Fin de l'Age de Pierre*, Prague, 205–20.
BANNER, J., & KUTZIAN, I. B. (1961), Beiträge zur Chronologie der Kupferzeit des Karpatenbeckens', *Acta. Arch. Hung.*, XIII, 1–32.
BATOVIČ, S. (1966), *Stariji Neolit u Dalmaciji* (early neolithic in Dalmatia), Zadar.
BEHM-BLANCKE, G. (1962–3), 'Bandkeramische Erntgeräte,' *Alt Thüringen*, 6, 105–74.
BENAC, A. (1961), 'Studien zur Stein- und Kupferzeit in nordwestlichen Balkan', *Ber. R.G.K.*, 7–170.
BERCIU, D. (1960a), 'Asupra Protoneoliticului Europei Sud-estice' (The Proto-neolithic of S. E. Europe), *Omagiu lui C. Daicoviciu*, Bucharest, 15–30.
——(1960b), 'Neolithic Figurines from Rumania', *Antiquity*, XXXIV, 283–4.
——(1961a), *Contribuţii la Problemele Neoliticului în Romînia în lumîna Noilor Cercetări* (Contributions to the Problem of the Neolithic in Rumania in the light of new research), Bucharest.
——(1961b), 'Les nouvelles fouilles de Salcuţa et le problème des groupes Bubanj et Krivodol', *Le Fin de l'Age de Pierre*, Prague, 125–35.
——(1961c), 'Chronologie relative de Néolithique du Bas Danube à la lumière des nouvelles fouilles faites en Roumanie', *Le Fin de l'Age de Pierre*, Prague, 101–24.
——(1966), *Cultura Hamangia*, Bucharest.
——(1967), *Rumania*, London.
BIBIKOV, S. N. (1953), 'Rannetripolskoye poseleniye Luka-Vrublevetskaya' (The early Tripolye settlement of Luka Vrublevetskaya), *MIA*, 38.
BÖKÖNYI, S. (1969) 'Archaeological problems and methods of recognising animal domestication', in UCKO, P., & DIMBLEBY, G. (Eds.), *The Domestication and Exploitation of Plants and Animals*, London, 219–30.
——(1970), 'Animal remains from Lepenski Vir', *Science*, 167, 1702–4.

P

——(1971), 'Zoological evidence for seasonal or permanent occupation of prehistoric settlements', in UCKO, P., TRINGHAM, R., & DIMBLEBY, G. (Eds.), *Settlement Patterns and Urbanization*, London.

——(in press). *The Historical Development of Animal-Keeping in Central and Eastern Europe*, Budapest.

BORDAZ, J. (1970), *Tools of the Old and New Stone Age*, New York.

BORONEANŢ, V. (in press), 'La période épipaleolithique sur la rive roumaine des Portes de Fer du Danube', *Prähist. Zeitschr.*

BRIUSSOV, A. (1957), *Geschichte der neolithischen Stämme im Europäischen Teil der USSR*, Berlin.

BRUKNER, B. (1968). *Neolit u Vojvodini* (Neolithic in Vojvodina), Belgrade.

BUTTLER, W. (1938), *Der Donauländische und der Westische Kultur Kreis*, Berlin.

BUTZER, K. (1965a), 'Physical Conditions in E. Europe, W. Asia and Egypt before the period of agricultural and urban settlement', *Cambridge Ancient History*, I.

——(1965b), *Environment and Archaeology*, London.

CHILDE, V. G. (1929), *The Danube in Prehistory*, London.

——(1949), 'Neolithic Houses—Types in Temperate Europe', *PPS*, XV, 77–86.

——(1957), *The Dawn of European Civilisation*, London.

CLARK, J. G. D. (1952), *Prehistoric Europe—the Economic Basis*, London.

——(1958), 'Blade and Trapeze Industries of the European Stone Age'. *PPS*, XXIV, 24–42.

——(1956). 'Radiocarbon dating and the expansion of farming culture from the Near East over Europe', *PPS*, XXI, 58–73.

——(1969), *The Stone Age Hunters*, London.

CLARKE, D. L. (1968), *Analytical Archaeology*, London.

COMŞA, E. (1957), 'Quelques données relatives à la periodisation et à l'evolution de la civilisation de Boian', *Dacia*, N.S., I., 61–73.

——(1959a), 'La civilisation Criş sur la territoire de la R.P. Roumanie', *Acta Arch. Carp.*, I, 173–84.

——(1959b), 'Betrachtungen über die Liniarbandkeramik auf dem Gebiet der Rumänischen Volksrepublik und der angrenzenden Länder', *Dacia*, N.S., III, 35–75.

DANILENKO, V. N. (1969), *Neolit Ukraini* (The Neolithic of the Ukraine), Kiev.

DIXON, J., CANN, J., & RENFREW, C. (1968), 'Obsidian and the Origins of Trade', *Scien. Amer.*, 218:3, 38–46.

DOMBAI, J. (1960). *Die Siedlung und das Gräberfeld in Zengővárkony*, Budapest.

DRIEHAUS, J. (1955), 'Zur Datierung und Herkunft donauländischer Axtypen der frühen Kupferzeit', *Archaeologica Geographica*, II: 3, Hamburg, 1–3.

DRIEHAUS, J., & BEHRENS, H. (1961), 'Stand und Angaben der Erforschung des Jungneolithikums in Mitteleuropa', *Le Fin de l'Age de Pierre*, Prague, 233–76.

DUMITRESCU, V. (1932–3), 'Anthropomorphic sculpture in clay of the eneolithic Balkano-Danubian culture of Gumelniţa', *IPEK*, VIII, 49–72.

——(1958), 'Observations sur certains problèmes du néolithique de l'Europe sud-orientale', *Dacia*, N.S., II, 35–58.

——(1959), 'La Civilisation de Cucuteni', *Bericht van der Rijksdienst voor het Oudheidkundig Bodemonderzoek*, 9, Amersfoort, 6–48.

——(1964a), 'Figurines from Gumelniţa', *Antiquity*, 38, 221–2.

——(1964b), 'Synchronisme des civilisations de Cucuteni et de Gumelniţa', *Dacia*, N.S., VIII, 54–66.

——(1965), 'Cascioārele: a late neolithic settlement on the lower Danube', *Archaeology*, 18: 1, 34–40.

——(1966), 'New discoveries at Gumelniţa', *Archaeology*, 19: 3, 162–72.

——(1967a), 'Quelques remarques au sujet de la culture néolithique Precucuteni et de la station de Traian (Dealul Viei), *Dacia*, N.S., XI (1967), 39–46.
——(1967b), *Hăbășești*, Bucharest.
——(1969), 'Betrachtungen zur chronologische Ansetzung der Cucuteni-Kultur in Verhältnis zu den Nachbarkulturen', *Štud. Zvesti*, 17, 87–104.
EHRICH, R. (1965), 'Geographical and Chronological Patterns in East Central Europe', in EHRICH, R. (Ed.), *Chronologies in Old World Archaeology*, Chicago, 403–58.
FIRBAS, F. (1949), *Spät- und nacheiszeitliche Waldgeschichte Mitteleuropas nördlich der Alpen*, Jena.
GALOVIĆ, R. (1964), 'Neue Funde der Starčevo Kultur in Mittelserbien und Makedonien', *Ber. R.G.K.*, 43–4, 1–29.
——(1966), 'The monumental prehistoric clay figurines of the middle Balkans', *A.J.A.*, 70, 370–1.
GARAŠANIN, D. (1954), *Starčevačka Kultura* (The Starčevo Culture), Ljubljiana.
GARAŠANIN, M. (1951), *Hronologija Vinčanske Gruppe* (The Chronology of the Vinča group), Ljubljiana.
——(1956), 'Die Bestattungsitten im balkanischen-anatolischen Komplex der jüngeren Steinzeit', *Glasnik Z.M. Sar.*, XI, 205–36.
——(1958), 'Neolithikum und Bronzezeit in Serbien und Makedonien', *Ber. R.G.K.*, 39, 1–131.
——(1961a), 'Der Stand der Neolithikumforschung in Serbien und Makedonien mit besonders Rücksicht auf die neuen Ergebnisse in der Agais und in Ostbalkan', *Vth Congress ISPP Hamburg 1958*, Hamburg, 307–11.
——(1961b), 'The Neolithic in Anatolia and the Balkans', *Antiquity*, 35, 271–81.
GARNETT, A. (1945), 'The loess regions of central Europe in prehistoric times', *Geographical Journal*, 106, 132–41.
GAUL, J. (1948), 'The Neolithic Period in Bulgaria', *BASPR*, 16.
GAZDAPUSZTAI, GY (1962), 'Sur quelques problèmes de la recherche de la préhistoire hongroise', *Arch. Ert.*, 89, 3–15.
GEORGIEV, G. (1961), 'Kulturgruppen der Jungstein- und der Kupferzeit in der Ebene von Thrazien', *Le Fin de l'Age de Pierre*, Prague, 45–100.
——(1956), 'The Azmak Mound in Southern Bulgaria', *Antiquity*, 39, 6–8.
——(1969), 'Die äneolithische Kultur in Südbulgarien im Lichte der Ausgrabungen von Tell Azmak bei Stara Zagora', *Štud. Zvesti*, 17, 141–58.
GIMBUTAS, M. (1956), 'The prehistory of Eastern Europe. Pt. I: Mesolithic, Neolithic and Copper Age Cultures in Russia and the Baltic area', *BASPR*, 20.
——(1965), 'The Relative Chronology of Neolithic and Chalcolithic Cultures in East Europe north of the Balkan Peninsula and the Black Sea', in EHRICH, R. (Ed.), *Chronologies in Old World Archaeology*, Chicago, 459–502.
GRBIĆ, M. (1957), 'Pre-classical pottery in the Central Balkans', *AJA*, 61, 141.
HIGGS, E., & JARMAN, M. (1969), 'The Origins of Agriculture: a reconsideration', *Antiquity*, 43, 31–91.
HÖCKMANN, O. (1968), *Die menschengestaltige Figuralplastik der sudosteuropäischen Jungsteinzeit und Steinkupferzeit*, Hildesheim.
HOOD, S. (1967), 'The Tărtăria tablets', *Antiquity*, 41, 99–113.
INDREKO, R. (1948), *Die mittlere Steinzeit in Estland*, Stockholm.
——(1964), *Mesolithische und frühneolithische Kulturen in Osteuropa und Westsibiren*, Lund.
JAŻDŻEWSKI, K. (1965), *Poland*, London.
JOVANOVIĆ, B. (1964), 'La céramique anthropomorphe de l'eneolithique des Balkans et du Bas-Danube', *Arch. Iug.* V.

KAHLKE, H. (1954), *Die Bestattungssitten des donauländischen Kulturkreis der jüngeren Steinzeit,* Berlin.

KALICZ, N. (1969), 'Einige Probleme der Lengeyl Kultur in Ungarn', *Štud. Zvesti,* 17, 177–206.

——(1970), *Clay Gods,* Budapest.

KALICZ, N., & MAKKAY, J. (1966), 'Die wichtigste Fragen der Linearkeramik in Ungarn', *Acta Ant. et Arch.,* X, 35–47.

KOWALCZYK, J. (1961), 'Die Trichterbeckerkultur und Tripolye', *Le Fin de l'Age de Pierre,* Prague, 201–4.

——(1969), 'Początki neolitu na ziemach polskich' (The beginning of the neolithic in Poland), *Wiad. Arch.,* XXXIV, 3–69.

KUTZIAN, I. B. (1947), *The Kőrös culture,* Budapest.

——(1961), 'Zur Problematik der Ungarischen Kupferzeit', *Le Fin de l'Age de Pierre,* Prague, 221–32.

——(1963), *The Copper Age Cemetery of Tiszapolgár-Basatanya,* Budapest.

——(1966a), 'Das Neolithikum in Ungarn', *Arch. Aust.,* 40, 249–80.

——(1966b), 'A contribution to the Chronology of the Lengyel Culture', *Sbornik N.M.,* XX: 1–2, Prague, 63–70.

——(1971), *The Copper Age of the Great Hungarian Plain,* Budapest.

LETICA, Z. (1964), 'The Neolithic figurines from Vinča', *Archaeology,* 17:1, 26–32.

LICHARDUS, J. (1964), 'Beitrag zur Linearbandkeramik in der Ostslowakei', *Arch. Rozh.,* XVI: 6, 841–81.

——(1969), 'Ein Beitrag zur Chronologie der Bükker-Kultur auf Grund der Forschungsarbeiten in Südslowakischen Karst', *A Mora F. Muz. Evk.,* 2, 23–8.

——(in press), 'Beziehungen der älteren östlichen Linearkeramik in der Ostslowakei zu den westlichen donauländischen Linearkeramik', *Alba Regia,* Szekesfehervar.

LICHARDUS, J., & PAVUK, J. (1963), 'Bemerkungen zum präkeramischen Neolithikum in der Argissa-magula und zu seiner Existenz in Europa', *Slov. Arch.,* XI: 2, 459–76.

MAKKAY, J. (1969), 'Zu Geschichte der Erforschung der Körös-Starčevo Kultur und einiger ihrer wichtigsten probleme', *Acta Arch. Hung.,* XXI, ?–31.

MAKKY, J., & TROGMAYER, O. (1966), 'Die Bemalte Keramik der Körös-Gru, ne', *A Mora F. Muz. Evk.,* Szeged, 47–58.

MELLAAR, J. (1960), 'Anatolia and the Balkans', *Antiquity,* 34, 270–8.

——(1965), *The Earliest Civilisations of the Near East,* London.

MIKOV, V. (1939), 'The Prehistoric Site of Karanovo', *Antiquity,* XIII, 345–9.

——(1959), 'The Prehistoric Mound of Karanovo', *Archaelogy,* XII: 2, 88.

MILOJČIĆ, V. (1949a), *Chronologie der jüngeren Steinzeit Mittel- und Südosteuropas,* Berlin.

——(1949b), 'South-eastern Elements in the Neolithic Cultures of Serbia', *Proceedings of the British School at Athens,* XLIV, 258–99.

——(1950), 'Körös-Starčevo-Vinča', *Reinecke Festschrift,* Mainz, 108–17.

——(1951), 'Die Siedlungsgrenzen und Zeitstellung der Bandkeramik in Osten und Südosten Europas', *Ber. R.G.K.,* 33, 110–24.

——(1952), 'Die frühesten Ackerbauer in Mitteleuropa', *Germania,* 30, 315.

——(1956), 'Die erste präkeramische bäuerliche Siedlung der Jungsteinzeit in Europa', *Germania,* 34, 208–10.

——(1958), 'Zur Anwendigkeit der C14-Datierung in der Vorgeschichte', *Germania,* 36, 409.

——(1960), 'Präkeramisches Neolithikum auf der Balkanhalbinsel', *Germania*, 38, 320–5.

——(1965), 'Die Tontafeln von Tărtăria und die Absolute Chronologie des mittel-europäischen Neolithikums', *Germania*, 43, 261–8.

MODDERMAN, P. J., & WATERBOLK, H. (1958–9), 'Zur Typologie der verzierten Tonware aus den bandkeramische Siedlungen in der Niederländen', *Palaeohistoria*, VI–VII, 173–83.

MODDERMAN, P. J. (in press), 'Zur Typologie der Linearbandkeramischen Gebäude', *Alba Regia*, Szekesfehervar.

NANDRIS, J. (1968), 'Lepenski Vir', *Science Journal*, 1, 64–70.

——(1970), 'The Development and Relationships of the Earlier Greek Neolithic', *JRAI*, V: 2, 192–213.

NEUSTUPNY, E. & J. (1961), *Czechoslovakia before the Slavs*, London.

NEUSTUPNY, E. (1968a), 'Absolute chronology of the Neolithic and Aeneolithic periods in Central and South-East Europe', *Slov. Arch.*, XVI: 1, 19–60.

——(1968b), 'The Tărtăria tablets: a chronological issue', *Antiquity*, 42, 32–5.

——(1969), 'Absolute Chronology of the Neolithic and Aeneolithic periods in Central and South-east Europe', *Arch. Rozh.*, XXI: 6, 783–810.

PASSEK, T. S. (1949), 'Periodizatsiya Tripolskikh poselenii' (Periodisation of the Tripolye settlements), *MIA*, 10.

——(1961a), 'Rannezemlyedelčeskiye [Tripolskiye] plemena podnestrovya' (The early agricultural [Tripolye culture] population of the left bank of the Dniester), *MIA*, 84.

——(1961b), 'Problèmes eneolithiques du Sud-ouest de l'Europe orientale', *Le Fin de l'Age de Pierre*, Prague, 148–160.

——(1962), 'Relations entre l'Europe Occidentale et l'Europe Orientale à l'epoque néolithique', *Atti del VII Congresso ISPP*, Rome, 126–44.

PASSEK, T. S., & ČERNYŠ, E. K. (1963), 'Pamyatniki kulturi linieno-lentočnoi keramiki na territorii SSSR' (Linear Pottery culture sites in USSR), *Arkheologiya SSSR*.

PĂUNESCU, AL. (1970), *Evoluţia uneltelor şi armelor de piatră cioplită descoperite pe teritoriul Romaniei* (The evolution of implements and weapons of chipped stone in Rumania), Bucharest.

PAVUK, J. (1969), 'Chronologie der Želiezovce Gruppe', *Slov. Arch.*, XVII: 2, 269–368.

——(in press), 'Linearbandkeramische Gräberfelder', *Alba Regia*, Szekesfehervar.

PETRESCU-DÎMBOVIŢA, M. (1959), 'Contributions au Problème de la Culture Criş en Moldavie', *Acta Arch. Hung.*, IX, 53–68.

——(1966), *Cucuteni*, Bucharest.

PIGGOTT, S. (1960), 'Neolithic and Bronze Age in East Europe', *Antiquity*, 34, 284–94.

——(1965), *Ancient Europe*, Edinburgh.

PITTIONI, R. (1961), 'Southern Middle Europe and South-east Europe', in BRAIDWOOD, R. (Ed.), *Courses towards Urban Life*, Edinburgh.

POUNDS, N. (1969), *Georgaphy of Eastern Europe*, London.

QUITTA, H. (1960), 'Zur Frage der ältesten Bandkeramik in Mitteleuropa', *Praehist. Zeitschr.*, XXXVIII, 1–38, 153–88.

——(1964), 'Zur Herkunft des frühen Neolithikums in Mitteleuropa', *Festschrift H. Unverzagt*, E. Berlin.

——(1967), 'The C14 chronology of the Central and South-east European Neolithic', *Antiquity*, 41, 263–70.

RAPOPORT, A. (1969), *House form and culture*, New Jersey.

RENFREW, C. (1969a), *The Art of the First Farmers*, Sheffield.

——(1969b), 'The Autonomy of the South-east European Copper Age', *PPS*, XXXV, 12–47.

——(1970a), 'New Configurations in Old World Archaeology', *World Archaeology*, II, 199.

——(1970b), 'Trade and Culture Process in European Prehistory', *Current Anthropology*, 151.

——(1970c), 'The Tree Ring Calibration of Radiocarbon', *PPS*, XXXVI, 280–311.

RENFREW, J. (1969), 'The Archaeological evidence for the domestication of plants: methods and problems', in UCKO, P., & DIMBLEBY, G., *The Domestication and Exploitation of Plants and Animals*, London, 149–72.

RODDEN, R. (1965), 'An Early Neolithic Village in Greece', *Scientific American*, 212: 4.

——(1968), *Pottery and Flint-working traditions in the Early Neolithic of South East Europe; and the spread of the farming economy*. Unpublished Ph. D. Thesis, University of Cambridge.

ROSENFELD, A. (1965), *The Inorganic Raw Materials of Antiquity*, London.

ROWLANDS, M. (1970), 'The Archaeological Interpretation of Metallurgy', *Research Seminar on Archaeology and Related Subjects*, London (6 May).

SANGMEISTER, E. (1943–50), 'Zum Charakter der bandkeramischen Siedlungen', *Ber. R.G.K.*, 33, 89–109.

SCHMIDT, H. (1932), *Cucuteni*, Berlin and Leipzig.

——(1945), *Die Burg Vučedol*, Zagreb.

SCHROLLER, H. (1933), *Die Stein- und Kupferzeit Siebenbürgens*, Berlin.

SCHUBERT, F. (1965), 'Zu den südosteuropäischen Kupferäxten', *Germania*, 43: 3/4, 274–95.

SEMENOV, S. A. (1964), *Prehistoric Technology*, London.

SKUTIL, J. (1940), 'Die neolithischen Plastiken aus den Kreise der mährischen bemalten Keramik', *IPEK*, XIV, 36–56.

SONNENFELD, J. (1962–3), 'Interpreting the Function of Primitive Implements', *American Antiquity*, 28: 1, 56–65.

SOUDSKY, B. (1962), 'The Neolithic site of Bylany,' *Antiquity*, 36, 190–200.

——(1965), 'Genèse, periodisation, et économie du Néolithique ancien en Europe centrale', *Atti del VII Congresso ISPP*, Rome, 276–80.

——(1966), *Bylany: osada nejstarších zemědelců z mladší doby kamenné* (Bylany, a settlement of the earliest neolithic farmers), Prague.

——(1968a), 'Criteria to distinguish cultural phases—methods employed in the excavation at Bylany', *Research Seminar on Archaeology and Related Subjects*, London (25 October).

——(1968b), 'Application de Methodes du Calcul dans l'étude d'un site néolithique', *Calcul et Formalisation dans les Sciences de l'Homme*, Paris, 131–42.

——(1969), 'Étude de la Maison Néolithique', *Slov. Arch.*, XVII: 1, 5–96.

SOUDSKY, B., & PAVLŮ, I. (1971), 'The Linear Pottery culture settlement patterns of Central Europe, in UCKO, P., TRINGHAM, R., & DIMBLEBY, G. (Eds.), *Settlement Patterns and Urbanization*, London.

SREJOVIĆ, D. (1964–5), 'Neolithic Anthropomorphic figurines of Yugoslavia', *IPEK*, XXI, 28–41.

——(1966), 'Lepenski Vir—a new prehistoric culture in the Danubian region', *Arch. Iug.*, VII, 13–18.

——(1969), *Lepenski Vir* (in Serbian with a French summary), Belgrade.

STIEREN, A. (1943–50), 'Bandkeramische Grossbauten bei Bochum und ihre Parallele in Mitteleuropa', *Ber. R.G.K.*, 33, 61–88.

SULIMIRSKI, T. (1970), *Prehistoric Russia*, London.

TELEGIN, D. JA. (1968), *Dnipro-Donetzka Kultura* (Dnieper-Donetz culture), Kiev.

——(1969), 'Das Mitteldneprgebiet und die östlich anschliessende Ukraine in der Epoche das Neolithikum und der frühen Metallzeit', *Zeitschr. für Arch.*, 3, 1–15.

TICHÝ, R. (1961), 'Einige Bemerkung zum Neolithikum in der Tschechoslowakei, nach den Forschungsergebnissen seit 1945', *Arch. Aust.*, 29, 96–122.

TOMPA, F. (1929), *Bandkeramik in Ungarn*, Budapest.

TRIGGER, B. (1968), *Beyond History: the methods of prehistory*, New York.

TRINGHAM, R. (1966), *The Early Neolithic of Central Europe*, Ph.D. thesis, University of Edinburgh.

——(1968), 'A preliminary study of the early neolithic and latest mesolithic blade industries in south-east and central Europe', in COLES, J., & SIMPSON, D. (Eds.), *Studies in Ancient Europe*, Leicester, 45–70.

——(1969), 'Animal domestication in the neolithic cultures of the south-west part of European USSR', in UCKO, P., & DIMBLEBY, G. (Eds.), *The Domestication and Exploitation of Plants and Animals*, London, 381–92.

——(1971), 'Territorial demarcation of prehistoric settlements', in UCKO, P., TRINGHAM, R., & DIMBLEBY, G. (Eds.), *Settlement Patterns and Urbanization*, London.

——(in press), 'The function, technology and typology of the chipped stone industry at Bylany', *Alba Regia*, Szekesfehervar.

TROGMAYER, O. (1966), 'Ein neolithisches Hausmodellfragment von Röszke', *Acta Ant. et Arch.*, X, 11–26.

——(1967), 'Bemerkungen zur Chronologie des Frühneolithikums auf dem süd-Alföld', *A Mora F. Muz. Evk.*, 2, Szeged., 35–40.

——(1969), 'Die Bestattungen der Körös-Gruppe', *A Mora F. Muz. Evk.*, 2, 5–16.

UCKO, P. (1968), *Anthropomorphic figurines of Predynastic Egypt and Neolithic Crete with comparative material from the prehistoric Near East and mainland Greece*, London.

——(1969a), 'Ethnography and archaeological interpretation of funerary remains', *World Archaeology*, II: 2, 262–80.

——(1969b), 'Penis Sheaths: a comparative study', *Proceedings of the Royal Anthropological Institute*, 27–67.

UCKO, P., & DIMBLEBY, G. (Eds.) (1969), *The Domestication and Exploitation of Plants and Animals*, London.

VALOCH, K. (1968), 'Paleolithic in Central and Eastern Europe', *Current Anthropology*, 9: 5, 351–90.

VAJSOVA, H. (1969), 'Einige Fragen über die Chronologie der Gumelniţa-Kultur', *Štud. Zvesti*, 17, 481–96.

VASSIĆ, M. (1930–6), *Preistorijskaya Vinča* (Prehistoric Vinča), 4 vols, Belgrade.

VENCL, Sl. (1960), 'Kamenné nastroje prvnich zemědelců ve středni Evropě' (The stone implements of the first farmers in central Europe), *Sbornik N.M.*, XIV, 1–91.

——(1968a), 'Zur Frage der Bestehens eines präkeramischen Neolithikums in der Slowakei', *Acta Arch. Carp.*, X: 1–2, 39–61.

——(1968b), 'K Otazce Interpretace pravěkych staveb' (The problem of interpreting prehistoric houses), *Arch. Rozh.*, XX: 4, 490–510.

VERTES, L. (1960), 'Die Altsteinzeit der Südlichen Donaugebiete', *Quartär*, XII, 53–105.

VLASSA, N. (1963), 'Chronology of the Neolithic of Transilvania in the light of the Tärtäria settlement's stratigraphy', *Dacia, N.S.*, VII, 485–94.

VULPE, R. (1957), *Izvoare; săpăturile 1936–48*, Bucharest.

WATERBOLK, H. (1968), 'Food production in Prehistoric Europe', *Science*, 1093–102.
WATERBOLK, H., & BUTLER, J. (1965), 'Comments on the use of metallurgical analysis in prehistoric studies', *Helinium*, V, 227–51.
WATERBOLK, H., & MODDERMAN, P. (1958–9), 'Die Grossbauten der Bandkeramik', *Palaeohistoria*, VI–VII, 163–71.
ZOTZ, L. (1932), 'Kulturgruppen des Tardenoisien in Mitteleuropa', *Praehist. Zeitschr.* 23, 19–45.
——(1941), 'Die Beziehungen zwischen Altsteinzeit, Mittelsteinzeit und Donaukultur', *WPZ*, XXVIII, 1–20.

INDEX